Veronika Jungwirth • Ralp

Solution-Focused Coaching for Agile Teams

A guide to collaborative leadership

solutions books

First published in Great Britain in 2021 by
Solutions Books
20 Atholl Crescent
Edinburgh
EH3 8HQ
Scotland
United Kingdom

No part of this publication may be reproduced, stored in a retrieval system, or
transmitted in any form, or by any means, electronic, mechanical, photocopying, recording, or
otherwise, without the written permission of the publisher

Copyright © Veronika Jungwirth and Ralph Miarka 2021

The moral right of the contributors to be identified as the authors of this work has been asserted
in accordance with the Copyright, Designs and Patents Act, 1988

Rights enquiries should be addressed to Solutions Books
via info@sfwork.com or by post to the address above.

ISBN 978-0-9933463-4-7

Cover design: Irene Neumayer

Cover photo by Liam Quinn, Macaroni Penguins at Cooper Bay, South Georgia, January 2011,
see: https://www.flickr.com/photos/liamq/5892415211.

Design, typesetting and production by The Choir Press, Gloucester

"Highly practical. You'll find new ideas and applications about guiding and encouraging teams. You'll also find insights and recommendations for working with team members and leaders as individuals. You'll learn about handling team conflict and designing meetings. I predict this book will become one of those critical few resources that every coach recommends to their peers."

Diana Larsen, co-author of Liftoff: Start and Sustain Successful Agile Teams

"What got us to where we are won't get us to where we are going. So how do we, as leaders, grow and coach effective teams? We need guides!
Veronkia Jungwirth and Ralph Miarka are two of the best. In *Solution-Focused Coaching for Agile Teams*, they share the wisdom they've gained over years of coaching in many different settings. The practical guidance they provide within these pages will make this one of the most referenced books in your library. Buy it and read it. Read it again. And again. Your professional and personal life will improve as a result."

Richard Sheridan, CEO and Chief Storyteller, Menlo Innovations, author, Joy,Inc. – How We Built a Workplace People Love

"This book is pragmatic, full of useful approaches and techniques to help with coaching Agile teams – a valuable asset for anyone using or wishing to use Solution Focus as a team coaching or individual coaching resource. I highly recommend it."

John Brooker, author of Jump Now: Lead Solution Focus Collaboration to Accelerate Sustainable Results

"Leaders and project managers will get a very comprehensible impression of what agile principles and methods mean and how they work. For consultants and coaches, the book is a backup for their methodological toolbox. Anyone who wants to form or train agile teams will find here one of the best manuals currently available."

Berliner Morgenpost

"Veronika Jungwirth and Ralph Miarka are your ideal guides for combining Solution-Focused and Agile, two effective, pragmatic and iterative practices, into a powerful overall way not just to do work but to do it as well as possible in the most challenging of circumstances."

Dr Mark McKergow, author of The Next Generation of Solution Focused Practice

Contents

Acknowledgements ... xi
Preface ... xiii
Foreword by Diana Larsen ... xv
Foreword by Mark McKergow ... xvi

1. **Introduction** ... 1
   1.1 Why this book and for whom? ... 1
   1.2 What is this book about? ... 2
   1.3 The structure ... 3
   1.4 History of the solution-focused approach ... 4
   1.5 Solution Focus and the Agile world ... 5
   1.6 The Agile Team ... 7
   1.7 The Agile Coach ... 8
   1.8 Team coaching ... 11

2. **Solution-focused coaching** ... 14
   2.1 Problem and solution ... 15
   2.2 Six fundamental coaching attitudes and positions ... 16
      2.2.1 The not-knowing position ... 16
      2.2.2 Everyone is an expert in their situation ... 18
      2.2.3 Patience and confidence ... 21
      2.2.4 Focus on resources ... 22
      2.2.5 Omni-partiality ... 26
      2.2.6 Confidentiality ... 26
   2.3 Eight important principles ... 27
      2.3.1 Focus on the preferred future ... 27
      2.3.2 If it works, do more of it ... 28
      2.3.3 If it does not work (anymore), do something different ... 29
      2.3.4 Small steps can lead to big changes ... 30
      2.3.5 The solution is not necessarily related to the problem ... 31
      2.3.6 Solution-talk creates solutions – problem-talk creates problems ... 32
      2.3.7 No problem occurs all the time – use the exceptions ... 34
      2.3.8 If it ain't broken, don't fix it ... 35

	2.4	Attitudes and principles at a glance	36
	2.5	Self-reflection	37
	2.6	Experiments and exercises	37
3.	**Questions and more**		**38**
	3.1	Everyday questions	38
	3.2	Coaching questions	41
		3.2.1 Scale-Question	41
		3.2.2 Coping questions	48
		3.2.3 Asking for exceptions	49
		3.2.4 The miracle question	49
		3.2.5 Circular questions	50
		3.2.6 Interposed questions	50
		3.2.7 Meta questions	52
	3.3	More linguistic interventions	53
		3.3.1 Appreciation	53
		3.3.2 Paraphrasing or summarising	54
		3.3.3 Normalising	55
		3.3.4 Reframing or reinterpreting	56
		3.3.5 Liquefying	58
		3.3.6 Meta-monologue	60
		3.3.7 Avoid *not* and *no* under all circumstances	61
		3.3.8 *And* instead of *but*	61
		3.3.9 Patience and the courage to endure silence	62
		3.3.10 Breaks	62
		3.3.11 Prescribing experiments	63
	3.4	Self-reflection	64
	3.5	Experiments and exercises	64
4.	**The Solution Pyramid**		**66**
	4.1	The ground – the topic	66
	4.2	The first level – goals and impact	69
		4.2.1 Defining goals	69
		4.2.2 Asking for meaning	77
	4.3	The second level – what works	78
	4.4	The third level – the next steps	79
	4.5	The fourth level – review of the results	81
	4.6	Taking conversational needs into account	83
		4.6.1 The conversational partner who is searching for a meaning	84

		4.6.2	The conversational partner who is searching for a goal	85
		4.6.3	The conversational partner who is searching for a way	88
	4.7	The follow-up conversation in the Solution Pyramid		90
	4.8	Self-reflection		91
	4.9	Experiments and exercises		91
5.	**Individual coaching – the team and its individuals**			93
	5.1	What needs to be considered in individual coaching		93
		5.1.1	Confidentiality and trust	93
		5.1.2	Voluntary participation	94
		5.1.3	Setting	95
		5.1.4	Corridor conversations	96
		5.1.5	Dealing with resistance to coaching	97
	5.2	Feedback talks		99
		5.2.1	The four steps of Nonviolent Communication	100
		5.2.2	Potential-focused communication	108
	5.3	Supporting further development		110
	5.4	Self-reflection		114
	5.5	Experiments and exercises		115
6.	**Team development**			116
	6.1	Goals of team development		116
		6.1.1	High-performance teams	116
		6.1.2	Self-organisation in agile teams	120
	6.2	Our R.E.S.U.L.T. model for team development		122
	6.3	Tools for team development		129
	6.4	Working with timelines in a solution-focused way		135
		6.4.1	From the past to the future	136
		6.4.2	From the future to the presence	138
	6.5	Developing a team vision		140
	6.6	Team development with large groups		143
	6.7	Self-reflection		147
	6.8	Experiments and exercises		148
7.	**Dealing with Conflicts**			149
	7.1	The concept of conflict		149
	7.2	The nine stages of conflict escalation		151
	7.3	The benefits of conflicts		154
	7.4	The comprehensible intention		156
	7.5	The SCARF model		157

	7.5.1	The five factors	158
	7.5.2	SCARF – and why change projects fail	164
	7.5.3	Making SCARF usable	167
7.6	Solving conflicts in a solution-focused way		168
	7.6.1	The ground of the conflict	168
	7.6.2	The first level – goals and impact	173
	7.6.3	The second level – what works despite the conflict	176
	7.6.4	The third level – the next steps and their impact	178
	7.6.5	The fourth level – review of the results	180
7.7	Conversational needs in the conflict		181
	7.7.1	The conflict partner searching for a meaning	181
	7.7.2	The conflict partner searching for a goal	182
	7.7.3	The conflict partner searching for a way	182
	7.7.4	The challenge	182
7.8	Self-reflection		184
7.9	Experiments and exercises		184

8. Solution-focused meeting design — 186

8.1	Considerations for solution-focused meeting facilitation		187
	8.1.1	Active involvement of all participants	187
	8.1.2	Monotony versus variety	188
	8.1.3	Dealing with "unstoppable speakers", "those keeping silent" and "troublemakers"	189
	8.1.4	Making decisions	194
	8.1.5	Handling objections	198
	8.1.6	Working with large groups	199
8.2	Preparation for meetings		200
8.3	The planning meeting		201
8.4	Solution-focused Daily Stand-ups		206
8.5	The review meeting		211
8.6	The solution-focused retrospective		213
	8.6.1	Step 1: Opening	215
	8.6.2	Step 2: Clarify the goal and impact	218
	8.6.3	Step 3: Collect what works	226
	8.6.4	Step 4: Initiate actions	228
	8.6.5	Step 5: Review confidence	232
	8.6.6	A retrospective with Ralph	234
	8.6.7	A solution-focused short retrospective	237

		8.6.8	Between retrospectives	237
		8.6.9	Retrospectives in a large project	238
	8.7	Facilitating Backlog Refinement Meetings		238
	8.8	Follow-up to meetings		240
	8.9	Self-reflection		242
	8.10	Experiments and exercises		242
9.	**Tips for the coach**			**244**
	9.1	Your role(s)		245
	9.2	When to act as a coach?		246
		9.2.1	What is your assignment?	246
		9.2.2	Contracting	247
		9.2.3	Can you stay out of anything content-related?	248
		9.2.4	Are you omni-partial?	249
		9.2.5	Do you have support?	249
		9.2.6	The appointment agreement and its effects	250
	9.3	The coach as host		251
	9.4	Setting and defending boundaries		251
		9.4.1	Your non-negotiable framework	252
		9.4.2	First of all, take care of yourself	253
	9.5	The Scrum Master – a unique role		254
		9.5.1	Role clarity	254
		9.5.2	Appreciation, wishes and further development	256
	9.6	Self-reflection		257
	9.7	Experiments and exercises		257

Bibliography	259
Tool Index	271
Index	272

About the authors

Veronika Jungwirth MC (fka Kotrba) has been working independently and enthusiastically since 2006 as a consultant in change processes, as a coach, mentor, trainer for solution-focused coaching, sparring partner in leadership issues and as a facilitator of team development processes in various industries. In doing so, she integrates her professional experience in education and business, as well as the exciting insights from solutions-focused brief therapy, Viktor Frankl's theory of meaning, modern brain research and positive psychology. She is a co-founder of the Austrian Solution Circle and is internationally networked in both, the agile and solution-focused communities.

Dr Ralph Miarka MSc works as an independent coach, consultant and trainer. He has been leading companies and their teams to a successful agile way of working for years. Previously, he worked for Siemens AG Austria as project manager, project consultant and department head in the support centre for project management. In his own projects he was able to convince himself and his customers of the advantages of agile working. Ralph is a trained business coach with a master's degree. He is thrilled to observe how a group of people changes into a team wanting to achieve a common goal. Ralph also enjoys sharing his knowledge and experience with others at conferences, workshops and training sessions.

Together they live in Vienna. As sinnvollFÜHREN they act under the sign of the penguin and want to support people in fulfilling their leadership work with ease and more effectiveness. Since 2012 they have been carrying the solution-focused approach into the agile community. They have appeared as speakers and workshop facilitators at numerous conferences and Agile Coach Camps. In addition, they have been and continue to be actively involved in the organisation of XP2013, EBTA 2015, Agile Coach Camps Austria since 2014, the Agile Tour Vienna 2011 and the Host Leadership Gathering 2021 and 2023 as well as the SOLworld Conference 2021 and 2023.

Acknowledgements

It is not at all easy for us to list all those people who have helped us in many ways in the making of this book. Nevertheless, we would like to make an attempt here:

First of all, we would like to thank Marc Löffler. He invited us to write a contribution for his book *Retrospektiven in der Praxis* [Löffler 2014] (in English: *Improving Agile Retrospectives* [Löffler 2018]). And because this chapter was well received by the readers – it is about solution-focused retrospectives – the German publisher *dpunkt.verlag* approached us with the idea of writing our own book. So somehow Marc is "to blame" for our writing this book in the first place.

Thanks also to all our clients, to the teams and individuals with whom we have walked part of the way together so far and from whom we have already been able to learn so much. They are the ones who have significantly influenced the content. It is their stories that we tell. And many thanks to Rolf Dräther, Klaus Schenck, Christa Preisendanz and so many others that made the German book such a success.

We would like to thank Moni Lexa for translating our book in a very professional way and being patient with us when discussing about all the little phrases that are dear to our solution-focused hearts. Furthermore, we send a wholehearted thank you to Jenny Clarke, who has made her linguistic talent as well as her expertise as a solution-focused thought leader available and is partly responsible for the hopefully good readability. Moreover, we like to thank Nathalie Karasek for taking her time to offer so many improvements.

Thanks to Diana Larsen for her foreword – and her prediction for this book.

A big thanks also goes to Mark McKergow who supported the birth of this English book by great means – offering a foreword as well as publishing it as part of the Solutions Book series and putting much effort into it.

Dearest reader, we hope you enjoy reading this book, gain numerous insights when applying the content and we look forward to your feedback on this piece of work.

Preface

On the cover of this book, you see penguins overcoming a rocky path together. And even though this is not a book about these animals, we think they fit well here thematically. They are team-oriented individual fighters. When it comes to survival in the icy winter months, to the safety of their offspring and to organising food, they stick together ironclad. Then they are a team. A team that relies on each other blindly – no matter what happens. Everyone knows their job and accepts their responsibility to the fullest extent.

Penguins have incredible talents! At first glance, they may look as if a few serious mistakes have been made in their construction – stocky stature, wings that are far too small, plus neither neck nor knees – but when such a penguin jumps into the water, it moves smoothly, elegantly and as fast as an arrow [Hirschhausen 2009, p. 355 ff]. It can wait for weeks – braving the icy wind – for its offspring to hatch without taking any food. And they never lose confidence that their mate will return from their search for food in time to take over from them. Penguins stand close together in a snowstorm to keep each other warm. With perfect self-organisation, they constantly change their positions so that everyone is in the middle to warm up and then on the outside again to protect the others.

Even though they don't stand a chance against a jaguar in a sprint and can never reach the top of a tree, penguins are naturally tough, trusting, dedicated and team players. They manage to cope with the demands of life together and with a clear division of tasks. That is what impresses us about these animals. In many ways, they can stand as role models for teams and also for the fact that it is better to look closely before making rash judgements about colleagues, employees or even bosses.

The penguin's element is water. There, they need no knees to glide smoothly and agilely through the waves of their lives. If the members of a team are allowed to work in their own element and in their own way, their potentials can unfold and contribute to a common team success. Coaching can support both the development of individuals and their cooperation.

It is the special form of cooperation – internally and externally – that particularly characterises agile teams. For this cooperation to be beneficial for everyone, it needs successful communication – and we would like to promote this with solution focus.

Agility, in our view, is no end in itself, it is a path to a goal. What that goal is must be worked out in each company by its people and in cooperation with its customers. An agile way of working can only be successfully developed when the communication between the participants works well – similar to how the birth of a child can enrich a previously happy partnership. That is why we want to recommend solution focus as an agile enabler.

Veronika Jungwirth and Ralph Miarka
Vienna, Austria, April 2021

Foreword

By Diana Larsen

When I first met Ralph Miarka, we had immediate rapport. We found a shared interest in Agile software development. Then we became even more interested in each other's ideas. Ralph – together with Veronika Jungwirth – explored and shared Solutions-Focused ideas to his coaching practice. I shared and applied Appreciative Inquiry thinking to my consulting practice. We found the confluence of the two streams with similar roots and mindsets.

A few years ago Ralph let me know that he and Veronika had begun writing a book. They intended to explore the intersection of agile teams and solutions-focus. And, now the book is in our hands. Yours and mine.

The roots of Agile run deep into the history of organisational development, design, and behaviour. Advances in technology and software development, nurtured it. It fed on Japanese management techniques like quality circles and a devotion to customer value. It adopted humanised work, like Deming's views on driving fear out of the workplace. Mix it all together and you get a human-centred, yet technical approach. This rich mixture forms the foundation for Ralph and Veronika's ideas about solutions-focused coaching for teams.

This book moves beyond the philosophical to the highly practical. You'll find new ideas and applications about guiding and encouraging teams. You'll also find insights and recommendations for working with team members and leaders as individuals. You'll learn about handling team conflict and designing meetings. The RESULT model shares a great mnemonic for keeping your coaching on track.

I predict this book will become one of those few critical resources that every coach recommends to their peers. I'm happy for you. You have a head start!

Onward,
Diana Larsen

co-author, Agile Retrospectives: Making Good Teams Great
co-author, Liftoff 2nd ed: Start and Sustain Successful Agile Teams
co-founder, Agile Fluency Project, LLC

Foreword

By Mark McKergow

I am delighted to welcome the publication of the important book from Veronika Jungwirth and Ralph Miarka. I say 'important' because the connections, parallels and mutual power between Solution-Focused (SF) and Agile approaches have gone underexamined for far too long. I remember first discussing these connections with Agile Manifesto co-author Alistair Cockburn over lunch in London more than a decade ago, and I am very pleased to see a much more complete account appearing in print.

Both SF and Agile approaches are interested in promoting emergent working, embracing change as it (inevitably) happens. Both are concerned with making progress in an iterative manner. Both are concerned with taking small steps (easier to do) rather than getting too involved in giant plans which lead nowhere. So why should Agile practitioners be interested in adding SF ideas to their options?

Put simply, because SF is very useful when things are tough. The Solution Focused approach was originally developed as a brief therapy method to help people who don't even know what to think, let alone know what to do, to rapidly regain a sense of what is important to them, what is working and (most importantly) what they might do next. It has been proven over decades in the roughest of settings. Moreover, it promotes co-operation, respect, acknowledgement and mutual connection.

When put together, SF tools and approaches provide a new dimension to Agile working. Veronika Jungwirth and Ralph Miarka are skilled in both. They are your ideal guides for combining these two effective, pragmatic and iterative practices into a powerful overall way not just to do work but to do it as well as possible in the most challenging of circumstances. I recommend the book whole-heartedly as an excellent next step for coaches, agile teams and consultants.

Mark McKergow PhD MBA
author, The Next Generation of Solution Focused Practice

1 Introduction

1.1 Why this book and for whom?

The world is changing faster than ever. New technologies are contributing significantly to these changes. More and more effort is required in increasingly shorter periods of time to stay ahead of economic competition. Today, making important decisions is often just a matter of emotional judgement [Kahneman, 2011] because there is too much information, which is often contradictory as well; in addition, time is limited, so it is impossible to give everything deliberate consideration. Communication lines are becoming increasingly faster and, therefore, more impersonal. This development has a negative impact on cooperation in the corporate context at all levels.

The use of coaching techniques can effectively support mutual understanding and add to safety and trust within the team. This increases the willingness to cooperate and the success of the joint effort in the long term.

This book is about solution-focused coaching of agile teams. We have been active in this field for years and owe our experience to our clients and to all the teams we have been working with. They keep showing us what works and how team coaching processes can be improved. We want to use our knowledge to show you ways of handling situations differently, so it becomes easier for you to act and also react quickly and in a confident manner.

We are enthusiastic about finding out how well the two worlds – the solution-focused and the agile worlds – go together with their values and principles. In this book, we want to share our enthusiasm with you and make our findings available to you as well.

Experience shows that the consistent and continuous use of solution-focused thinking and behaviour improves agile working. Although this book refers to coaching, we are convinced that this approach also provides an answer to the question of leadership in an agile environment.

Last but not least, this book is meant to be a reference book. We want to provide you with helpful ideas and tips for dealing with challenging situations. It is up to you which of the content and techniques in this book you will find suitable for you and which not. Since some of the methods and exercises we describe can be applied in various situations, and because we also want you to be able to read single chapters of this book, you will often find minor repetitions and cross-references.

So, if you are involved with teams in one way or another, this book will be helpful and useful for you. Whether you are a Scrum Master, Product Owner or Project Manager, Department Head or Agile Coach – we hope and believe that this book will provide valuable and practice-oriented suggestions which you can use in your daily work. We will be glad if this works out for you.

In this book, we will often address you directly, dear reader. We hope you are okay with that.

Perhaps you would also like to talk to us directly while reading this book. If you have any questions, want to share your thoughts or tell us about your experiences, please send an e-mail to:

office@sinnvoll-fuehren.com

1.2 What is this book about?

Our idea is to show you how the specific use of solution-focused coaching can lead to more success in your everyday professional life, with the content of this book focusing on working with teams. Solution-focused coaching of individuals is also part of this book. After all, the concerns of individuals have a significant impact on teamwork.

There are a lot of different coaching approaches which are successfully used today; we specialise in solution-focused brief coaching. Our main goal is to support people in finding their own solutions quickly and directly. In this, we also use helpful findings from positive psychology, modern neuroscience, logotherapy, communication and economic sciences and, last but not least, from our own experience.

Solution-focused coaching might be new to you. However, it is an approach which makes it possible for you, your colleagues and your employees to be even more successful. We hope that you – whatever your current role or position is – will find relevant ideas in this book to help you with your everyday situations. After all, the principles of the solution-focused approach can be applied to various fields. Please always bear in mind what Steve de Shazer, one of the founders of the solution-focused approach, said about applying his findings: "It's simple, but not easy." The best thing to do is to find out to what extent this statement applies to you personally.

1.3 The structure

This book is divided into nine chapters. Depending on how much time, previous knowledge and interest you have, you can either decide to do it the traditional way and read one chapter after the other, or you search for specific answers to your current question. You will find some questions for self-reflection as the second last part at the end of each chapter, so you can review the content of the specific chapter if necessary. After the self-reflection part, we have compiled experiments and exercises to enable you to put the content directly into practice.

- In chapter 1, *Introduction*, we tell you about our motivation for writing this book, and we present the book's structure. You will get to know the terms we use in this book.
- Chapter 2, *Solution-focused coaching*, describes the cornerstones of the solution-focused approach in team coaching. In this chapter, you will find attitudes and principles which, from our point of view, are the basis for the following chapters. If you do not know this approach yet, we recommend reading this chapter first.
- Chapter 3 includes a compilation of questioning techniques and other linguistic interventions, some but not all of which are based on solution-focused coaching. We like to use them when working with teams and individuals.
- Chapter 4 is all about the procedure and the structure of solution-focused conversations in team coaching. For your orientation, we have developed a graphical model, *the Solution Pyramid*, which you will meet again in the subsequent chapters.
- Chapter 5 includes some thoughts about *Individual coaching*. In this chapter, we have compiled practical tips for you when talking to individuals. You will learn what to observe in order to give feedback or criticism, so your conversational partner can make use of what you say in the best possible way. We will tell you how you can support individual development effectively.
- In chapter 6, we will introduce our R.E.S.U.L.T. model for *Team Development*. You will find tested and approved interventions and tools which you can directly put into practice with your teams.
- Chapter 7 examines the major topic of *dealing with conflicts* in a team.

Our aim is to provide you with both theoretical ideas and practical tools to support you in challenging situations.

- Chapter 8 is titled *Solution-focused design of meetings* and will introduce you to ideas and exercises for a variety of agile meeting formats. We will also provide you with tips for working with large groups or for dealing with special circumstances like unforeseen disturbances you might encounter in meetings.
- The ninth and last chapter, *Tips for the coach*, is of special concern to us. It is about how you can pay attention to your own resources in your role as a coach. Since you are reading this book, we assume that you want to be highly effective when working with teams or individuals. To be able to do that in the long term, it is important to reflect on your individual practice, treat yourself to downtimes regularly and not lose sight of your own needs.

1.4 History of the solution-focused approach

The solution-focused counselling approach comes from family therapy and was developed by Steve de Shazer, his wife Insoo Kim Berg and a team of therapists in Milwaukee, Wisconsin, in the 1970s and 1980s. In numerous therapy sessions with patients, they had observed that some patients were quicker than others when it came to their willingness and readiness to find solutions for their respective situation. The therapists focused on finding out how those patients did this and what they did differently compared to those who stuck in their problem for a longer period of time.

Their observations led to linguistic interventions – the solution-focused questions. With these, they managed to exert a positive influence on the patients' thinking processes towards goal and solution focus. The result was shorter therapy as the patients' situations improved faster with a longer lasting effect.

Solution focus in therapy might have been what agile development was for the software industry – a small revolution. The result was an approach which provided success in therapy faster than before. Gingerich and Peterson [2013] compiled and evaluated an overview of studies and their results showed the effectiveness of this new way of working. The solution-focused approach was – and still is – regarded as radical because it avoids focusing on and analysing the problem. You can probably imagine that this idea is disconcerting to the traditional psychotherapeutic world.

The collected findings have been described in literature many times and have also been applied in other areas. Examples include, among others, de Jong and Berg [2012] in brief therapy, Lueger and Korn [2006] in leadership, Meier and Szabó [2008] in coaching, Bamberger [2010] in counselling, Lueger [2014] in pedagogy and even in software testing [Schirmer, 2014].

1.5 Solution Focus and the Agile world

On closer examination, agile thinking and solution-focused coaching share some similarities.

- We have already mentioned the statement Steve de Shazer often made about the solution-focused approach in his workshops: "It's simple, but not easy". Sutherland [2013] made a very similar statement on Scrum: "Scrum is easy to understand, but hard to implement".
- The tenth principle of the Agile Manifesto [AgileManifesto 2001] is: "Simplicity – the art of maximising the amount of work not done – is essential". Steve de Shazer, who was also looking for simplicity leading to success, might have turned this sentence into: "Simplicity – maximise the number of words not said", therefore making it usable for solution-focused teaching.
- Both agile and solution-focused approaches derive from observing successful behaviour. Both are revolutionary in the sense that new and radical views and practices replaced prevailing ones. Values and principles are in the centre of both approaches.
- Both are about the interaction of two parties – of a client or coaching client and a service provider, i.e. the agile team or the coach. The two parties influence each other and, as a result, a unique relationship forms between them.
- For successful cooperation, the parties need to trust each other. The coaching client relies on the coach's support, methodical leadership and discretion. The client trusts the agile team to perform high-quality work which corresponds to the existing professional possibilities.
- In both the agile and the solution-focused world, people are in a dynamic environment which they also influence with each other's behaviour. In this sense, both solution focus and agility are systemic. If, for instance, new features of the software are published, both competitors and users react to

those features, and thus change the future path of software development. This is similar to the solution-focused approach. If the coaching client changes their behaviour, their fellow human beings will react to this change, which will then in turn have an influence on the coaching client's behaviour.

- The focus of both approaches is on the client's success. The client's needs and concerns are paramount. The client is responsible for the goal and is the only one who can say whether they have achieved it. Close cooperation with the client is a fundamental component of success, both in the agile and the solution-focused world.

- Continuous dynamics influence the way of working as well. Koerner [2005] writes that representatives of both approaches work in coherent units, for instance. In the agile world, those units are called iterations or Sprints which last typically one to four weeks. In coaching, however, such units take only one to several hours. In both approaches, each unit has its own goal which contributes to achieving a higher goal.

- Both models are strongly empirical. The first step is to find out where you are at the moment and where you are headed. Then, the next steps are planned. The clients are trusted to execute the steps. Afterwards, the cycle starts all over again, until there is no need for further improvements on the way towards the goal. The client finally decides when cooperation comes to an end. Therefore, each session could also be the last one. In coaching, this means that the client feels confident that they can take further steps on their own.

1.6 The Agile Team

AgileManifesto [2001] postulates four values and twelve principles for successful agile software development. It states:

"We are uncovering better ways of developing software by doing it and helping others do it. Through this work we have come to value:

- individuals and interactions over processes and tools,
- working software over comprehensive documentation,
- customer collaboration over contract negotiation,
- responding to change over following a plan.

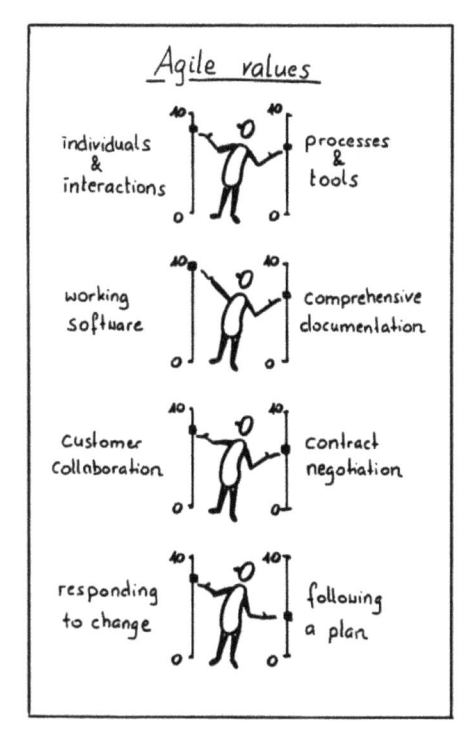

That is, while there is value in the items on the right, we value the items on the left more."

A lot of companies and teams already work in an agile way according to these values and the twelve principles, or want to do so.

> ### *Depicting agility*
>
> Often, only one slider is used for depicting the value pairs that belong together. This gives the wrong impression, which is that if there is more of one value, there must be less of the other value. 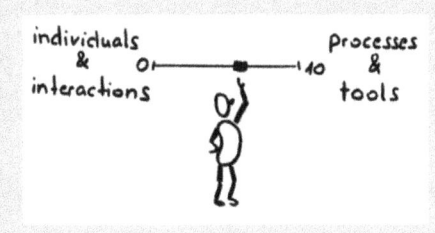
>
> This is not what it means, however. To make it clear that these values are independent, we suggest using two single sliders as you can see in the figures Agile values figure above.

One of the characteristics of *agile teams* is that they operate independently within a given setting. This means that they have the skills required to carry out an assignment and that they are able and enabled to effectively combine these skills in their joint work without external influences or directives. They rely on each other, fill in for each other if necessary, and both know and follow their own rules for optimum cooperation.

This is a good idea but not new. In sectors other than the software industry, such as automotive engineering, autonomous teams have also been established more or less successfully. The question is, however: how do *agile teams* work best? What conditions are necessary to work successfully as a team with its own authority? How can such conditions be created? Our experience with solution-focused coaching is very helpful for us when we work with *agile teams*. We will show you how we work with such teams to promote cooperation, agility and success.

1.7 The Agile Coach

The term Agile Coach is increasingly used as a professional title. On 16th March 2019, there were 716 job advertisements for Agile Coaches in the United Kingdom on LinkedIn. Often, companies also search for a Scrum Coach at the same time and some companies use the two terms as synonyms. The advertisements describe the tasks of an Agile Coach as follows:

- Promoting the agile mindset
- Implementing agile methods
- Supporting and counselling the Scrum teams and developers concerning the use of agile methods
- Supporting cooperation with the Product Owner
- Being available with answers in case of questions from the departments
- Steering several teams
- Being a strategic business partner
- Providing assistance in conflict situations
- Professional management of meetings for optimum goal achievement
- Analysing and supporting the improvement of (agile) development processes
- Ensuring transparency in the quality of results delivered

- Further developing the agile approach in the company
- Leading by example
- Actively contributing to agile development beyond organisational boundaries and in various hierarchical levels, acting as a change agent of sustainable cultural change
- Designing and carrying out training courses and workshops
- Acting as a mentor for new employees
- Coaching on agile methods.

Agile Coaching is a form of consulting. In Champion et al., [1990], the authors distinguish the following consulting roles:

- Reflective observer
- Technical adviser
- Hands-on expert
- Facilitator
- Teacher
- Modeller
- Counsellor
- Coach
- Partner.

An *Agile Coach* observes, gives feedback, promotes learning and teaches others. They support the team in its effective communication, cooperation and managing difficult situations [Davies & Sedley, 2010]. In doing so, they are repeatedly challenged as a content expert. According to Adkins [2010], you can call yourself an *Agile Coach* if you

- have introduced agile practices in teams,
- have formed new agile teams,
- have accompanied single team members,
- have accompanied an entire team,
- have accompanied Product Owners,
- have supported outsiders,
- have accompanied a team through changes,

- have put a team on the road to top performance,
- put the ideas of a team above your own,
- can control yourself,
- have led through conflicts,
- have improved yourself,
- contribute to society.

If you reconsider this description of what an Agile Coach should do and be able to do and if you take it seriously, you might conclude that one person alone can hardly meet all of the requirements. Professional Agile Coaches know their strengths and limits, will be transparent about them and will seek support if necessary.

So how does a content expert for agile, strategic, technical and conflict-solving procedures fit the image of an omni-partial coach, with the unintentional attitude of not-knowing and the decision-making strength of a leader acting as a role model? If, for instance, a conflict over the introduction of pair programming arises, how will the Agile Coach behave when they have been hired to introduce eXtreme programming in the company?

We want to take this opportunity to present our personal view of the Agile Coach profession and leave it up to you to what extent you agree with us:

> ### *The Agile Coach*
>
> is an expert for agile methodologies, their principles and their components. The coach puts this knowledge into service for organisations and teams to sustainably support them in their development towards higher effectiveness and satisfaction. In doing so, the coach's goal is to strengthen independent solution competence as well as to trust in this competence and, therefore, the clients' self-confidence. The coach builds upon the knowledge and expertise of the clients appreciatively and develops an individual approach together with them. If the coach experiences a role conflict or is not able to meet the requirements, they will immediately acknowledge this circumstance and actively arrange support.

Solution Focus for the *Agile* Coach

Adkins [2010] as well as Kaltenecker & Myllerup [2011] argue that Agile Coaches can learn essential skills from coaches working systemically. The solution-focused approach we present in this book, which is a systemic approach as well, can be helpful for Agile Coaches in a lot of their roles.

Some tasks require additional knowledge. For the role of a teacher, for instance, the idea of the potential-focused pedagogy can be exciting and useful [Lueger, 2014].

For Adkins [2010], the Agile Coach is also a problem solver and conflict navigator. However, in our view it is up to the team and other people involved to solve problems, while the coach has a supporting role only. When resolving conflicts, the coach acts as a facilitator while the content-related expertise remains with the conflicting parties.

1.8 Team coaching

Since this book is about team coaching, the first question is: what exactly is meant by the term *coaching*. There are a lot of different descriptions in literature and on the internet. In this book, we use the following definition:

> ### *What is coaching?*
>
> Coaching is an individual, interactive, time-limited, and trusting cooperation of experts that takes place voluntarily and in a professional context. The coach, as an expert for the coaching process, has no role concerning the content and always handles the information received carefully and discreetly. The coaching client, who is, in turn, the expert on the content and the goal, is supported by the coach with specific methods aiming to utilise the coaching client's existing resources. Coaching can be used to help individuals, groups and teams.

Perhaps you do not want to be a coach in the sense of this definition? Maybe you want to get to know coaching tools to support your colleagues and teams in the professional environment in the best possible way? Or you are already a coach and would like to find out whether you can learn something new here? With this book, we want to make all of this possible for you.

The challenge in team coaching

To describe the differences between working with a team and coaching a person, we first would like to focus on what a team is. According to Hochreiter [2012], a team is characterised as follows:

- Teams develop around a common goal which can only be achieved together. This goal is the team's purpose.
- Each team member expects a personal benefit from their participation, a benefit they would not be able to achieve without being part of the team.
- In high-performance teams, we can observe that they have fun working together and that they experience joy and ease at work and in their cooperation.
  The result is positive dynamics, a team spirit [Owen, 2008], which ensures that success seems to come automatically.

The conclusion is: only the pursuit of a common goal turns a group into a team. It is therefore essential that all team members agree the desired future state together. A lot of companies, departments or teams which show less personal drive and motivation among the employees lack a common goal. This does not mean that management dictates the goal. Rather, a vision must be created together. This is the only way employees can be sure that they are integral members of the whole organisation, not just performing assistants.

One way to achieve this is Agile Chartering [Larsen & Nies, 2016], a workshop which aims to develop a joint vision of the product and of cooperation. The result is a lightweight document (sometimes a few flipcharts only) which describes the cornerstones of the project, the meaning of the work and the cooperation. This includes, among other things, the name of the project, the names of the team members, the product vision, the project mission, common values and principles, working agreements as well as project limits and mutual expectations [Larsen, 2004].

It is difficult, however, to find – and maintain – common goals. Merl [2012] writes that each system – that also means every team – strives to improve its processes at all times. This has an unfavourable effect on finding the common goal because each team member tries to harmonise their personal goals with the team's goal. So, whenever the system changes something, the individual person is challenged to adapt, and vice versa. This requires strength and endurance. Therefore, a team member sometimes renounces the fulfilment of their own needs in favour of the team's goals. Another possibility is that personal goals are pursued without consideration of the team's goals. Both ways cause damage – to the team and to the individual person. As a result, the achievement of common goals is impeded in both scenarios.

Merl sees the key to the solution in the knowledge that every human being strives for recognition of their own abilities and as a person. The higher the appreciation of the single team members is perceived, the greater is their willingness to cooperate and their energy for productive participation in the system. As a result, it is more frequently possible for individual team members to harmonise their own goals with team goals and, therefore, to contribute to the team's success.

So, team coaching is primarily about honest appreciation and recognising the needs and abilities of the team members. Only when this is successful, can other issues such as negotiating team goals and team rules or defining concrete next steps be dealt with successfully.

Rules of team coaching

The rules of team coaching basically follow the rules of individual coaching; however, due to the number of people present (>1), several other things must be taken into account. When working with groups or teams, the coach needs to keep an eye on additional focus points and also needs to use different intervention methods.

After all, demands placed on team coaching are high: an attractive goal needs to be found. For this, an appreciative and open atmosphere and discussion culture are required. Team members' problems are to be given space, without exceeding the time limit set for the meeting. All team members are to participate actively – on a voluntary basis. Finally, it is also about defining steps which are implemented so improvements can be made. Only, who exactly is to implement these steps? The distribution of tasks must be fair, of course, whatever that means…

You can see: successfully coaching a team is often challenging. This book aims to provide you with some tools which have served us well in a lot of situations.

2 Solution-focused coaching

> *"Our wishes are presentiments of the abilities that lie in us, harbingers of what we will be able to accomplish. What we can do and want to do is projected in our imagination quite outside ourselves and in the future; we feel a desire for what we already have inwardly. Passionate anticipation thus transforms what is really possible into dreamed reality. If such a way lies decidedly in our nature, every step out of development will fulfil a part of the first wish; under favourable circumstances on a straight path, under unfavourable circumstances in an indirect way, from which we will always come back to the other."*
>
> [Goethe 1812, p. 419]

The solution-focused approach is about what Goethe described as early as 1812, namely to imagine the preferred future. Anyone who wants to achieve a goal knows instinctively that they can achieve it. A clear idea of what exactly needs to be different makes it easier to achieve the goal. Coaching then only has to focus on how to take the first steps. After all, anyone who really has a clear desire will head towards it anyway – with or without coaching.

Thus solution-focused thinking concentrates on as many details of the preferred future as possible, while the problem focused approach spends a lot of time and energy on the origins of a current situation. Therefore, the question *why* a situation is like it is is replaced by the questions *which goal* is to be achieved and *what purpose* the achievement of the goal will serve. Attention is especially paid to all the small instances from the past which point towards the preferred future. If you recognise that a lot has already worked well, the confidence needed to make the next steps concrete and to implement them will increase.

Avoiding analysis of the origin of a problem saves a lot of time. Therefore, Solution Focus is a so-called *brief approach* which allows for effective results in a shorter period of time.

2.1 Problem and solution

Solution Focus is not problem-phobic at all! The problem[1] itself is of great importance and significance. Without problems, we would live in a world without any reason for change or improvement. There would be no research and, therefore, no progress. Reflecting on goals and how to achieve them would be redundant if everyone was satisfied with everything. Last but not least, without problems, there is no need to focus on solutions. Problems and difficulties are the engine for improvement, modernisation and progress. The word *solution* is used in a special sense in this approach, meaning what is wanted instead of the problem, which we like to call the *preferred future*.

Steve de Shazer said that anyone who has a problem also has an idea of what could be better – that is, an idea of the solution. If this person did not have this idea of a solution, they would not have a problem, but a fixed condition which they would have to come to terms with [de Shazer, 1988].

If a Product Owner, for example, thinks that a development team is working too slowly, this means that the Product Owner thinks the team can work faster. The Product Owner might even have a concrete idea what needs to change in the team, so the team can develop its full potential. It is not relevant whether the Product Owner's assumptions are correct or not. If the Product Owner had a reasonable explanation for the current speed of work, however, this speed would be an acceptable condition and not a problem. As a result, the Product Owner might reduce the number of orders accordingly or extend the time for carrying them out.

So, what is the best way to deal with a problem once it has been discovered? You can put it on a pedestal and use it as an excuse for a lot of other problems which appear in the shadow of the first problem and which make you feel as if you were at the mercy of the situation. You can also talk about the problem again and again and in detail, to receive confirmation that your problem is indeed particularly difficult and leaves you powerless – you probably know such a situation. Another popular way to treat a problem is to dig into the problem's origins and search for a culprit. Unfortunately, however, none of these strategies will provide a solution to the problem.

Solution Focus takes a different approach: the problem – as well as its effects – is appreciated as a catalyst for defining a solution. The presence of the problem

---

[1] Borrowed from the Latin word problema in the 16th century – an undecided task proposed for solution; a controversial question. From the Greek word problēma (pro+bállein) which means to put forth, to throw forward, to put forward (see: en.wiktionary.org & en.oxforddictionaries.com).

is unconditionally accepted as a harbinger of change – an improvement – which will take place. Working with a solution-focused approach means, first and foremost, to take a different perspective.

We invite you to discover this new perspective with the six attitudes and positions as well as eight principles we describe below. Please check how well this perspective suits you or whether you have already taken it – consciously or unconsciously.

2.2 Six fundamental coaching attitudes and positions

First, six basic attitudes of solution-focused team coaching are described below. They are helpful in many situations of interpersonal communication.

2.2.1 The not-knowing position

Everything we have experienced in our lives so far makes us feel like experts in many areas. What we hear or see reminds us of a similar situation we have already experienced in the past. Therefore, we classify the new experience as *"just like back then – I already know this situation"* in our brain and react accordingly.

This classification is helpful and important in many situations; when it comes to being able to act fast in dangerous situations, for example. In other situations, or in conversations, however, this classification often prevents us from being open to and curious about the new situation. Old experiences mask the fact that they are different and, as a result, are misinterpreted as truth.

Solution-focused people are aware of this fact. They accept their memories, put them aside and, when asking questions, remain open to and curious about answers they did not expect. As a result, they switch from questions which force the answers they expect, to open questions, which give their conversational partners the opportunity to think and find their own answers. This requires confidence, restraint and patience – and, therefore, is the most difficult inner attitude to acquire.

So, if someone reaches out to you with a problem, we recommend not offering the answer immediately. Instead, ask first what the goal of the person with the problem is.

Practical example of the not-knowing position

Let us take, for example, a team which has repeatedly failed to reach their Sprint goals. As an Agile Coach, you could hand out good advice based on your own experience on how – from your point of view – the performance of the team could be improved. You could suggest, for instance, that the team includes pair programming and test automation more often. It is possible but not very likely that something will actually change.

With the not-knowing position, however, you would probably ask instead what the team needs from *their own* point of view to be able to achieve the Sprint goals better. In this case, the team's goal does not necessarily involve working faster.

When asked how they could achieve their Sprint goals better, the team members might answer that they need more details about the requirements and a view of the customer's overall picture into which the present product needs to be embedded. It would therefore be helpful for the team to be able to talk to the customer more often.

The team usually knows very well what they need right now. You can rely on that. Asking about their needs saves time, energy and nerves – especially if your advice is not implemented because the team considers it inappropriate or not useful enough to improve their situation.

The longer you have known someone, the harder it is to adopt a not-knowing position. The more experience we share with other people, the more we believe that we know the other person well and know what they mean or need for their problem. In new teams, which do not have a shared history yet, you can successfully avoid misunderstandings with the not-knowing position.

Agile Coaches are experts in agile approaches. They are familiar with the interrelated effects of different meetings, techniques and procedures; they can provide their knowledge. However, it is worth paying close attention to customer wishes, team needs and general circumstances and taking them seriously instead of focusing on known responses. The not-knowing position helps to learn all relevant details.

2.2.2 Everyone is an expert in their situation

You may be familiar with the following situation: someone gives you well-meant advice; instead of taking it gratefully and being happy about it, you get angry because the advice does not suit you and will not improve your current situation. This does not come as a surprise. Only you know what your circumstances are and what you need. And only you know what is right for you and what is not.

In an agile environment, the Prime Directive of Retrospectives [Kerth, 2001] is an established approach to recall this attitude:

> **The Prime Directive**
>
> "Regardless of what we discover, we understand and truly believe that everyone did the best job they could, given what they knew at the time, their skills and abilities, the resources available and the situation at hand."

Do you believe in this attitude? If not, just try for once acting "as if". What would be different? With this attitude, you would acknowledge the team's expertise. This promotes the dedication and motivation of individual team members. And your intention would be to change inappropriate conditions – not the people.

You can rely on the fact that everyone who has a problem also has an idea that there must be some kind of better. Otherwise, they would probably consider a situation unpleasant but not problematic. Consequently, any advice you offer can only be suitable for others in absolutely exceptional cases and purely by chance.

In solution-focused work, you can ask questions in many ways. Questions help others to find their own solutions. When the person who has the problem has an idea of a solution, it will meet all the requirements to be effective. The probability of success increases.

Practical example of "Everyone is an expert in their situation"

Backlog refinement meetings are probably a suitable example here. In such a meeting, team members are to give tentative information on the scope and the expected duration of the upcoming product development. For this purpose, they rely on their experience and knowledge. They consider given conditions, possible delays such as holidays which are already known, competencies existing or missing in the team and much more. Nobody else can make a better estimate. Only the team that will actually do the work afterwards has all the information needed and can include it into their considerations.

Those working with teams must make sure that standards and guidelines are met. Within these defined limits, however, they can and should give the employees enough space to develop and implement their own suitable responses to their problems. Mainly in phases of intense work, it seems to be easier and more efficient to provide answers or even implement them so that work can continue. However, we recommend deciding in such situations what is economically more profitable in the long term: to correct all mistakes or to support others so they can deliver better results in terms of quality.

With the following metaphor, we want to explain the not-knowing position and the concept of everyone being an expert in their situation.

The Coconut Model

Metaphorically speaking, every one of us lives on an island. Each island is shaped by what the respective inhabitant has learned and experienced so far. Also, the island is constantly changing – because the inhabitant is constantly learning.

Who do you think knows *your* island best? Exactly! *You* know your island best – and even you might discover new corners on your own island! It is therefore completely absurd to think *somebody else* might know what *you* need. And vice versa, it is impossible for you to know what others need. All you can do is make assumptions.

We want to tell you a short story about a young girl living on a coconut tree island. She loves coconuts more than anything! A young man lives on a neighbouring oak tree island. He has never seen a coconut before. The young girl feels sorry for him and throws one of her beloved coconuts over to his island. What do you think will happen? What will the young man think when he sees the brown coconut hurtling towards him?

Right! There is a good chance he will feel threatened and take cover. In the worst case, he will even counter-attack.

On her island, the girl is completely confused and disappointed when she observes the man's unexpected behaviour. She may decide that the young man is not worth contacting again. A sad end to a story with quite a promising start.

Let us go back to the beginning. What else could the girl have done to influence what happens in a positive way?

People can build bridges between islands by asking questions. The questions help them find out enough about the other island, so they can communicate with the other person in an appropriate way.

In this story, a helpful question for building a bridge could have been: "Hello neighbour! I have wonderful coconuts! Do you want one? May I throw it over to you?" This question and the subsequent answer would have prevented a lot of misunderstandings.

Please note, however, that even if the answer to the question is "Yes, please!" and the girl throws the coconut over to the other island, she will not be entitled to decide what the young man does with the coconut! Whether he plays ball with it, sits on it or eats it – it is not the girl's decision. She can only make recommendations on how to make use of the coconut. The decision how to use the coconut is to be made by the inhabitant of this island only!

The bridge, moreover, does not entitle the girl to walk over with a spade and plant a coconut tree on the other island – even if she is convinced that the young man will benefit from the tree in the long term and does not see it yet.

Last but not least: the answer to the girl's question might also be "No!". Instead of being personally offended, the girl should assume that the young man has a good reason for his decision. He might be on a kiwi diet at the moment or allergic to coconuts. Who knows? Exactly. The young man on his island. And the best way to find out about the reason for his decision is to ask him – which would be another step towards a stable bridge for a good neighbourhood.

This story results in some important statements:

- None of us can really understand another person.
- Therefore, just hearing about a problem or a goal another person has will not make us understand them the same way the person concerned does.
- It is therefore not possible either to tell someone else what to do or to be sure that this is right for this specific person.
- The only one who really knows the problem – the goal – is the person concerned!
- The only one who knows the suitable solution and appropriate way is the person concerned, too!
- The solution is on the island of this specific person.
- Any other person can help find the solution by asking questions.

2.2.3 Patience and confidence

Patience in the context of coaching refers to patience when asking questions. Have you ever asked questions and the reaction was silence? How did you feel? What were you thinking in that moment?

Questions trigger thinking – and it might take a while until an answer is given. Sometimes it is difficult and uncomfortable to wait. However, breaking the silence by asking another question means interrupting the process of thinking which has previously been set off so skilfully. As a result, you might not receive important information. We can also see the difference between *patience* and *waiting* here.

Being patient means that, deep inside, you are hopeful and confident that there will be an answer and that the respondent just needs time to find it. The question obviously addressed an important issue or was thought-provoking. Patience and confidence make it easier to bridge the time until an answer is provided than just waiting for an answer.

People waiting for something or even *expecting* something specific are usually disappointed that nothing has happened so far – as for instance that the required code has not been written yet. This inner dissatisfaction is often perceived as a problem which needs to be solved. *Im-patience* spreads, followed by not so helpful attempts to actively find a way out of this unpleasant situation.

Therefore, an important rule for working with teams and individuals is: when you ask a question, be patient, confident and curious until you get an answer – no matter how long it takes. Maybe you want to try it! You will see that sooner or later a well-considered, sometimes even surprising, response will be given. Only if you are sure that your question was not understood or cannot be answered, will it be the right time to restate the question or change the direction of your questions. It might even feel good to have endured the silence. Enjoy it – if you want!

> ### *Practical Tip*
>
> When you ask a question, count to 20 in your mind. When you are done, start again. Be confident that the other person will say something.
>
> By doing so, you will not interrupt the other person's process of thinking. Also, as long as you are counting, you cannot hypothesise why you have not received an answer – yet.

2.2.4 Focus on resources

Pay attention to everything that works. The main aim here is to focus on the strengths and abilities instead of the flaws and weaknesses of your conversational partner or colleague. Human beings are able to decide for themselves at any given moment what they want to focus on: what is good – or what is bad.

This decision is based on expectations influenced by our own experiences. A newcomer at work might cause positive expectations (*Finally, a breath of fresh air!*) or trigger negative ones (*Great, another one who has no idea how we do things here!*).

The focus on existing skills and abilities also makes your conversational partners see what they have to change. The following exercise helps you find out resources, skills and abilities of your conversational partner within three minutes.

> ### *Sparkling Moments – after McKergow [2008a]*
>
> Ask the participants to form pairs. First, each pair decides who is *A* and who is *B*. In the first round, *A* is the speaker and *B* is the listener. The listener will have to listen attentively to what *A* says. We use the image of the giraffe by Marshall B. Rosenberg. He established the giraffe as a symbol for listening with the heart in *Nonviolent Communication* since the giraffe, in organic terms, has the biggest heart of all land animals [Rosenberg, 2015]. It is best to introduce the exercise as follows:
>
> For three minutes, *A* tells *B* about a sparkling moment in their life. Please make full use of the three minutes and explain the moment in as colourful and detailed a way as possible. *B* will listen attentively and without interruption for the whole time.
>
> After three minutes, I will give you a signal. *B* will thank *A* for sharing their sparkling moment and will then have three minutes to give feedback: *B* will tell *A* which strengths, abilities, resources and values *A* seems to have so that this sparkling moment was possible.
>
> There will be a second round with reversed roles later on. *B* will have a different task then. I will keep an eye on the time with the stopwatch, so you can determine afterwards whether finding strengths and resources is possible at all in three minutes.

> As soon as all *A*s have found the sparkling moment they want to talk about, start the exercise with "Go!" After three minutes, stop this first part of the exercise and ask all *B*s to thank the *A*s for sharing their sparkling moments. Then start the feedback round with the following words:
>
> "*B* now has three minutes to report back which strengths, abilities, resources and values *A* seems to have so that this sparkling moment was possible. Maybe start with 'It seems to me that you are the kind of person who …'. Please make full use of the three minutes. If nothing else comes to your mind, imagine I am standing behind you and ask you 'And what else?'. I am sure this will help you think of something else. *A* will listen attentively and without interruption for the whole time. Ready? Go!"
>
> Take the time again. After three minutes, end the first round and ask all *A*s to show you with their hands how much everything they just heard about themselves actually fits. For this purpose, introduce a way of working with scales:
>
> "On a scale from the upper thigh", place your hand on your upper thigh, "to the head", now lift your hand above your head. "How far would you agree to what you just heard about yourself?"

Experience has shown that a lot of resources are discovered and reported. Most hands are usually above the chin when asked for their evaluation.

We often hear about problematic and annoying stories in everyday work life. Instead of being drawn into a negative suction, it is now about paying attention to positive and helpful aspects. This makes it possible to show more understanding of the one telling their situation and, as a result, react in a more constructive manner as well.

For this purpose, the participants talk about an annoying moment in the second round. This adaptation of the exercise was developed based on Ghul [2005] and Lamarre [2005].

The scales after the second round often show an even better result than the scales after the sparkling moments. Most hands can be found above the nose.

Annoying moments

Introduce the second round as follows:

"Well – that was easy, wasn't it? When someone talks about a sparkling moment, they virtually hand their resources to you on a silver platter, right? However, what do you hear more often than sparkling moments in your professional life from your colleagues, superiors or clients?"

Get some answers and then continue as follows:

"We will exchange roles now. *B* will complain to *A* about a moment in their life for three minutes.

Again, please make full use of the three minutes and describe the moment in as much detail as possible. *A* will listen attentively and without interruptions.

After three minutes, I will give you a signal. *A* will then thank *B* for sharing the annoying moment – after all, it takes a lot of trust – and then has three minutes to report back about which strengths, abilities, resources and values *B* obviously has that they were annoyed to such an extent. What is important to *B*? What does *B* care about? Which of their values has been violated?

When the time is over, we will again determine how well finding strengths, resources and values worked."

During the reflection after the exercise, participants often say that they were able to hear the resources because they had been given the order to report them back. As a result, they were intentionally focusing on the strengths, abilities and values of the other person. What we see here is that it is possible to draw positive conclusions about people from a negative story.

> **Practical Tips**
>
> Pay attention to positive and helpful aspects even when you listen to other people describing a problem or a troubling moment!
>
> For team development processes, we recommend sparkling moments in both rounds, as intended in Mark McKergow's original version.

2.2.5 Omni-partiality

When there are disagreements in your team, the time has come for you as a facilitator to help find a way forward. People need to feel safe to be able to open up to others. It requires trust to disclose our thoughts, needs and wishes without putting ourselves at a disadvantage. Only if all the team members are willing to share what they think and feel will team coaching be successful in the end.

A lot of people have had negative experiences in their lives with team or group situations. Some had the experience of their statements not being appreciated or taken seriously. Others had to surrender to loud or dominating people during discussions. And yet others found themselves in a situation where suddenly everyone turned against them – and not even the coach was willing or able to provide the necessary protection against verbal abuse.

The coach has a key position in team coaching processes and is the one who has to make sure that all statements are *equally valid*. To do this, the coach needs to adopt the attitude of omni-partiality and needs to be convinced that each contribution is correct and justified from the point of view of the participant concerned. This way, the team members will learn quickly that it pays to actively contribute to a way forward, and that the coach will also perceive this contribution as positive. This is how openness and trust develop. Establishing mutual understanding and consensus-building will then work well.

2.2.6 Confidentiality

The issue of confidentiality is very important in team coaching as it provides for safety, trust and openness. Everything the team discusses stays in the room and is not passed on by either the coach or other participants to the outside world – unless otherwise agreed before the discussion.

Even one single violation of this important rule can destroy the trust and openness among the team members beyond repair. Future team coaching situations will then be ill-fated. Even if another coach intends to work with the team later on, the team will react with mistrust at first, making the coach's work significantly more difficult.

Individual content can be passed on only as an exception to the rule and only with the consent of all participants. This could be the case when keeping important pieces of information a secret would seriously harm people or the company. If there is no consent in the team on passing on the information, however, it will be necessary to find a different way together to prevent the imminent damage.

2.3 Eight important principles

These attitudes are now complemented by eight important principles of the solution-focused approach. The better we succeed in acting according to these principles, the faster and more easily we will achieve our goals.

2.3.1 Focus on the preferred future

The word *focus* has a significant meaning in this principle. It reminds us to paint the picture of a preferred future with high intensity. The more detailed and colourful this picture of our future is, and the more knowledge we have of what will be different and better in the future and what impact that will have, the more likely it is that we will get there. This is what is meant by the word *solution* in this approach.

A vague idea of the preferred future is like a thin red elastic thread. It shows the direction but can easily tear as soon as an obstacle needs to be overcome. A clear picture, however, is like a thick elastic rope. It will not tear even if it is stretched; it makes sure that we keep connected with our preferred future.

The solution-focused approach helps to clarify our vision by using a lot of questions. Formulating directions and goals constitutes a fundamental part of the coaching process, also in terms of time.

This focus, however, might sometimes involve the discovery of undesirable effects. This is important, because now the goal can be adjusted in good time and resistance can be prevented.

In practice, this principle is helpful in all conversations which are about describing the goal. Think of planning meetings, team development processes or change projects, for example. Requirement talks held with clients are another good example: the detailed description of the preferred future, which the client hopes to achieve by using a certain product, can lead to relevant information which otherwise might not have been taken into consideration.

> **Practical Tip**
>
> Transport your employees mentally into a better future with solution talk. By doing so, they will pretend that the desired goal has already been achieved. This method allows for a more comprehensive idea of what is to be achieved and of possible effects.

2.3.2 If it works, do more of it

What has worked well before will probably work again. This principle aims to build confidence that the way towards the goal does not start from scratch; instead, we can build on what we already know. Three implicit aspects are behind this principle:

- Apparently, things have been done properly in the past. So, it is obviously possible to achieve improvement actively and by oneself.
- No major creativity is required for developing initial ideas on how to achieve the desired goals. After all, we already know some things about what works well.
- It is actually not necessary to do everything differently to reach the preferred future. A lot of what has already been done can and should remain unchanged.

To find out what works well, however, we have to focus on exactly that. If we always look for mistakes, we will have difficulties finding and using these valuable resources.

> **Practical Tip**
>
> Whenever you try to find an answer to a problem, ask yourself what is already working. Collect as many small, well-working aspects as possible and build your next steps on this information.

A practical example of "If it works, do more of it"

Do you know about the origins of eXtreme programming? In 1996, Kent Beck was brought in to consult on a project which, at that time, was beyond the originally given limits regarding both time and budget. Beck knew from his own experience which factors were helpful in software development. He dared to dial them to the extreme – hence the name eXtreme programming.

He knew that sub-step testing provides valuable information for continued work. Taken to the extreme, this means that tests are written even before the code. As a result, the occurrence of new functions as well as design-related problems with regard to linking and cohesion was reduced, and trust in other people's work was built. Another successful measure to improve quality in software development was to carry out code reviews. Driven to extremes, this could be done by working constantly in pairs. *Pair programming* was born.

Kent Beck clearly focused on the well-working areas of his work. He made use of them and the result was a completely new way of working [Beck, 1999; Beck & Andres, 2004].

2.3.3 If it does not work (anymore), do something different

You may wonder: 'And if what worked in the past no longer works? Can this way of thinking be a depressing deadlock?'

There are, of course, circumstances which prevent working strategies being repeated. And yet, this is about learning from the past, too. It rarely makes sense to repeat an attempt at something which did not work once – or no longer works – because you hope that the good idea might prove right again at some point.

Maybe you know the situation: if it seems logical that a certain approach has worked, we are very willing to repeatedly attempt the same thing even if it does not work, blaming random circumstances for failure. Only when we get a bloody nose – metaphorically speaking – are we more willing to think about taking a completely different path towards the desired goal.

To find a new way, it is, of course, necessary to know the desired goal. And it is helpful to be brave and open to creative and completely new lines of thoughts. Actually, such thoughts do not need to sound realistic at first – they can even be crazy, irrational or fantastic. The wildest ideas often conceal creative and practical options.

> **Practical Tip**
>
> Whenever a chosen path does not work out, make yourself aware of your goal again. Then it will be easier for you to find a new way and see the first failure as *learning*.

> **A practical example of "If it does not work, do something different"**
>
> The history of projects proves the truth of this statement. Ways have been developed to improve the accuracy of project planning. There were Change Control Boards to manage change. Increasingly heavyweight processes were designed to make projects more controllable and predictable. However, all this and more did not have a significant impact on the goal of making projects more successful and thus increasing customer satisfaction.
>
> Only abandoning the well-trodden path and focusing on the actual goal made a rethink possible. Essential success factors of projects were rediscovered. The focus shifted to increased cooperation with customers and employee satisfaction. This is how agile work came about.
>
> Today, the establishment of agile approaches is too often regarded as a goal in its own right. However, these ways were developed individually and were tailored to the respective context. So, if the known paths of others do not work for you, take a step back. Inquire about your current goal, then find the style that suits you, your teams, and your organisation.

2.3.4 Small steps can lead to big changes

The agile approach uses small steps and frequent feedback loops to adjust product development and teamwork constantly; this allows for reaction to changes. Agile processes make use of changes for the competitive advantage of the client [AgileManifesto, 2001]. A lot of small adjustments can lead to big changes when, for example, features are left out or new ideas are integrated into a product.

The same applies to communication and relationships: it is often the small things that lead to big changes. A different seating position, for instance, or different light conditions or other changes in a room can lead to a different discussion atmosphere. Just sincerely saying thank you can change relationships. An honest smile can make the whole day better. We will describe a lot of small changes in the course of this book; you can try and test them and see which impact they have.

> **Practical Tip**
>
> In his book *2 Second Lean*, Akers [2016] recommends finding a way to save only 2 seconds in your daily routine every day. Ralph is diligently doing it. He might not find an opportunity to save 2 seconds every day, but he has managed to save many resources so far.
>
> In chapter 4 of his book *59 Seconds: Think a little, change a lot*, Wiseman [2009] shows how even small things can increase human creativity considerably. Hang up appropriate modern pictures, have plants in your office, offer your employees a desk at the window and a view of trees or grass, or provoke unusual thoughts, for instance of a punk with a colourful Mohawk hairstyle, before a problem is to be solved.

2.3.5 The solution is not necessarily related to the problem

Technical systems essentially require searching for the root cause of an existing problem to find lasting solutions. Working with people, however, is different. In solution-focused work with people we build on the assumption that problems and solutions are not directly related to each other. Steve de Shazer used to say that the solution does not care about the problem. This means that the exact knowledge of the origins of a problem, conflict or unsatisfactory situation does not help define steps towards improving the situation. Questions such as "Who is to blame?", "How could this happen?", "What mistakes have been made?" etc. will not improve the current situation.

You may wonder how the sentence "*We should learn from our mistakes*" fits in here? We can, of course, learn from mistakes made in the past when we think about what would have to change to make something work better today. This is how we learn from the past for present situations.

A developer who is not ready for pair programming might be a good example here. We could try to find out why the developer does not want to do pair programming. Maybe they had a conflict with their programming partner or negative cooperation experiences which they have not come to terms with yet; or they might simply have an ongoing bet with a colleague about whether they can get away with it. None of this, however, will solve the problem of the *developer rejecting pair programming*.

We might ask them, however, what would have to be different in the current situation, so they could commit to pair programming. We would probably find out that the developer needs clear information on when and for how long the pair programming is to take place, so they know when they will have time to pursue their own agenda again.

Maybe the answer is that the developer wants to pick their own partner to make sure that the two of them are more or less on the same page when it comes to know-how.

Whatever the reason for the current problem, what we need to know to make progress is only the desired goal, so we are able to describe ways to achieve this goal. Ideas regarding possible ways mostly come from experiences, namely the experience of the person who describes the problem and wants to achieve the goal.

> **Practical Tip**
>
> Yet, in many situations, most people like to start talking about their problems first. We recommend that you listen to their explanations, take them seriously and appreciate the problem. The art lies in not asking questions to understand the problem – such questions would only lead further into the problem; instead show some understanding for the misery first and then ask what would be different if the problem were solved.

2.3.6 Solution-talk creates solutions – problem-talk creates problems

The most important instrument in solution-focused work is language. "The limits of my language mean the limits of my world", Wittgenstein [1922] wrote. This means that we can change the limits of our world with language and, as a result, also the limits of our own reality. After all, language creates reality.

The more detail you give in describing a situation, the more it seems as if you were right in the middle of it. Maybe you have already experienced the following: when you talk about a negative situation from the past and explain it in detail, you start having the same physical sensations you had back then. Even the reactions of your body are similar to the reactions in the past. It is as if you are in the same situation once again.

This also works for situations you have never experienced before. When you give it a try, however, focus on positive things; the more detail you include in the picture of your preferred future, the better you can feel in your body how you will feel in your preferred future. Your breathing may get calmer and you will adopt a relaxed posture.

This sensation will then pull you towards your goal, like a magnet. Only if we define what the goal, i.e. the preferred future, should look like, we will also find a way towards this goal and the preferred future and eventually reach them.

> **Practical Tip**
>
> Always ask for details regarding the goal and its effects. Never ask for details regarding the problem. In doing so, you will make your employees adopt a positive and solution-focused attitude.

False memories

When someone is asked about the details of a problem, they are at risk of developing false memories as a result [Loftus, 1998]. There will be different answers depending on how the questions on the details are framed.

As early as 1974, Loftus and Palmer [1974] published a study in which participants had to describe a car accident. They were shown a film about an accident. After watching the film, the participants had to answer several questions about the accident. Their answers about the cars' speed were different, depending on whether they were asked about the cars' speed when they *smashed* or when they *had contact* with each other. During interviews held later on, some participants even remembered broken glass on the ground although there was no glass in the original film.

Loftus' research results further encourage us to prefer solution-talk over problem-talk whenever possible. However, if it is necessary to stick to problem-talk, for instance, when a team is to be given the opportunity to get their problems off their chest, please be careful about how you formulate the questions.

2.3.7 No problem occurs all the time – use the exceptions

The language describing a problem often contains words such as always, never, constantly, permanently. These and similar terms indicate an unchanging existence, a stability of the problem described. However, there is no such thing as stability in life. Each moment is unique and cannot be repeated. The intensity of an existing problem therefore varies from moment to moment. The problem might seem huge and serious at one point, while it might be barely perceived at another.

Searching for moments in which the problem was smaller and easier can indicate which circumstances were responsible for the experienced *better*. This includes solution approaches which can be used for achieving the preferred future, that is a permanent *better* of the current problematic situation.

Usually, the solution-focused view is directed towards the future rather than the past. It is worth making an exception here.

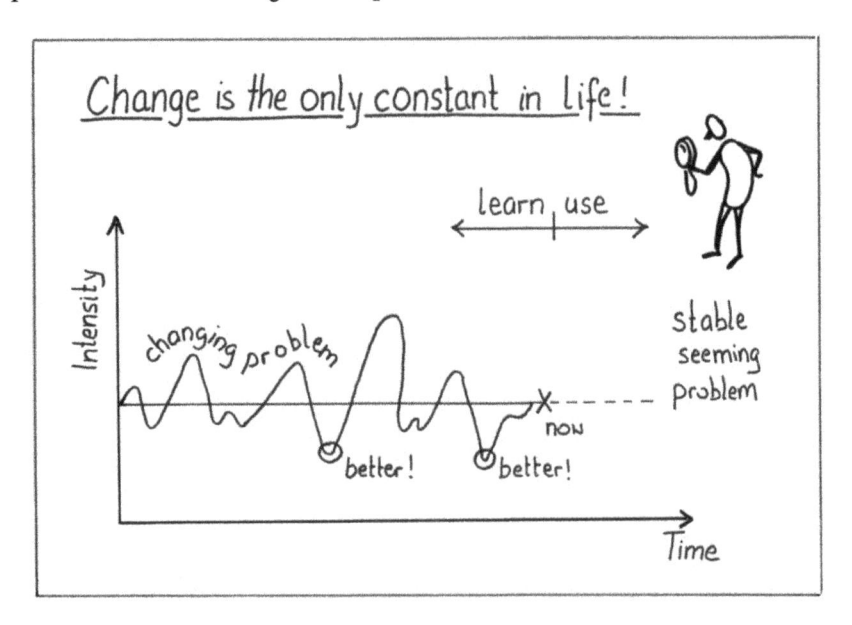

Practical Tip

Whenever you describe a problem, use words such as *so far or still* instead of stabilising words such as *always* or *never*. By doing so, you will incidentally initiate much more willingness to change – not only within yourself.

> **A practical example of "use the exceptions"**
>
> Successful projects are a particularly interesting exception in software development. How are they different to failing projects? An example: in his article, Coplien [1994] writes that the *Borland Quattro Pro® for Windows project* was successful because, among other things, the development was designed based on daily meetings in which all team members participated.
>
> Sutherland [2014] writes that these findings led him to the idea of the daily stand-up in scrum.

2.3.8 If it ain't broke, don't fix it

Sometimes we observe something that we think is wrong. A programmer, for example, may find double entries of a method in the system. They may then try to remedy the problem as quickly as possible. In this case, that means that they have to carry out refactoring. The problem is that they can only see the alleged mistake from their own perspective and, therefore, do not know all motivations which led to it. If they had asked about the double entries, they would have probably been told that the respective developer had good reason to act like that, for example, to remove dependencies.

Not everything that seems to be broken or wrong at first glance actually is. Often there is good and understandable explanation for a certain procedure. This explanation, however, is only given to somebody who asks for it. And if there is no understandable explanation, with a good team culture the joint development of a way forward will be more successful in the long term.

So, if the mistake is simply fixed, at least one new problem arises: either the developer feels misunderstood or ignored, which might lead to an argument or even a conflict between the two people involved, or the developer does not learn what needs to be done instead and will probably make the same mistake again.

This is also about identifying our own assumptions and asking what is behind the observed actions. In doing so, we can avoid misunderstandings and prevent individuals from being hurt.

> **Practical Tip**
>
> Whenever you find a mistake in the actions of others, the assessment *mistake* is an assumption. Please ask what is behind the observed action to avoid misunderstandings and prevent individuals from being hurt.

2.4 Attitudes and principles at a glance

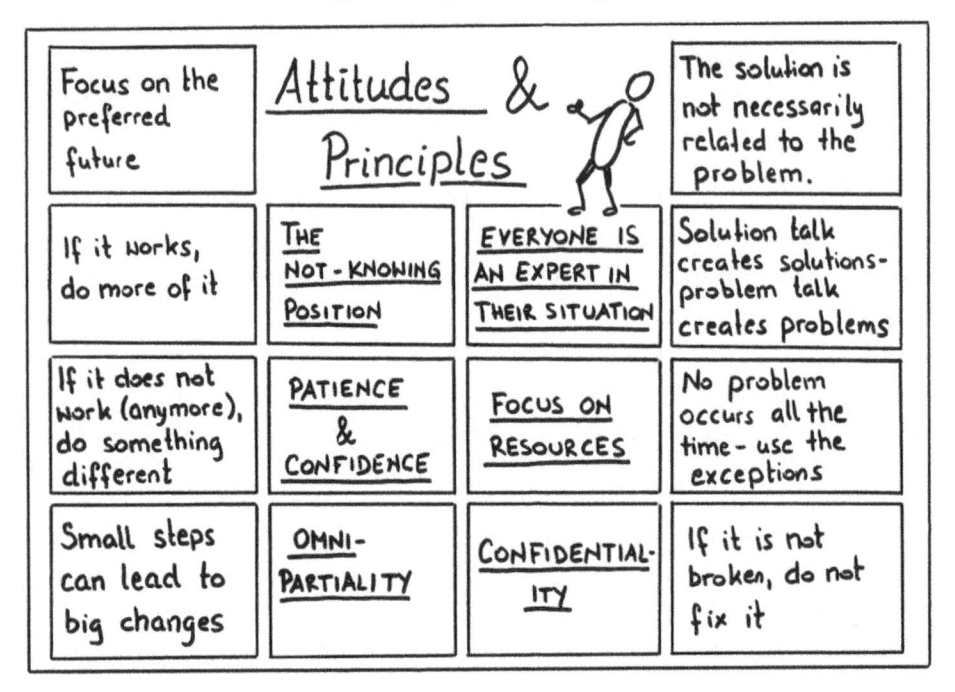

Focus on the preferred future	**Attitudes & Principles**		The solution is not necessarily related to the problem.
If it works, do more of it	THE NOT-KNOWING POSITION	EVERYONE IS AN EXPERT IN THEIR SITUATION	Solution talk creates solutions - problem talk creates problems
If it does not work (anymore), do something different	PATIENCE & CONFIDENCE	FOCUS ON RESOURCES	No problem occurs all the time - use the exceptions
Small steps can lead to big changes	OMNI-PARTIALITY	CONFIDENTIALITY	If it is not broken, do not fix it

The attitudes, positions and principles of the solution-focused approach form the basis for the effective use of the coaching techniques described later. No matter how brilliantly a coaching question may be posed – if, for example, the not-knowing position is missing – we will not hear the answer provided by our conversational partner, but the answer we expect.

Speaking of coaching questions – the most common form of intervention in solution-focused coaching is the question. Framing questions in a way that they are actually solution-focused, i.e. directing the coaching client's thoughts towards their preferred future, what is working and positive differences, is almost an art form. The following chapter will give you an insight into asking solution-focused questions. You might already use some of the mentioned questioning techniques or similar ones in your working life.

2.5 Self-reflection

- What was exciting/new/helpful in this chapter?
- When and with whom would you like to focus on existing strengths and abilities in the near future? What effects will that have in the best-case scenario?
- When, specifically, can you use the not-knowing position? What will you probably get out of it? What benefits might others have?
- What does the Coconut Model mean for your work routine?

2.6 Experiments and exercises

- First thing tomorrow morning, find at least five opportunities to thank somebody and do it. The aim is to focus on small things like somebody holding the lift doors open for you, handing you the pen you are looking for or offering you a seat on the bus.
- Start the next meeting by making a list together about what is working well in your cooperation, the current working phase or whatever the meeting is about. Do you observe a difference to other meetings in the course of this meeting?
- Choose any day in the next week and try, whenever you ask a question, to be curious and confident until you get the answer – no matter how long it takes. What impact does this attitude have on you and your conversational partners?

3. Questions and more

"You can tell whether a man is clever by his answers. You can tell whether a man is wise by his questions."

(Nagib Mahfuz)

Questions are a powerful communication tool. They almost always lead to a reaction from the other person. This reaction, however, might not be what we expect. Questions might trigger not only answers but also resistance, fear, anger, incomprehension or withdrawal. Rephrasing one single word in the question can make a difference. The aim of this chapter is to show you how to determine the different effects questions have and how to choose which question is suitable for a certain situation.

The types of questions we present here have been developed by many coaches, therapists, linguists and others over time and were also described in many works, such as Berg and Szabó [2005]; Meier and Szabó [2008]; Prior [2009]; Hargens [2011]; Kindl-Beilfuß [2011]; de Jong and Berg [2012]; Burgstaller [2015].

In this chapter, we will discuss everyday questions in detail and present solution-focused questioning techniques which can be used in any type of conversation. Take your time to consciously think about the questions you ask. You may want to rephrase some questions, so they suit you and your language.

3.1 Everyday questions

First, consider the questions which you probably already ask every day. Have you thought about when, why (for what purpose) and how you ask your questions? Asking questions thoughtfully makes a huge difference to how coaching and team situations evolve.

Open (open-ended) questions

Open or open-ended questions serve to receive information from your conversational partner. Those questions invite the other person to share their thoughts. Therefore, we recommend open questions over closed ones, which allow for *yes* or *no* or *don't know* as answers:

- What do you think of this idea?
- What do you want to achieve?
- What might be the answer to this problem?

Closed (close-ended) questions

Closed or close-ended questions can only be answered with *yes* or *no* or *don't know*. They are important when you want to end a specific part of a conversation, when you aim to reach an agreement or when other clear decisions are to be made:

- Do you agree to what I said?
- Do you think we can do this?
- Are you ready to do what you want to do within the agreed time frame?

Directed questions

With the directed question, you address a person specifically. The answer inevitably begins with *I ...* or *We ...* This type of question is suitable for asking about a concrete next step, an agreement or direct expertise:

- What is your approach in this case?
- What can you contribute to the improvement?
- How much time would you need to achieve it?

Non-directed questions

Non-directed questions are more general. Their aim is to collect as many different answers as possible; those answers are then the basis for selecting a suitable one. When you use a *neutral form* or choose a *passive form* instead of *you*, replies will be without commitment. Non-directed questions therefore allow for a lot of creativity.

"How could this problem be solved?" allows for openly expressing ideas without the need of being worried that those ideas will have to be implemented immediately. Your conversational partner will feel like an expert asked for their opinion.

The phrase "How could *you* solve this problem?" (directed question), however, sounds like an invitation to put into practice what is being answered. This is why non-directed questions, especially in delicate situations, will often produce more answers and ideas that provide for a broad basis of options for further work:

- What approach might work in this case?
- What would it take to improve work performance?
- What is needed to increase the chance of implementation?

Clarifying questions

Clarifying questions serve, as the name suggests, to clarify incomprehensible or incomplete information or observations:

- What exactly do you mean?
- What is that supposed to mean?
- What do you want to achieve?

> **Practical Tip**
>
> There is a second practical field of application. If you feel personally offended, you can choose this type of question instead of a counter-attack, a retreat or the feeling of powerlessness: "What exactly do you mean?" This question will buy you a few seconds to think of an appropriate reaction.

We found two more clarifying questions in *Clean Language* [Sullivan & Rees, 2009], the so-called *Lazy Jedi Questions*. They help specify terms and learn more about them. The questions are:

- What kind of X is this X?
- What else can you tell me about X?

Examples:

- What kind of 'happiness' is this 'happiness'?
- What else can you tell me about 'happiness'?
- What kind of 'book' is this 'book'?
- What else can you tell me about 'the book'?

Hypothetical questions

This type of question fits the solution-focused coaching approach perfectly. Hypothetical questions focus on the preferred future and ask what this preferred future might look like hypothetically. As a result, they support the formulation of the preferred future and can therefore be used very well, in the development of goals:

- Assuming we achieved the goal, what impact would that have on our customers?
- Supposing the colleague behaved differently, what would your reaction be?
- If we had a positive culture dealing with mistakes in our team, what would be possible which is not possible now?

3.2 Coaching questions

Solution-focused coaching questions follow a certain pattern. They focus on what works, are usually future-oriented and increase the number of options. They help specify and refine the respective goal.

3.2.1 Scale-Question

The scale question is an excellent way to make progress visible and to identify the next steps towards the goal [Szabó, 2007]. Scales can be used in many different ways. They work just as well with individuals as with teams. You can draw them on a piece of paper or on a flipchart, display them on the floor in any size to stand on, or work with hand signals – from thigh to above the head, for example.

We will explain each step of this multi-step type of question below.

Step 1: Show a scale from 0 to 10
Both in literature and in practice, you will also find scales from 1 to 10 (the goal). Since we are working with differences, which are visible on the scale, it does not matter whether the scale starts with 0 or 1.

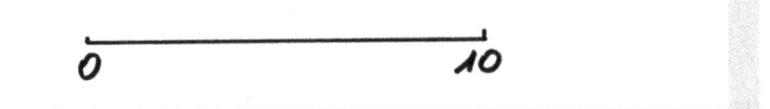

Step 2: Define the current position
Please ask your conversational partner to mark their current position).

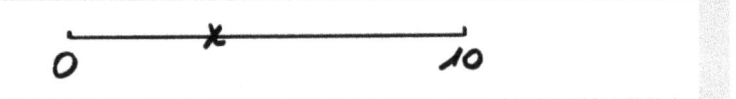

- Where are you currently on the scale, with 0 meaning you just started to deal with the issue, and 10 meaning you have achieved your goal?

Step 3: Collect what works
The response provides you with many clues for finding out what already works. Focusing on what works increases both confidence and trust in abilities. You can also point out and utilise positive differences.

- How come you are already there (and not at 0)? How did you do that?

Step 4: Specify the goal

The next step is to specify the goal – it is not always the case that 10 must be achieved and a lower number may be good enough for the purpose.

- Which value on the scale would you like to reach?

Some people would like to reach 10, while others achieve their goal with a 7 or an 8. Often, people realise that reaching 10 would require too much effort while a smaller step is actually sufficient.

This is also the right time to refine the goal once again:

What is different there (goal) compared to the current position?
How will you recognise that you have reached your goal?
How will others recognise it?
Assuming you have reached your goal, what does that make possible for you?

Step 5: Scale the next step

Recognising the next small step very clearly will help to make progress on the way towards the goal.

What will help you to recognise that you made progress on the scale?
And how else will you notice this?
How will you have managed to take that step?

These questions are to draw attention to the small signs of progress. It is also about opening up many options and ideas, so the respondent can choose concrete actions they consider appropriate. These actions are best written down, so the respondent can refer to them whenever necessary.

The simple scale structure provides for three different points of focus for the conversation [Iveson et al., 2012]:

1. a realistic description of the preferred future
2. a list of all the things which already lead towards the preferred future – including the success made so far
3. recognition potential progress in the immediate future.

> ### *Practical Tip*
>
> When working with teams, scales are also used by positioning team members in the room. The individuals physically stand on the current situation and the preferred future. This makes them feel whether a position is right for them or not. They are also able to perceive the differences between the different positions better. So, this is also about *gut feeling*.
>
> The team members' points of view become so clear that they are able to discuss those differences. It is often noticed that – despite different positions on the scale – the statements on what is already working or what the preferred future should look like are very similar. This insight helps team members to show more mutual understanding resulting in fewer conflicts.

Before we finish this section, we would like to tell you a small anecdote from Ralph's practice. He was invited to a team coaching by one of his customers. First, Ralph and the team agreed the coaching goal. Then, they used a scale to find the current position on the way towards the goal. The team members also told Ralph a lot of details about what had worked in the past. Ralph then asked which value on the scale they would like to achieve in the future. The team members chose values between 5 and 7 and were also able to tell a lot about what would be different then.

Following his intuition, Ralph wanted to know where on the scale they had been when they thought the situation had been best. The team members actually took a step forward towards 10! So, there had been a moment in the past when the situation had been better than the situation they were now striving for. Ralph had not expected that, so he came up with a lot of new questions regarding existing resources, competencies and differences. Do not be unsettled by such unexpected moments but remain curious and solution focused. The behaviour of the team members could perhaps be explained by the fact that this best moment in the past had cost the team too much energy to sustain it permanently.

Multi-scaling

It makes sense, especially with complex goals, to make various aspects visible and, therefore, usable. In case of multi-scaling [Meier & Szabó, 2008, p. 96 ff.; Szabó, 2017], this is done with a main scale to present the progress made towards the respective goal, and about five subscales. We have used this method only with individuals so far, to support Scrum Masters or Product Owners, for example. If you can imagine it, we are sure it will also work with your team.

Use the already known question technique of the progress scale and start with the question:

- On a scale from 0 to 10, with 10 meaning that the goal has been achieved completely, and 0 the opposite, where are you at the moment?

After your conversational partner has chosen a value and marked it on the scale, proceed as follows:

- Which five aspects have contributed to the fact that you are already at X and no longer at 0?

Write down five aspects and prepare more scales, one for each of them. The next step is to ask your conversational partner how well each single aspect already works. The answer is then put on the respective scale.

Afterwards, ask your conversational partner what improvement they consider the minimum necessary; these values are marked on the respective subscales, too.

Once all the preliminary work has been done, turn back to the main scale and ask how an improvement of the single aspects would affect a change in the main scale.

Your conversational partner will receive a clearly visible point of reference to which topic is particularly worth working on with regard to achieving the goal.

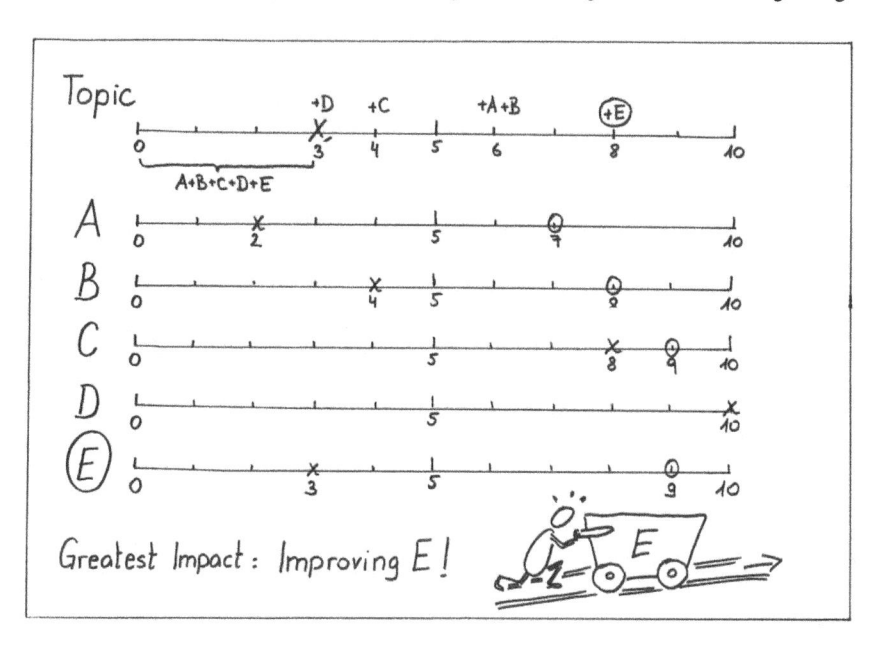

Crossed Scales

Crossed scales are a simple and effective form of multi-scaling, i.e. the simultaneous use of several scales. For this purpose, two ten-part scales – one vertical and one horizontal – are crossed so they meet at value 5.

The advantage of using crossed scales is that two questions can be asked at the same time. This method is of great value particularly when you start a workshop topic or a team coaching process. Please make sure, however, that the team consists of a maximum of ten people. For larger groups, other methods to start the coaching process are more time-efficient (you will find possible alternatives for starting an intervention in large groups in section 6.6 "Team development with large groups").

In practice, crossed scales work well when you fix the two scales – using as much space as possible – to the ground with masking tape. Put a sticky note with a 0 at the left end of the horizontal scale and another one, also with a 0, at the lower end of the vertical scale. Then put a sticky note at the right end of the horizontal scale, and one at the upper end of the vertical scale, each with a 10. Moreover, prepare a flipchart with the two questions and two additional reflection questions.

You can ask about trust in a team on a scale, for example:

- How important is trust in a team for you?

And on the other scale:

- How much trust do you think the team has at the moment?

Ask the team members to position themselves on the point where their two answers meet. Usually, it is advisable that the facilitator demonstrates this process. To be on the safe side, point out that it is not necessary to oust others from their respective position to assume a position. If a position is already taken, it will be free again after the reflection questions have been answered and the next person can follow.

Once all team members have assumed their positions, those who are exactly where they want to be are asked the reflection questions. After answering the two questions, the each team member will be asked to sit down. Suitable reflection questions are, for example:

- How come you are standing exactly there?
- What is supposed to happen here today so that this coaching/this workshop makes sense to you?

Of course, you can also draw the crossed scales and display the respective positions by using adhesive points. However, the huge advantage – all team members taking a stand with their whole bodies – might get lost. Taking the position with their bodies makes it easier for all participants to get started with the coaching or workshop.

The second reflection question is often used to address any discrepancies. For example: "This coaching makes no sense to me. I have lost faith in the team and I am sure it will not be possible to restore it in two hours, no matter what." Such information, or similar, is important for you as coach or facilitator, for various reasons. On the one hand, it is always better to know what bothers the participants so you can assess their reactions better. On the other hand, the person can say right at the beginning what bothers them and is then able to concentrate on other thoughts. Moreover, you have the opportunity to thank them for being so open and for participating, nevertheless. And you can invite him or her to let you know whenever an idea comes up about how this workshop may contribute to an improvement of the situation.

The confidence scale

You can take a look at the various measures at the end of a coaching session in the same way. By doing so, you can address any remaining doubts about the implementation of the measures and eliminate those doubts as far as possible. As a result, internal resistance can be avoided, and the probability of implementation increases significantly.

- On a scale from 0 to 10 – with 10 meaning you are very confident about implementing what has been agreed, and 0 meaning that you consider it almost impossible – what, would you say, is your level of confidence at the moment?

The confidence scale helps to:

1. review whether the measures have what it takes to actually be implemented,
2. address any doubts that may still exist and find ways to deal with those doubts,
3. increase the binding nature of the agreement.

If necessary, it may be helpful to talk about ways to increase the confidence among all participants to disclose identified obstacles and to find solutions for them:

- What else do you need to be a little more confident?
- What needs to happen in the next few days to keep your confidence on the same level?

3.2.2. Coping questions

Sometimes, someone places the current situation at 0 on a scale from 0 to 10, with 10 meaning that everything is as it should be, and 0 meaning the opposite. So, this person sees nothing positive in their current situation. Coping questions can help make at least very small differences visible here.

With this type of question, you may succeed in getting your conversational partner's attention away from failures or worries and reservations. Their attention will instead return to what they are already doing to cope with their situation. It is all about focusing on the small positive differences:

- How have you managed so far to ...?
- What keeps you going?
- What gives you strength?
- What was helpful in making it?
- How come things are not worse?

3.2.3 Asking for exceptions

According to the solution-focused principle *There is no problem without interruption – there are always exceptions, make use of them*, asking for exceptions focuses on positive exceptions and differences in the past. Often, you can find useful ideas for achieving the current goal in the past:

- When have there been times in the past few weeks during which the problem did not exist/was not a burden/was not so bad?
- Who did something so this exception could happen?
- What led to this exception?

3.2.4 The miracle question

The miracle question was developed when Insoo Kim Berg had a client who was convinced that only a miracle could help her [de Shazer & Dolan, 2007, p. 37; de Jong & Berg, 2012, p. 90 ff]. Berg was very creative in formulating solution-focused questions; the miracle question was born. Adapted to a team situation, a miracle question can be, for example:

- Suppose you go home tonight and do what you usually do in the evening. Maybe you eat something, read a little bit, or watch TV and finally go to bed. You quickly fall asleep because you are pleasantly tired. While you are asleep, and your house is quiet, a miracle happens. The miracle is that your current problem has disappeared. You do not know, however, that the miracle happens because you are asleep. So, when you wake up tomorrow morning, what will be the first thing that makes you realise that a miracle has happened and your current problem has gone?

This miracle question is the introduction to a conversation about the preferred future. The following questions should be added subsequently to increase the miracle question's effect:

- What will you notice first? and: What else?
- What will you do in response to this miracle?

- Who else will notice?
- How will they know?
- When they notice, what will their reaction be?
- And what will your reaction be?

Let the team members tell you everything in detail. Encourage them to tell even more details by asking "What else?". Also, focus on what the people involved would do after the miracle happened. Let the team members describe any possible actions and reactions of others to the miracle. Involve the whole team, other departments, superiors, customers etc. For a lot of people, the preferred future will be much clearer and more tangible after this exercise than before. Often, the answers already contain a lot of concrete references to potentially realisable actions.

3.2.5 Circular questions

Circular questions allow for looking at a situation from a different angle; they increase the individual scope of possibilities [Simon & Rech-Simon, 2009]. It is not relevant whether the perspective of a person, an animal or an object is taken. Circular questions often lead to an aha-experience and can be used in a lot of different situations:

- Who knows you particularly well?
- How will this person know the problem has gone?
- What would this person say about this issue?

3.2.6 Interposed questions

Interposed questions are probably the most frequently used type of questions. We will start with our favourite question:

- What else?

People tend to be as sparse as possible with their energy reserves. That is a good thing. Not knowing what the day will have in store for us, we use just as much energy as needed and as little as possible when we perform a task. So, if you ask someone a question, it is absolutely natural and understandable that their first answer will be as energy-saving as possible, in the hope that this answer will meet the requirements. Only when you add the question "What else?" will the respondent have to reflect more. This will work, however, only if you – the one asking the question – actually believe in the idea that more answers will follow.

> **Practical Tip**
>
> Pay attention to the wording:
>
> - What else? is an open question, leading to a flow of information.
> - Anything else? is a closed question which might lead to "yes" but more often to "no" as an answer.
>
> When you ask questions, also include nonverbal communication: look at your conversational partner in an expectant and inviting – and maybe even curious – way.

The next interposed question aims to get to the bottom of negative statements (see section 3.3.7 "Avoid not and no under all circumstances"). This question is helpful when you want to express what should be instead of what should not be. We always try to establish a *towards* language instead of an *away from* language.

You can ask this question anytime a statement contains words such as *not* or *no*. For example, if an employee explains that they are not willing to participate in team meetings in the current form, the question "What would you want instead?" will contribute to receiving valuable ideas on how to improve the situation:

- What would you like instead?

The third interposed question is about the meaning of a statement or an observed behaviour. It also encourages the respondent to think about what they intend to achieve with their behaviour or statement – i.e. what their goal is (see section 4.2.2 "Asking for meaning"):

- For what purpose?

The question "Why?" is often asked here. This question, however, easily leads into the centre of the problem to search for reasons and possible culprits. Therefore, we recommend avoiding the question "Why?" to a large extent and replacing it with the question "For what purpose?". This question directly leads to the preferred future and is helpful for understanding and finding meaning.

3.2.7 Meta questions

In the previous chapters, we considered the coach an expert in asking questions. The team members, however, can also formulate helpful questions. After all, they are the experts in their own situation.

There are several occasions when team members can be involved through meta questions. Firstly, this allows the team to become more involved in the process. Additionally, the team is encouraged to ask questions and answer them to develop new insights and solutions – even beyond the coaching session. Sometimes, the coach might not have a suitable question; then it also makes sense to involve the team.

A question which concerns the coaching process and not the content is referred to as meta question. Such questions can be, for example:

- What question would be helpful for you now?
- What else could I ask you to help you see the situation from a different perspective?
- What could I ask you now to make you leave your familiar thought patterns and develop new, creative ideas?
- What else could I ask you to support the development of new ideas?
- What else could we do now to help you take another step?
- What else could we look at, to see the impact of the next steps better?

After team members have developed questions or ideas, the coach takes them up and uses them. We recommend repeating the question to invite the team members to provide an answer.

Some questions also serve as a reflection of the earlier discussion with the aim of finding new points of reference, for example:

- How do you feel about the questions I have asked so far? What was helpful for you?

Solution-focused coaching always builds on what already works. So, if there were any helpful moments in the conversation you can go back to them. Afterwards, you could ask for another suitable question.

Another type of meta questions helps the coach reflect on the coaching interview for themselves. This often happens quietly in the background, with thoughts such as:

- How has the conversation been going so far?
- What questions have been helpful so far?
- What other questions could I ask?
- Did the answer match my question? If not, does it make sense to repeat the question?
- Which points of reference do the answers provide?
- What is my attitude towards these people?

3.3 More linguistic interventions

In addition to questioning techniques, various forms of linguistic interventions are also common in coaching. Most of those interventions can be helpful in any kind of conversation, just like the questioning techniques. Some of the linguistic interventions introduced below can also be found in Prior [2009].

3.3.1 Appreciation

Is appreciation really an intervention? Or is it rather an attitude? Appreciation as intervention will only have the desired effect if it is accompanied by an appropriate inner attitude. Therefore appreciation always has to be sincere. If you use it purely as an intervention method to achieve a particular form of cooperation, for example, your intention will be exposed immediately in most cases. To a great extent, you will achieve exactly the opposite of what you wanted to.

To express appreciation, we recommend using the personal pronoun *I*

- I am impressed with how you dealt with the issue.

instead of *you*: "You have done a good job of dealing with this issue." The difference is that the personal pronoun *I* expresses a personal opinion or feeling.

Using the personal pronoun *you*, on the other hand, creates the impression of a judgement rather than appreciation. Performance is no longer appreciated but assessed – from a position of objective knowledge. In this case, you would unconsciously place yourself above the person to be appreciated. This makes it look as if you could say and determine for certain what is *good* and what is not.

In practice, appreciation has many faces. Addressing someone by their name, for example, is often considered appreciative. Asking for help or advice from an expert also is an opportunity to express appreciation. Thanking others – even for trivialities or obvious things – is another of many ways to show appreciation.

Rising [2010] wrote a moving article on the value of appreciation. In this article, she also mentioned examples of how teamwork was improved when appreciation was expressed. Positive psychology research also shows that appreciation has a health-promoting aspect for the person who is appreciative [Fredrickson, 2010].

3.3.2 Paraphrasing or summarising

It may happen sometimes that a person describes a negative situation with a lot of details. Since language, as we know, creates reality, the problem described in detail might seem bigger than it actually is. When you provide a short and concise summary of the story you were told, you can find out whether you managed to get the core of the message. Moreover, such a summary can make the problem seem smaller and more manageable.

> ***Practical example of "Paraphrasing"***
>
> Such a description of a problem could read as follows: People are complaining about their team communication...
>
> "Communication does not exist in this team at all. Whenever I ask something, they roll their eyes instead of answering. Well, most of the time there is no one available who could even answer my questions."
>
> "Exactly. And if there is communication for once, it will not take a minute for the first argument to break out. Everyone is offended personally when a mistake is made."
>
> "Not only then. Some people here need constant standing ovations for every small thing they do. I dare not say anything any more!"
>
> "Wait – who are you talking about? Yourself?"

> At such moments, paraphrasing interrupts the description of the problem. An example of paraphrasing might be:
>
> "If I understood you correctly, you are not content with the current culture of discussion in your team."
>
> Wait until the team members confirm your statement with a nod before asking further questions. The next step would be to clarify the goal and its impact:
>
> "What should it be like instead and what would be different then?"

3.3.3. Normalising

Similar to paraphrasing, normalising is about de-emotionalising the impression of a situation which is dramatically described with a lot of emotion. For this purpose, the coach repeats the statement of the person describing the problem.

The introductory question "Do I understand correctly that …" shows that the coach is willing to be corrected regarding the content. When the coach continues, they should omit all words expressing emotion and describe only factual content. This objectification helps the team put aside their own blocking emotions. Only then, they can continue working on their goal definition.

> ### Practical example of "Normalising"
>
> A team might describe their cooperation with a customer as follows:
>
> "You cannot imagine how many truly incompetent people can be in one single office! They only seem to drink coffee and dream of their next holiday. We cannot explain it in any other way!"
>
> "Exactly – they are not even willing to provide us with the most basic information. I guess they do not have that information at all. A classic case of 'I do not know what I want but I want it the day before yesterday and, of course, with as many extras as possible at half price'!"

> When you normalise these statements, you can turn the tide towards defining a goal. You could ask the following question, for example:
>
> "Do I understand you correctly that cooperating with this customer is difficult for you because you do not get important information which you need to continue your work?"

3.3.4 Reframing or reinterpreting

Reframing means "giving something a new frame". In the coaching context, this means gaining a new perspective on a situation which increases the possibilities for action. Reframing works by changing the place, the time, certain people, values or similar with regard to a situation in our thoughts; the aim is to see how the situation would change as a result.

Reframing is to help see the possible advantage in the supposed disadvantage – along the lines of: "Who knows what good is in what is happening right now?" A suitable reframing to the statement: "I always have to deal with the most difficult customer!" could be, for example: "So, your boss seems to put a lot of trust in you."

We basically distinguish two types of reframing. One is called *context reframing* and the other *meaning reframing* [Wilhelm, (n.d.); Bandler & Grinder, 1982].

Every behaviour is justified – according to the context. In context reframing, a behaviour that is perceived as undesirable is freed from the current context and transferred to a new framework in which it is useful. The "problem" is not solved but moved to a useful place. Two questions are helpful here:

- When would this behaviour be useful?
- Where would this behaviour be a resource?

Or, put differently:

- In which context does this behaviour, this ability or this problem make sense?
- Imagine this situation happened somewhere else (or at another time/with other people). What would be different then?

Practical examples of "Context Reframing"

The following example illustrates context reframing:

A team has decided to include fewer stories than usual in their Sprint Backlog. The Product Owner is not content with their decision. The coach talks to the Product Owner and asks when such a behaviour would be useful. The Product Owner answers that the team would be able to pay more attention to quality. Also, the team members might not have fully understood the reason for the requirements yet and, therefore, wish to protect themselves as well as the customer from a huge amount of future reworking. The Product Owner might think of even more situations in which the team's behaviour is useful and makes sense. This reframing can lead to a constructive discussion between the Product Owner and the team.

Another example: a mistake leads to a delay. The coach asks under which circumstances the mistake could have been good and helpful. The team can use the answers to this question to adjust their working environment in a way that they can detect and fix mistakes earlier.

A behaviour or a situation is sometimes associated with a negative meaning. *Meaning reframing* looks for a different and positive meaning. *He is stubborn*, if seen more positively, might also mean *he is reliable, consistent or assertive*. The aim of this intervention is to help people involved develop new, more helpful perspectives or at least reconcile with a behaviour or situation. Helpful questions can be:

- What else could it mean?
- Could it also mean …?
- What is the advantage/benefit of this behaviour?

> **Practical Tip**
>
> The following exercise can help understand meaning reframing: The build process again takes longer than expected and you are annoyed at first. How could you use this situation for you or the team in a positive way? Try to find ten positive aspects.

Getting a new perspective on an unpleasant situation or undesired behaviour allows for identifying resources and utilising them. This paves the way for the preferred future.

> **Practical Tip**
>
> Do not explain reframing. Usually, the team knows what to do. If not, consider it an attempt and just continue the conversation. If it works, however, you will often see a smile, some irritation or even speechlessness.

3.3.5 Liquefying

Similar to reframing, liquefying is about repeating your conversational partner's words in a slightly modified form with the aim of turning a seemingly unchangeable situation into a changeable one [Simon & Weber, 1988; Simon & Rech-Simon, 2009, p. 271; Simon & Weber, 2012, p. 73 ff.]. The result is new linguistic dynamics and, therefore, the possibility of change.

In problem descriptions, people often tend to use solidifying words such as always or never. You have probably heard sentences such as:

- He is always late.
- He never listens to me.
- This team is always dissatisfied.
- You can never please him.

The solidifying words indicate that there is a – seemingly – unchangeable situation. As long as this is the case, it will be difficult for the team to work on their goal. The team members will not believe in the possibility of change.

It helps to include words such as *until now* or *at the moment* when you repeat the other person's words. This leads to liquefaction which is at least the linguistic possibility of change. It is also necessary to formulate the repetition as a question, so your conversational partner has the option to contradict you in terms of content.

If somebody says, for example: "I am too stupid. I will never understand it!", you could ask:

- That means you do not understand it at the moment? or That means you have not understood it yet?

Asking such a question makes the focus shift to the possibility of future change; also, the view of the current situation changes. Phrases such as *so far* or *not yet* work well for putting an inflexible thought into motion:

- Does that mean your colleague has always been late so far?
- Did I understand correctly that you are under the impression that your colleague has never listened to you so far?
- So, this team has always been dissatisfied so far?
- Did I understand correctly that you think you have not been able to please your boss yet?

Practical Tip

Make sure that your rewording is a question which can also be answered with "No". It is all too easy for the coach to misunderstand the conversational partner's goals.

Liquefying the problem leads to confidence that the current situation can be changed. We are not victims of the situation but can instead become creators of our own future: "I have not understood it yet and that is what I can change as soon as I find the right way."

3.3.6 Meta-monologue

Experienced coaches also have the courage to look at the coaching process and the further procedure in a meta-monologue in front of all participants. It is absolutely vital to appreciate all the participants in the meta-monologue, so they feel that they are in good hands. Ask them for a short reflection break. Tell them that you will say what goes on in your mind out loud, so everyone who is interested can hear it. An example of a meta-monologue might be:

"I think it is remarkable how the team is reacting to the situation. The team members show so much commitment and want to achieve the best for the company." Please note that you should say only what you are actually convinced of. Remember: Appreciation must be honest. When you say "You already have so many resources such as …", name specific resources. Start with "I wonder …" so you can raise one or more questions. "What if …" is possible, too. It will help if the monologue ends with another starting point for the team, such as: "I would like to ask you which path we should take now." Then ask the question directly. After all, you cannot assume that everyone has listened to your monologue.

A meta-monologue serves as orientation for the coach and also as a short break in the coaching process for the team. Often, it leads to new ideas among the team members when the coach talks about their thoughts. If you have a co-coach, a reflection between the two of you can also work well as a meta-dialogue.

> **The virtual reflecting team**
>
> Rolf Dräther mentioned the idea of a meta-dialogue with the whole team – a method we would like to introduce as well. All team members get up and stand behind their chairs. In this meta-position, they will discuss what they had observed while seated in the earlier discussion. The advantage of this intervention is that everyone present is directly involved in the process.
>
> Their altered positions make it easier for the team members to distance themselves emotionally from the discussion they had before. This view from above enables them to reflect on the conversation without starting a content-related discussion again.

3.3.7 Avoid *not* and *no* under all circumstances

To achieve a goal, you have to know what it is. Knowing that you will certainly *not* go to China for your next holiday is not enough to book a flight at the travel agency. The travel agent will expect you to make clear what you really want – just like when you place an order at a restaurant. For example: "I would like to travel through New Zealand by rental car." Or: "I would like to eat fish and chips."

Negative wording often has the opposite effect of what we actually want. The human brain can process words such as *not* and *no* only with great effort. So, if you tell the travel agent that you do *not want to visit China*, it is very likely that the first image appearing in the agent's head is *holiday in China*. The agent then has to delete the image with some effort before they can apprehend what you actually want [Wales & Grieve, 1969; Clark & Chase, 1972; Kaup, 2001; Budiu & Anderson, 2005; Hasson & Glucksberg, 2006].

In coaching processes, a lot of people find it difficult at first to say what they actually want. It is often easier to describe what they do *not* want or *no longer* want. Reformulating the negative goal to turn it into a positive goal is necessary to achieve an improvement. "I do not want to be fat any more," will help gain more and more weight in the long term rather than achieve the desired state of being slimmer.

There are questioning techniques which help your conversational partner define their goals in a positive way. Be consistent in cases of negative wording and do not give up until your conversational partner expresses a positive goal:

- What should be achieved instead?
- So, you no longer want this? What do you want instead?

Pay close attention to your own language. How often do you use the words *not* or *no*? It will also be easier for people in your environment to follow your wishes if you use a positive wording. If, despite all caution, you ever make a negative statement and – should you notice it – just add "and instead I want ...".

3.3.8 *And* instead of *but*

The small word *but* can very quickly turn a positively meant statement into a negative one. If somebody says: "You did a good job, but you need to change the method", the reaction will seldom be "Ok"; usually, such a statement will lead to a discussion. How the word *but* is ultimately received depends on the individual recipient.

Some people forget the first part of the sentence which comes before the *but*. They erase it in their mind and only perceive the second part of the sentence. For the example mentioned above, it would be: "You need to change the method." Too bad they did not get the appraisal "You did a good job", right?

Other people interpret the word *but* as a negation of what has been said. In this example, they would understand that they did not do a good job at all. The appraisal becomes counterproductive. Even worse, the recipient might offer resistance and get too angry to hear the second part of the sentence.

In his trainings, Marshall B. Rosenberg says "[...] never to put your 'but[t]' in the face of an angry person!" [Rosenberg, 2015, p. 119]. You would not want to do that, would you?

We therefore recommend replacing the word *but* with the connecting words *and* or *furthermore*. By doing so, the first statement can exist next to the second without being negated.

3.3.9 Patience and the courage to endure silence

Again, we address an attitude of solution-focused work here. It is important to stay patient and curious when your conversational partner takes their time to answer a question. Otherwise, there is a great risk of interrupting a line of thought and, as a result, devaluing the question you have just asked. In addition, your patience will signal to your conversational partner that you firmly believe that they will find an answer. These two aspects together form a good basis for answers. Only if your conversational partner says that they did not understand the question or that they cannot provide you with an answer, has the time come to ask a new question or rephrase the first one.

3.3.10 Breaks

Whenever a process seems to be stuck, when you wish for a change in the course of the conversation or when you require a new idea of how to proceed further, we recommend taking a break.

No matter whether you are in a single or a team setting, a decisive break leads to movement. Participants get up, maybe even leave the room for a while, talk to each other or quickly check their e-mails on their mobile phones. Whatever people do during a break, they will change positions both intellectually and physically. Meanwhile, you as the coach can sort your thoughts, catch some fresh air or generate new energy and creativity in another way. Then, when everyone is back, you can continue with fresh energy.

3.3.11 Prescribing experiments

It is common to recommend to your coaching client an experiment at the end of a solution-focused coaching session. The experiment is based on the topic of the coaching session and can be either logically derived from it or creatively developed [Scheel et al., 2004]. You can find such experiments at the end of each chapter in this book, including recommendations for both type and duration, similar to a doctor's prescription. That is why the coaching jargon often refers to the *prescription* of experiments.

An experiment, however, is not an assignment, the completion of which you check later. Rather it suggests how to transfer the results of the coaching process as efficiently as possible to the professional or private everyday life. We distinguish various types of experiments [de Jong & Berg, 2012, p. 125ff].

Observation experiments

The aim of *observation experiments* is – as the name suggests – to observe what changes positively in a certain situation in the near future and what patterns can be discovered in the process. Observation is the only thing the conversational partner needs to do. For example:

- Observe in the next few days in which situations pair programming is helpful to you and what these situations have in common.

This type of experiment is suitable for people who are good observers and who notice many details. You can use this kind of experiment to use their strength and only direct the focus of observation from the negative to the positive.

Action experiments

Actions experiments aim to change your conversational partner's behaviour. In many cases, we rely on chance – by throwing a dice or tossing a coin – to make differences visible. For example:

- In the coming Sprint, toss a coin at the daily stand-up each morning. If it is heads, perform a person-centred daily stand-up (see also section 8.4 "Solution-focused Daily Stand-ups"); if it is tails, perform a task-centred one.

Ritual experiments

Ritual experiments aim to make the difference in individual experience visible. The idea is to regularly implement a change in behaviour for a certain period of time – like a new ritual – and to pay attention to the difference it makes in the personal experience. For example:

- From now on, start each daily stand-up by saying thank you. Do that for ten days at least. Every one of you will thank their neighbour for the support they provided: an open ear in a certain situation or something similar.

Most teams are very creative in finding experiments that they want to carry out and they consider useful on their own. Experiments found by teams are much more likely to be actually carried out than prescribed experiments.

3.4 Self-reflection

- What was exciting/new/helpful for you in this chapter?
- What questions do you ask in the course of a working day? Are there any favourite questions you use particularly often?
- To what extent do your customers or colleagues rely on you when it comes to finding answers to their problems? How often have you preferred questions over providing answers?
- Which of the questions or interventions presented in this chapter would you like to use and test their impact in the next few days?

3.5 Experiments and exercises

- If you feel like it, try to avoid "Why" on any day next week and replace it with "for what purpose". What effects can you observe?
- During your next contracting talk, experiment with the question "What else?". What impact does this question have on you or on your conversational partner and on the result of the talk?
- Have a talk with someone you know well this evening and tell them about your day. Make sure to replace any but with and. Perhaps you can also

count how many times your conversational partner uses the word but. From your perspective, what effect does the experiment have on you and your conversational partner?

- Write down the answers to the following questions right now:
  - What worked very well for you today? What are you proud of?
  - Whom did you help today? And how?
  - What – when looking back – could you possibly do differently?

4. The Solution Pyramid

Solution-focused coaching is based on adopting the fundamental coaching attitudes, following the principles and mastering solution-focused questioning techniques. However, solution-focused coaching also requires something else: structure. The "Solution Pyramid" described here aims to provide a simple structure for any solution-focused conversation.

Every solution-focused conversation essentially has four phases. The illustration to the right shows them in the form of a Solution Pyramid.

These phases can be used in various types of meetings, customer talks, performance interviews, conflict management talks etc. They serve as the coach's own preparation and as a guideline for the coaching session.

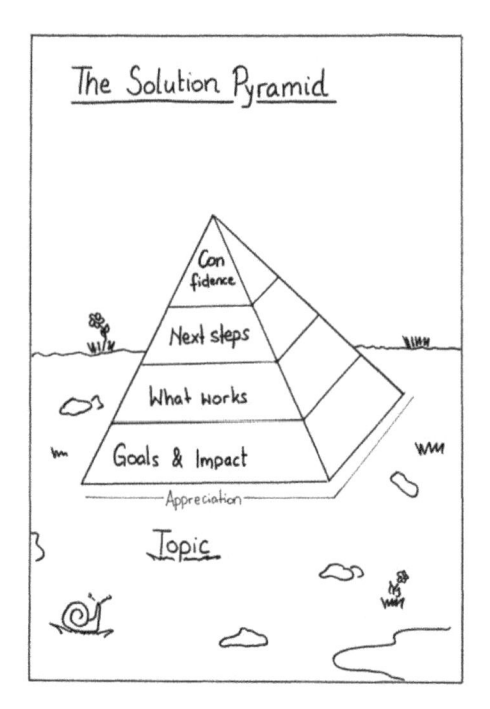

4.1 The ground – the topic

The Solution Pyramid stands metaphorically on the topic of the conversation. The ground contains the problem and all experiences made in this field. This is what is already known. The pyramid is built on that knowledge. Therefore, the ground is not part of the Solution Pyramid. This means that the topic needs to be given as much space as necessary but not more. Detailed questions are asked only at the first level of the Solution Pyramid to prevent sinking into the "problem swamp" and to keep the way forward open.

A good way to prepare the ground is to thank everyone present for coming and for taking the time. This kind of appreciation should not only be kindness; it should also make clear that everyone is there as a volunteer and is interested in working on the topic for the meeting.

Steve de Shazer emphasised this by often saying at the beginning of his sessions something like: "So, first, thank you for coming today. I hope that what we do together will be useful. There's no guarantees about that. Huh. I can guarantee I will do my best. I assume you guys will too. And we see what happens." [de Shazer & Dolan, 2007, p. 73]. With this statement, he made it very clear right from the start that the coaching session can only be successful if everyone contributes. After all, it is not the coach who works on the way forward. The coach's role is to guide the process towards it. Often, the description of a problem sounds different after such an introduction compared to starting without it. This makes it easier to jump to the first level of the pyramid.

The transition from problem-focus to goal-focus

The question is: how can we succeed in reaching the first level? How do we manage to escape the problem and turn to the preferred future in our minds?

The answer is once again: appreciation. Only those who have the feeling that their problem is understood and appreciated, i.e. consider themselves "in good hands", will feel safe enough to let go. Transitioning onto the Solution Pyramid is probably a key point in solution-focused conversations. Therefore, you need to attach great importance to this moment. Now is the time to be sensitive and go with your gut feeling. Empathy and authenticity belong together and can lead to success in this moment. Try to understand your conversational partner. Listen with your heart and think about what is important to this person at this moment and what they might want to achieve. React according to your gut feeling. There is no standard procedure.

One person will probably throw up their hands in horror and look concerned, while another might nod sympathetically, and the third says: "I can imagine that this is a burden for you," or similar. Whatever you do – honestly appreciate your conversational partner's openness in your own way.

If you fail to show appreciation, you are probably the wrong person to have this conversation in a solution-focused way. If you manage to give your conversational partner or team members a sense of safety, however, they will follow you to the first level of the Solution Pyramid. This paves the way for achieving the respective goal.

> **Practical Tip**
>
> At the beginning of the conversation, thank all participants for coming and taking their time. This kind of appreciation makes it clear that everyone is a volunteer and is interested in working on the topic. You might want to use a statement similar to the one Steve de Shazer would make:
>
> "I will do my best to obtain a good result and I am sure you will, too."
>
> Questions at the beginning of a conversation can be, for example:
>
> "What is it about? What is the topic?"
>
> "What should we talk about, so the conversation/meeting makes sense to you?"
>
> Instead of asking in-depth questions, the best way to react is with sympathy and appreciation – both verbally and non-verbally.

Disturbances take precedence

If the team members are preoccupied with a current topic, you need to give priority to that. Even if you were hired to work on another topic, it will not make sense to ignore urgent matters. The team members will not be able to focus. Dörner [2004], Wranke [2009] and others describe how negative emotions affect thinking. The basic rule therefore is *"Disturbances take precedence"* [Cohn, 2009; Hoffmann, 2017].

A company hires a coach, for example, to support working on the topic of *openness and trust in the team*. When clarifying the contract with the team, however, it turns out that new requirements stipulated by the management have caused quite a stir among the team members and there is not much room for the assigned topic. The team members' strong focus on improving their current situation based on the new requirements can be used for the coaching. Openness and trust emerge in such situations almost of their own accord. This is how you as the coach can meet both requirements – the company's wishes and the team's needs.

Systemic connections require that improvements in whatever field they are achieved have a positive impact on other topics. This is something you can rely on. Therefore, you can give priority to disturbances without violating your assignment.

4.2 The first level – goals and impact

> *Knowing the goal makes success possible. Understanding and feeling the goal makes success likely!*
>
> *(Veronika Jungwirth)*

The first level is the largest part of the pyramid. Defining the goal and its impact takes time, patience and perseverance; often, it takes as much as half of the entire time of the coaching engagement. Therefore, its importance is clear: without a well-defined goal, success can only be achieved by chance at best. In this context, a goal is seen as the preferred future and it sets a direction, not a destination.

For you as the coach or facilitator of the conversation, it helps to understand what your team wants; but above all, your team needs to know what they really need and want to achieve. They often only know what they do not want anymore. Knowing on which goal they should work together is an important basis for good cooperation. It is almost like with the navigation system in a car. It can only take you to the desired destination if you first tell it where you want to go.

4.2.1 Defining goals

As mentioned in the introduction, striving for a common goal is the basis for any team. Only if all team members understand where they are headed to and support the direction will reasonable cooperation be possible. The meaningfulness of the preferred future is of particular importance. Those who are confident that the efforts will ultimately pay off are more willing to show full commitment. Therefore, we recommend paying attention to the following details when defining goals.

Positive wording

Make sure that the definition says *what should be* instead of *what should not be* (compare section 3.3.7 "Avoid not and no under all circumstances"). A lot of teams find it easier to make negative statements because they are used to paying a lot of attention to what should no longer be happening. This knowledge can be useful for the positive definition of a goal. So, allow negative wording – as a starting point for your questions about *what instead*.

> **Practical Tip**
>
> When you hear a negative statement, these questions will help:
>
> - What do you want instead?
> - What should be instead of ... ?

Explicit, detailed and observable from the outside

The more comprehensive and diverse the definition of a goal is and the more visible the observable change is, the more colourful and real the image of the desired state in people's minds becomes. And it is all the more likely that the goal will actually be achieved. Maybe you have already experienced the following: the better you can imagine a situation, the more you believe in the idea that this situation will actually happen. A desire, or a vague hope, becomes a goal which can be achieved.

A good user story, for example, does not depend on someone writing about it in as much detail as possible. It is rather a matter of the Product Owner being able to describe the target scenario verbally and in such a vivid form that the development team can imagine clearly how, for what purpose and in which situations the customer will use the product eventually. People should be able to ask questions and have a discussion. It is all about the energy and the realistic description. If everyone has a vivid and comprehensible image in their minds, only keywords will be required in written form to trigger memories of the conversation later. Success is perceptible from the outside at the latest when the product is used by the customer.

> **Practical Tip**
>
> You can support the specific definition of a goal with the following questions:
>
> - What has to happen here today so you will be satisfied with the result?
> - How would your superior or other relevant people notice that you have successfully worked on your goal?
> - How would your superior notice that you have achieved your goal?
> - What, do you think, would be a major or a small change?
> - If I filmed you with a hidden camera, how would I notice, when watching the film, that you have come closer to your goal or already achieved it?

Using the language of the person who wants to achieve the goal – correct definition

When accompanying goal-finding processes, it can sometimes be observed that the coach repeats or writes down formulations differently from those actually said by the participants themselves. If a participant says: "I do not want to be constantly interrupted when working", it may happen that the coach asks: "Do you mean that you want to be undisturbed when you work?" If the person nods, the sentence: "I want to be undisturbed when I work" might be written down on the flipchart. Although the coach asked a question, words are put into the participant's mouth which they might have never said.

It would be better to ask: "If you do not want to be constantly interrupted, what do you want instead?" This gives the participant the opportunity to find their own wording which can then be written down. They might say: "It is not bad if someone comes and needs my help. It would be helpful, however, if I could work at least two hours per day without interruption so I can carry out difficult work steps." This statement is different to the one mentioned above: "I want to be undisturbed when I work."

An explanation for the fact that agreements ostensibly made together are broken might be that the original idea is lost when the coach or a superior rewords what has been said. Let the person who wants to implement an idea or achieve a goal write their statements down themselves. This makes sure that what was meant is written down.

> **Practical Tip**
>
> Use the exact words of your conversational partner to frame the next question.
>
> - I need more peace when I work. → What would be different if you had more peace when you work?
> - My colleague X is stubborn. I just cannot work with him. → How would you notice that your colleague X is less stubborn so you can work better with him?

One approach which makes sure that a statement is not influenced and no other words or information are used, is called *Clean Language*[2]. In this approach, it is important to keep your own content, words, assessments or interpretations completely out of the conversation. We would like to recommend the book written by Cooper and Castellino [2012], for example, if you want to learn and practise *Clean Language*.

Achievable and verifiable

Find out together with the team whether the chosen goal is actually achievable and whether it is within their sphere of influence – i.e. whether it is in the team's power to achieve the goal. Ask for *both* the goal of the current coaching session *and* for the overall goal to be achieved.

If achievement of the goal is outside the team's sphere of influence, the task is to redefine the goal in such a way that it can be directly reached by the people present. Those aspects that cannot be influenced by the team are accepted as given.

A travel ban declared by the company management could be an example of such a situation. For a team working in different locations, for example, such a travel ban can be a real challenge. The quality of the team's communication will decline if meeting in person is prevented. The goal: "We need to be able to travel again", however, is usually beyond the team's sphere of influence – especially in large companies. The travel ban must therefore be considered a given fact. To develop a new, reasonable goal in this case, the question: "For what purpose?" is

---

[2] http://www.cleanlanguage.co.uk/

helpful. The question "For what purpose do we need to be able to travel again?" will lead to a new goal, for example: "For continuing good and personal communication in the team in the future." The new goal, which is within the team's sphere of influence, has been found: "Despite the travel ban, we can continue good and personal communication in the team in the future."

A goal is verifiable when it has been defined in advance how progress towards achieving the goal or the achievement of the goal itself can be recognised. So, what does the team need so they can notice good and personal communication despite the travel ban? And what does "good and personal" actually mean? Making a small checklist, which helps see when the goal is achieved, is a concrete and motivating step. Such a list also helps the team members develop a largely similar picture of the desired target state in their minds. This makes it easier for them to achieve their goal together.

Practical Tip

You can support the definition of an achievable and verifiable goal with the following questions:

- How confident are you that you can actually achieve the goal as it is defined now?
- What resources do you have that guarantee you that you can actually achieve this goal?
- For what purpose would something which is beyond your sphere of influence have to change? What do you want to achieve with it?
- How could you redefine the goal so that you can actually achieve it?
- What else would be helpful for you now to make achieving the goal as likely as possible?
- How will you know in the end that you have achieved your goal?
- How will others know?"

Impact: Integration of the relevant environment – tolerable for others

> *"Of course, I cannot say whether things will get better if they change; what I can say is that they must change if they are to get better."*
> Georg Christoph Lichtenberg [Lichtenberg, 1796]

If something changes, the change will not only affect an individual or the team but will also have an impact on their environment (basic systems theory [de Shazer, 1991, p. 17ff.]). Perhaps there are other goals that stand in the way of the new goal. When defining a goal, it is therefore worth taking the environment into consideration as well checking or increasing the goal's actual feasibility.

Each achieved goal involves a variety of effects:

- effects on the individual members of the team
- effects on other teams or departments
- effects on the customer
- effects on the company
- effects on the team members' families and private environment.

Some of the effects are quite welcome. Others might become challenges or perhaps new problems. They could even be unfavourable for individuals in the team and therefore unwanted.

In that case, the goal will have to be modified in such a way that everyone who is to contribute to the achievement of the goal can support it unconditionally, based on their current knowledge. If this step – reviewing the potential impact of the goal – is left out, existing objections will often be kept a secret. They will lead to an unspoken barrier among those who bear fears or doubts. This barrier counteracts the achievement of a goal and therefore obstructs the entire undertaking.

> **Practical Tip**
>
> You can help review the impact of the goal with the following questions:
>
> - Assuming that you actually achieve the goal, what would be different for you?
> - What impact would achieving the goal have on you personally?
> - And what impact would achieving the goal have on important people in your environment/on other departments or teams in the company/on the company/ on customers/on your families?
> - Who will be the first person to notice that you have achieved your goal? What will make them notice?
> - What could this person's reaction be? What else could it be?

Reasonable and helpful – finding a meaning

So, we absolutely need to pay attention to possible negative effects of a goal. Those effects provide valuable information. We can use this information to reduce the likelihood of meeting resistance when we define the goal. After all, such resistance might interfere with the achievement of the goal.

Particular focus on the positive effects is just as important. This can be the answer to the question: "For what purpose are we actually doing it?" It therefore becomes a symbolic rubber rope that pulls the team towards the goal. When we focus on useful aspects of the goal we can find a meaning. Everyone will have to find their own meaning, however. There is no such thing as a team-meaning. This makes things more challenging because we cannot influence whether someone finds meaning in a goal.

If some team members consider the achievement of a defined goal reasonable – and this is always the case when the team itself has defined the goal – it will be helpful when they share their thoughts with the others. Firstly, one team member revealing their meaning can contribute to making it easier for others to find their own meaning. Secondly, one team member sharing their values and motives will help the team get to know each other better. This will further strengthen their cooperation and mutual support. Every team member finding their meaning in the achievement of the goal will have an extremely motivating effect on and be an invisible push for the whole team.

> **Practical Tip**
>
> You can help your conversational partner find a meaning in the achievement of the goal with the following questions:
>
> - What would you personally gain by achieving the team goal?
> - What would achieving the goal make possible for you and the team?
> - What other meaning could achieving the goal have from your point of view?

Goal = REACH TOP

We have summarised the factors for defining a goal with the acronym REACH TOP. The initial letters stand for the previously mentioned characteristics of a reasonable goal:

- **R** easonable
- **E** xplicit & detailed
- **A** chievable & verifiable
- **C** orrectly formulated
- **H** elpful
- **T** olerable for others
- **O** bservable
- **P** ositive (wording)

Different models for defining goals have been mentioned in literature. The best known and most frequently cited models are: SMART (specific, measurable, achievable, relevant, time-bound); CLEAR (challenging, legal, exciting, agreed, recorded); PURE (positively stated, understood, relevant, ethical). The respective adjectives in the brackets are only examples; different versions exist in literature.

Whitmore [2015, p. 64 f.] writes that all three models are necessary to describe a good goal. However, even the three models together lack fundamental aspects which are relevant for coaching. Using the language of the person who wants to achieve the goal, the meaning, including the relevant environment and the fact that the goal needs to be perceptible from the outside, is not explicitly taken into account. We therefore hope that REACH TOP is a more complete reminder for defining goals.

4.2.2 Asking for meaning

According to Viktor Frankl, Austrian psychotherapist and founder of logotherapy, humans are motivated by meaning and by striving for meaning [Frankl, 2012]. It is important to know that meaning cannot be given by anyone else – everyone has to search for it themselves. For working with goals in the coaching process, it is necessary to create opportunities so that everyone can find meaning in the goal. If everyone finds meaning in the goal, they will also be motivated to achieve the goal. Meaning can be found in the professional environment, service for a greater cause or service for humanity.

Meaning is always present and can therefore be found or discovered. However, it is in each case the concrete meaning of a concrete situation and a concrete person. That is to say, everyone can find a different meaning for themselves in the same situation.

Meaning and purpose can be easily confused. Purpose refers to a thing, an action or a task, while meaning describes their significance; purpose asks for the benefit while meaning asks for the significance (based on the assessment by the person concerned) [Böckmann, 1987].

"From a meaning-oriented point of view, people primarily want to realise meaning, and if they are in contact with their areas of meaning, they will deliver performance" [Spaleck, 2009, p. 78]. According to Lukas [1999][3], meaningful is

- what has an outstanding chance of doing something good and useful,
- what is in the best interest of everyone concerned,
- what is very concrete in the here and now,
- what is neither overwhelming nor sub-challenging,
- what is capable of consensus with experienced people,
- what gives someone the strength to want it.

Following Friedrich Nietzsche, Viktor Frankl said [Frankl, 1985, p. 97]:

He who has a why to live for can bear almost any how.

which we like to rephrase to:

He who has a meaning to live for can bear almost any how.

---
[3] as quoted by [Ostberg, 2007, p. 89]

> **Practical Tip**
>
> To promote motivation to achieve the goal, ask which meaning this goal has for the people involved.
>
> - What is your meaning in achieving the goal?
> - And what else?
> - What does achieving the goal mean to you?
> - For whom will achieving the goal be useful?
> - What will this person/these people gain?
> - To what extent will achieving the goal be useful to others?
> - When and how will the benefits of achieving the goal become visible?

4.3 The second level – what works

This level is about building a stepping stone for the third level where concrete next steps will be developed. The second level consists of important information about what should definitely stay the way it is, what works well, what is important to your team. For the team you work with, this level will be suitable as a stepping stone if the team has confidence that some progress has already been made on the way towards the goal. If the team members see that they have already made progress in the past, that they can build on this progress and that their own competencies are sufficient, their confidence that the next steps are feasible will increase. Once this confidence exists, it is easy to reach the third level.

The question about the current position on the scale from 0 to 10 for achieving the goal is rarely answered with 0 by single team members and almost never by the whole team. This is something you can rely on. The difference from 0 to the given value X is full of such smaller and larger achievements that have already contributed to getting closer to the goal. By addressing those past achievements and existing resources, they take the centre stage of consciousness where they will be of great help to the team.

If all team members answer the question with 0, they usually have another problem which needs to be dealt with first. The team might feel inhibited, collectively misunderstood, treated unfairly or insecure (compare section 7.5

"The SCARF model") and therefore incapable of action for the moment. Behind this collective discomfort, however, there often is a common goal that connects them, and which they can utilise. Figure out what this goal is and then start again on the ground beneath the Solution Pyramid.

> **Practical Tip**
>
> Questions that can help build a good stepping stone on this level are, for example:
>
> - On a scale from 0 to 10, with 10 meaning you have achieved your goal and 0 meaning the opposite, where are you now? And what is already working so you are at X and no longer at 0?
> - What did you do to get to X?
> - And how did you do that?
> - And if everything changes, what should definitely stay the way it is now?
> - Which of the things you need to achieve the goal is already there?
> - What else?
>
> The question "What else?" is of huge importance, especially on this level. We tend to focus on what is still missing or is not working yet. This question helps stay tuned and discover all essential, already existing details of what works. Therefore, ask "What else?" until your conversational partner has given all the possible answers. Whether there is another answer also depends on whether you as the person asking the questions believe there is another answer or not. So, stay confident that there is one.

4.4 The third level – the next steps

Once the first and second levels have been sufficiently processed, the next steps will happen almost automatically. Use the creativity and experience of your conversational partners, i.e. the team members. They alone know exactly what needs to be done to make progress on their way towards the goal. The team knows all their available resources, existing and potential obstacles as well as the resulting opportunities. A small but effective solution-focused trick can be used to make defining the next steps easier.

If you start at the current position on the scale towards the goal, i.e. at X, you can first define a smaller stage goal: X+1, just like on the first level of the Solution Pyramid. It helps here as well to discuss the effects of this interim goal in detail.

So, the whole team acts as if it they were already one step closer to the goal and exchange views on what is already different there compared to before. As a result, the meaning of the next stage goal will become clearer for the team members. When everyone feels comfortable at the new position of X+1, you can ask how they will have reached this next step. This will make them take a look at the present from the preferred future.

It is easier for our brain to describe in retrospect how a solution was achieved than to plan a way to the preferred, yet unknown future in advance. You can make use of this fact when you act as described above.

> ### *Practical Tip*
>
> First ask about the impact of the next steps:
>
> - Assuming that you are already one step further on the scale – that is X+1 – what would be different?
> - What difference would it make for you/for the team/for your superior/for the company/for the customer if you were already one step further?
> - Who else would notice that you are already one step further on your way towards the goal? And what would make them notice?
> - What would the reaction of this person be?
>
> Then ask for the next steps. On this level, use primarily action-oriented language. Words such as "do", "make", "manage" or "accomplish" are suitable for obtaining concrete, feasible steps as an answer:
>
> - When you are already at X+1, how will you have accomplished this?
> - Who will have helped you and how?
> - How will you have managed to make it work? And how else?

Finding the next concrete steps is a creative and often enjoyable task for the participants if achieving the goal seems meaningful. The probability of implementing the next step can occasionally be increased and for this purpose, you will now reach the top of the Solution Pyramid.

4.5 The fourth level – review of the results

We often think that we have achieved the goal of a meeting when we identify the concrete, feasible next steps and write them down. The coach or facilitator would be happy and proud that so many points have been found and that everyone has actively participated.

Since they are enthusiastic about their own performance, the coach or facilitator may often not understand why agreed steps are only partially implemented or not implemented at all. The reason might be that the ideas and agreements are based on common euphoria, sometimes even on fear or indifference – or maybe even on the attempt to please you.

Solution-focused coaching therefore involves some safety mechanism to increase the likelihood of implementation and to take any doubts into account. This is why we ask the question about how confident our conversational partners are that they can actually implement the agreed steps. If confidence is still rather low, this indicates that there are still doubts which have not been addressed so far.

These concerns and doubts must be taken seriously. They indicate that either the goal has yet to be redefined in a way that everyone can support, or that the measures you have developed together need to be assessed again for their likelihood of implementation. When you support the team in increasing their confidence that they will achieve the goal, you also increase the likelihood that the discussed changes will become reality after the coaching.

Practical Tip

We recommend using a scale as tool here again, the confidence scale:

- On a scale of 0 to 10 – how confident do you feel about actually implementing the next steps you have found?
- What would make you more confident? And what else?
- What would have to change in the definition of the goal/the next steps to increase confidence?
- And what would have to happen so that you believe in the implementation of the measures? And how could that be achieved?
- What will have to happen in the next few days so that confidence stays high? And what else?

When confidence is low...

At the end of a meeting the team might not be very confident that they can implement the next steps. Now you might think that all the work has been in vain. Perhaps you are also at a loss because the meeting is over, and you lack the time to start again.

There is usually a very special statement behind such a feedback from the team: "We have a huge problem here that burdens every one of us and we have not been ready to talk about it yet because, dear coach, we did not trust you sufficiently or because we did not think that this would help. Now we are ready. We are sufficiently confident that you understand us, and we have also learnt that you are able to handle difficult situations with appreciation and in a professional manner. We are sending a signal with our low position on the confidence scale. It is a cry for help and also an invitation to help us."

All of this is hidden in a low confidence value. Quite impressive, right? For you as the coach this means "back to the beginning". So: appreciate the problem (ground) and the fact that active work has taken place despite the circumstances. Then, ask for the goal and its impact (first level), for example:

- What would have to be different for you so that you could feel a bit better in this situation?
- And what exactly would be different for you then?

...and so on.

Do not worry – nobody expects you to tackle the issue immediately. For starters, it is enough to take a few minutes and let the team talk about what would have to be different, so they could be more confident. Appreciate the openness of the team members, listen carefully and show understanding for their situation. Make a new appointment so you have enough time for the new topic.

A low level of confidence at the end of a process is unexpected at first glance and therefore unpleasant. If you take a closer look, however, this new way of frankness opens up a lot of opportunities to further improve cooperation. In this sense, you should be glad about such a development and celebrate it like a small victory.

4.6 Taking conversational needs into account

In his writings, de Shazer [1988, p. 85ff] distinguishes between three types of clients with three different patterns of interaction in therapeutic conversations. They differ in the respective goals and needs they bring to the conversation.

1. The visitor:

    A client behaves like a visitor when they do not know whether they want to change anything and when it remains unclear whether they have a concern. Often, the visitor does not participate in the conversation voluntarily but has been made to participate in it.

2. The complainant:

    In contrast, the complainant provides a clear picture of their goal. They consider themselves a victim, however; they cannot act from this position. The complainant always finds the solutions on the outside. The others need to change something so the complainant can get closer to their goal.

3. The customer:

    The customer knows their goal and has ideas how they could achieve it. The more urgent the need to make progress is to a client, the more likely they are to become a customer.

In the solution-focused community, they say that Steve de Shazer and Insoo Kim Berg abandoned the concept of the three types of clients in the last few years of their professional activity. The reason is that someone identified as a *visitor* or *complainant* has an unfavourable starting position in the coach's mind. Those terms have a rather negative connotation with regard to coaching. From the linguistic point of view, they are considered *difficult* clients. The coaching success might therefore be obstructed by such a classification.

Identifying the individual needs of your conversational partners can be helpful in setting the focus on the respective levels of the Solution Pyramid. Therefore, we would like to provide you with new definitions which focus on the process and include the confidence that progress can be made.

4.6.1 The conversational partner who is searching for a meaning

They do not know yet what the conversation is about and what they can contribute to a good result. Two steps are necessary to clarify these two points.

First, meet your conversational partner on the ground beneath the Solution Pyramid in a gentle and appreciative manner. Only when they understand that they have been invited to this conversation because they are an important expert and play a significant role in this process will they drop their doubts and concerns. Only then will they be ready to cooperate on the first level – which is defining the goal and searching for the meaning.

Having arrived at the first level of the Solution Pyramid, it is time to invite them to contribute to defining the goal in a way they consider desirable and attractive, i.e. that makes sense to them. There lies the key which this conversational partner was missing at the beginning of the conversation and which they need in order to make a constructive contribution to reaching the preferred future. As soon as they define their goal and find a meaning in it, the *conversational partner who is searching for a meaning* becomes a *conversational partner who is searching for a way*. This ensures their active participation in the further process.

> ### *A practical example of a "conversational partner who is searching for a meaning" in coaching*
>
> C: "I am glad you are here. Welcome. What should happen here in this hour so this conversation will have paid off for you?"
>
> CP "I thought you could tell me. I have received an appointment entry for this conversation and I do not know why I am here."
>
> C: "Ok – well, thanks for being here. After all, you probably have enough to do and I can imagine that you are not pleased about having this appointment without knowing the purpose."
>
> CP: "That is right. Actually, I do have other things to do."
>
> C: "Do you have any idea who might have sent you here?"
>
> CP: "Sure, I do. My boss. His secretary has made the appointment."
>
> C: "And do you have any idea what your boss expects from this conversation?"

CP: "He summoned me to his office last week to tell me that I need to be more polite when handling customer complaints on the phone. Maybe this is what this appointment is about."

C: "So this is what he discussed with you? I suppose you have a specific intention when you talk to customers as you do?"

CP: "After all, we put a lot of work and brainpower in our products. So, if something does not work out as the customer expected, I still would like to be treated respectfully. We can talk about anything in the end. But I will not tolerate being shouted at. Not even by our customers. I can expect a certain sense of decency among adults, right?"

C: "Yes, I can well imagine that you might get angry. It is also important to me to be treated with respect. Even differences on the factual level are no excuse for becoming abusive or loud. What do you think your boss is concerned about? Does he understand you?"

CP: "I think he is worried we might lose the customer if they feel misunderstood."

C: "And do you understand his concern?"

CP: "Yes, sure."

C: "Hmmm ... What could you and I do now so that we can take a step forward?"

CP: "It is also important to me that our customers are satisfied. I do not want my boss to be worried, either. Still, I cannot tolerate the tone of some customers. Maybe this could be the basis for our conversation?"

The coach (C) has taken the conversational partner (CP) seriously, which made the CP feel understood. This contributed to the CP's willingness to cooperate with the coach. Together they looked at the meaning of the conversation. Now, the CP is ready to work on finding a goal.

4.6.2 The conversational partner who is searching for a goal

This conversational partner already knows a lot about what should no longer be happening. However, they cannot yet define the goal they want to achieve.

To bring this conversational partner into the solution process well, it is important to give them sufficient time on the ground beneath the Solution Pyramid to explain everything that concerns them. In many cases, their explanation will be very comprehensive because they have been thinking about their situation a lot.

The transition from the ground to the first level, goals and impact, is the important turning point in the conversation. Only if the *conversational partner who is searching for a goal* trusts you to take good care of their problem and to understand their pressure will they be ready to climb up to the first level of the Solution Pyramid with you.

What needs to develop in the mind of your conversational partner is the idea that they can influence their situation. The aim is to move away from undesired observations towards desired changes. Then, the conversational partner will consider it worthwhile to develop the idea of a goal they want to achieve in their mind.

A practical example of a "conversational partner who is searching for a goal" in coaching

C: "I am glad you are here. Welcome! What should happen in this hour so that the conversation will have paid off for you?"

CP: "I do not think that you can help me. My colleague said I should see you. To be honest, I do not know what I could get out of this."

C: "Hmmm... would you like to tell me what this is about? I promise I will do my best to make this conversation helpful for you and I am sure that you will do the same."

CP: "Alright. Where do I start ...? Okay. The main problem is that our communication goes totally wrong. I am the tester here, you know. My job is to find mistakes and report them back, so they can be fixed. Our star programmers are not interested, however. They do not want to hear about mistakes. It is as if I criticise a piece of art, as if this is none of my business. They ignore me, sometimes even call me names, only because I'm doing my job properly. I hardly dare to point out mistakes anymore. All I can do is change departments. Or the company. But I like being a tester. And I am really good at it. Somebody should explain to those guys what a tester does and what our purpose is. And ask for compensation for each bad word or evil eye. After all, I am only human. Do you understand now that you cannot help me?"

C: "Wow ... that sounds really intense. Do I understand you correctly that you have not found a way to make it clear to the programmers that your job is to help improve the quality of the product?"

CP: "Exactly. They do not get it. You, however, totally get it."

C: "Hmmm ... Are there any exceptions? Or are all programmers equal in their reactions?"

CP: "They are all the same. Only Ferdinand – he is a good guy. Unfortunately, it is not possible to work only with him ... That would be nice!"

C: "Yes, that sounds like a nice idea ... What is it that Ferdinand does differently so that you like to work with him?"

CP: "He sees me as a human being. He asks about my weekend and tells me about his motorbike tours. And when it comes to testing, it is all about testing, not personal. He understands what I want to tell him and tries to implement the changes. Then he asks me if I meant it like that. That is great!"

C: "And you would like the other programmers to act like him?"

CP: "I do not necessarily care about private conversation. I cannot force them into that. If they talked to me about necessary changes in an objective way and understood that I want to provide support, my situation would improve significantly."

C: "So, it would be an important goal for you that the other programmers understand that you, as a tester, want to provide support?"

CP: "Yes, exactly. That would help a lot."

The coach appreciated the negative experience of the conversational partner and took it seriously. The story of Ferdinand is a useful resource for the conceptual switch from problem-oriented thinking to goal-oriented thinking.

C: "What exactly would you gain if the programmers understood that?"

CP: "Well, then I would see that they consider my work a valuable asset instead of an annoying obstacle. Perhaps they would then come to *me* instead of the other way round. And who knows – maybe I would come to love my job again ..."

The CP is now talking about the preferred future and, therefore, can work on a concrete goal.

4.6.3 The conversational partner who is searching for a way

This conversational partner knows exactly what they want to achieve and what this conversation is about. From a brief description of the problem on the ground beneath the Solution Pyramid, this conversational partner will usually jump to the first level by themselves and tell you about their goal. If you then ask about the impact of the goal, you will probably get comprehensive answers very quickly.

Let this conversational partner find their own speed up to the second level to a large extent. You can support them with specific questions when describing the impact (compare section 3.3.7 "Avoid not and no under all circumstances").

This conversational partner probably develops new thoughts on the second level, which is about focusing on what works. The greater the awareness of already existing resources and positive aspects regarding the current situation is, the easier it will be for your conversational partner to develop next steps that build on those resources and aspects. Therefore, spend enough time and energy on the second level. Then harvest the benefits on the third level of the Solution Pyramid – the level for the next steps.

A practical example of a "conversational partner who is searching for a way" in coaching

C: "Nice to have you here. Welcome! What should happen in this hour so that the conversation will have paid off for you?"

CP: "Thank you for taking time. I would like to advance on a professional level and need support in finding my best options."

C: "That sounds like a nice challenge. What exactly do you want to achieve professionally?"

CP: "You know, I am currently working as a developer in a project which will end soon. In the past two years, colleagues have repeatedly approached me and asked for help – not only regarding project-related issues. I think I would make a good leader. I have ideas for the future of our company, I get along with people at all hierarchy levels and I would also like to contribute a little more strategically to the success of the company."

C: "So, you want to become a leader and make strategic contributions? What future position would you like to be in?"

CP: "Well, I know that one of the team leaders is expecting a child. She wants to stay at home with her baby for at least two years. I think being a team leader would be a good start for me to gather my first experiences as a leader and who knows where the road will lead to later on ..."

C: "And, assuming that you would take over as a team leader from your colleague – what would that change for you?"

CP: "I could then find out whether leadership works the way I think it does. I would do a lot of things differently from my current team leader – although I know he always gives his best. I would have much more personal talks with the team members, for example. I believe that team members would talk more about their troubles instead of swallowing them. We would probably have fewer misunderstandings in the team. I would also let the team members make more decisions on their own. They often have really great ideas which unfortunately nobody wants to hear. Stuff like that. Maybe I am completely wrong – but I will only see if I try."

C: "And what impact would such a position have on your private life?"

CP: "Hmmm ... I have not thought about that yet ... I assume my partner would understand more about the things I have on my mind than they do now. People would probably react differently when I tell them about my profession – developers still have the image of loners who are only interested in their computers and are not able to have a normal conversation."

C: "If there were any disadvantages, what could they be?"

CP: "Maybe the responsibility I would have to bear. After all, the team leader has to justify the team's failures before the department head. I would not mind, though. I can handle that."

C: "You told me you are good at communicating with people, that you have good ideas about how leadership works, that you are willing to make strategic contributions to the company's success, that the position of a team leader will be vacant soon. What else gives you the confidence that you can achieve your goal?"

CP: "I think that both the HR manager and my department head trust me. The project I am currently working on will end soon, as I said, and I have gained a lot of professional experience in the past twelve years. I am quite sure that there is a lot to be said in my favour which justifies my confidence."

> C: "I hear that you have given this a lot of thought. What you say sounds absolutely coherent and clear to me. From your point of view, what would be the next step to get closer to your goal?"
>
> With the coach's questions, the CP is now very confident that they will be able to achieve their goal. Their desire to do so has also increased as a result of defining the positive impact. Defining the next steps is probably easier for them now than it was before the conversation.

4.7 The follow-up conversation in the Solution Pyramid

Changes usually take place between individual coaching sessions and rarely during them. There, the coaching client mainly finds impulses for change and develops concrete steps for their implementation. As a result, there is a new starting point at the beginning of each coaching session. New topics might develop when the next steps are implemented, and current developments, which have nothing at all to do with the first session, might become the priority in the next session.

It is therefore necessary to start each coaching session with a new contracting phase, i.e. to start on the ground beneath the pyramid again. Only after the contract is clarified can the coach and the client decide together which goal they work on this time – the old goal or a new one. The Solution Pyramid will guide you through this conversation, too.

If no new topics come up, focus on the improvements achieved since the last meeting. On this basis, further steps towards achieving the goal can be defined. Typical questions for starting a follow-up interview are:

- What is different/better since the last time we talked?
- What have you achieved?
- What shall we work on today?

4.8 Self-reflection

- What was exciting/new/helpful for you in this chapter?
- When could you use the Solution Pyramid in practice?
- How could you support your colleagues/employees/customers in finding a meaning in their work or when completing their tasks?
- How would people react to the question about confidence?
- What difference could this question make for the goal achievement of your conversational partners?

4.9 Experiments and exercises

- Prepare yourself mentally for an upcoming conversation, in which you want to achieve a goal, with the help of the Solution Pyramid:
  - Ground:

    What is the topic? What is this about?
  - Level 1:

    Which goal would you like to achieve in the conversation? What impact would the achievement of the goal have on you/others? And what else?
  - Level 2:

    How far are you on your way to your goal? What is already working? What do you already have that helps you achieve your goal?
  - Level 3:

    Assuming that you were already one step closer to your goal, what would be different? And what else? How will you have managed to make this next step?
  - Level 4:

    On a scale from 0 to 10, how confident are you that you will be successful? What has to happen in the next few days so that your confidence remains high? What has to happen so that your confidence increases? How can you achieve that?

- Think of a goal you want to achieve: for example, a next step on the career ladder, exercising regularly, a healthier diet, spending more time with friends – it should be something that is really important to you. Now think of the preferred future, that is, the moment when you have achieved your goal completely.
    - Find at least 20 things that are now better for you than before and write them down. What will you do differently? What new opportunities would you have? What would others say about you? ...
    - Now find another 20 things that the achievement of your goal would improve for others and write them down as well.
    - Now call a friend, read your list to them and ask them to add another five things.
- In the next few days, observe what you are already doing to get closer to your goal. When you discover something, tell your friend about it.
- On any day of the next week, try to avoid using the words *not* and *no* and make positive statements instead. Be patient with yourself. Whenever you notice a *not* or *no*, it shows that you are already internalising the positive phrasing. You might also want to ask others "What instead?" when you hear a *not* or *no* from them.

5. Individual coaching – the team and its individuals

You might wonder why we write about individual coaching in a book about team coaching. Well, a team only becomes a team when the individuals work together towards the same goal. Therefore, the individual person is of great importance in the team. Even if only one team member is unhappy, excluded, in a personal crisis situation or in resistance to external circumstances, the entire team will be affected.

The use of the different skills and strengths of all team members is what makes a team successful. These skills and strengths include constant communication as well as celebrating success and solving upcoming challenges together.

The problems of individual team members have an impact on everyone and can lead to conflicts within the team. The reasons are often of a private nature and therefore cannot be resolved in the team. This is why individual coaching is important in the context of teamwork.

5.1 What needs to be considered in individual coaching

5.1.1 Confidentiality and trust

Whatever you are entrusted with in private during a coaching session – or in any other conversation – can be disclosed to third parties only with the explicit permission of the coaching client or employee. Confidentiality creates the space for trust. Only if there is trust can problems be discussed openly. One single violation of this important rule can lead to a loss of trust once and for all.

If you are hired to coach an employee by a company's HR department or the employee's superior, the confidentiality rule must be part of your contracting. Of course, the employer has the right to know whether the coaching session took place or not. Disclosure or even assessments regarding the coaching client, however, are to be strictly declined.

There are exceptional situations which require disclosure for urgent reasons such as the protection of an employee. In this case, it is necessary to obtain the explicit consent of your conversational partner. If they refuse to give approval, alternatives need to be worked out together.

The trust required for openness is based on mutuality in individual coaching. The coaching client must be able to trust that the coach wants to help them improve their current situation and that – as mentioned before – they keep information they discuss to themselves. The coach, for their part, must trust in the fact that the coaching client gives their best and is able to find the right solution for their problem.

Conversations between superiors and employees also need trust that a high degree of openness will not have a negative impact on the employee's career. No conversation will be successful if fear is involved. If fear exists, the focus will not be on the actual topic but on avoiding possible consequences of the conversation.

5.1.2 Voluntary participation

Coaching can only be effective if it is voluntary, i.e. if the coaching client wants to talk about something. If so, active participation in the conversation, openness and the intention to change something can be assumed. By adopting solution-focused attitudes and applying the questioning techniques, the way towards the goal is often quick and easy to master.

In reality, the client is not always a volunteer. Superiors recommend their employees to make use of coaching because they are not satisfied with the employee's performance or behaviour in some respects and expect improvement as a result of the coaching. Or HR managers prescribe coaching because they see it as part of the job after reaching a certain hierarchical position. And sometimes situations arise in which a person resorts to coaching because they think they owe it to their position.

How does a coach deal with such a situation? In many cases it is possible to have a good coaching conversation even if the starting position is unfavourable. This requires a great deal of appreciation, transparency with regard to the assignment and the coach's full concentration on the conversational partner and their current situation. The coach must be patient to gain the coaching client's trust and to clarify the contract appropriately. In principle, the coaching client is in control. They determine the speed and the direction of the conversation.

A practical example

Veronika experienced an example of this topic right at the beginning of her coaching career. She was working for a company which was commissioned to assist long-term unemployed people in their reintegration into the labour market. A homeless man came to an individual coaching session which he had to do to receive money from the Social Welfare Office. He asked Veronika to sign the attendance confirmation so that he could leave immediately afterwards. She agreed to sign the paper in 50 minutes. The man sat down and remained silent. Veronika was silent, too.

The silence lasted about 20 minutes. Then the man interrupted the silence and asked what would normally be discussed in such a coaching. Veronika asked him what would make sense to him. The bumpy beginning resulted in a good and appreciative coach-client relationship. From then on, the man came to his coaching sessions on time and voluntarily every week.

5.1.3. Setting

For the development of trust and openness in the conversation, it is necessary to create an undisturbed and pleasant environment. A well-prepared room, for example, with two chairs facing each other, a small table with a water jug, two glasses, writing pad and pens – these things make people feel welcome when they arrive. Pay attention to small important details that might distract from the conversation or may be helpful:

- Take your time before the meeting to prepare yourself for it. This means that you should put aside all your worries, the stress of the day, your later appointments, any work you still need to do, other people's bad mood, etc. for the duration of the meeting. Develop your own strategy which works well for you. For some, it is a cup of tea they drink consciously or the short walk around the block. Others like a short meditation or to put on different clothes which makes them assume the appropriate role. Be aware that your state is transferred to your conversational partners, which makes working with them easier or more difficult. Whatever helps you to be completely there for your conversational partner is the right thing to do.
- Make sure that you are ready to welcome your conversational partner 15 minutes before the coaching session starts. This means that the room needs to be prepared by then. It also means that you are ready for the meeting.

- Switch off your phone or redirect calls.
- Put a clock behind the chair of your conversational partner so you can keep an eye on the time during the coaching session without your conversational partner noticing it. The clock should be quiet and large enough so you can read the time easily.
- Just in case, put a box of handkerchiefs within your reach.
- Think about whether you might need a flipchart and, if you need it, organise it in time, with paper and good writing pens.
- Book the room for a little longer. This gives you the opportunity to overrun a little when the conversation has just reached a delicate point before the end and you want to continue. Also remember to plan your follow-up appointments accordingly.
- At a large table, it is best to place the chairs across the corner. A table seems to be a barrier between you and your conversational partner and often has a negative impact on openness and trust in the conversation.
- To establish a good working relationship, your conversational partner will need some time in the beginning to settle down. This is especially the case when you see each other for the first time. Do a little bit of small talk. Ask whether it was easy to get here, talk about the good weather or the current season. Whatever suits you right now is welcome. With the small talk, your conversational partner can adjust to your voice, your speech tempo and your manner – and you can learn quickly which behaviour is appropriate for your conversational partner.
- Before you start, agree on the conditions: the duration of the meeting, the possibility to take notes and the confidentiality of what you talk about.

5.1.4 Corridor conversations

It happens quite often that employees want to express their respective concerns during an accidental meeting in the corridor or in the coffee room. The opportunity to speak privately for a brief moment is rare, especially in open-plan offices, and is frequently taken whenever it arises.

The solution-focused coaching approach in particular has the right techniques for such a situation. With the correctly placed question about the goal and a subsequent scale, it is often possible to provide valuable help even in a very short time (see also Cooper & Castellino, 2012).

If it turns out, however, that the present topic needs a more profound consideration, the public space will be inappropriate for such a conversation. The risk of being suddenly interrupted is too high. Depending on the intensity and urgency of the matter, we therefore recommend using the moment to make a concrete appointment. If there is an opportunity and if the respective schedules permit it, you can, of course, go to an appropriate meeting room to continue discussing the addressed topic immediately.

Even if you are sometimes tempted to provide immediate help with suitable advice, allow yourself and your conversational partner the opportunity to have a clarifying conversation in peace and quiet. Then you can be sure that the ideas you develop together will fall on fertile ground.

5.1.5 Dealing with resistance to coaching

It can happen from time to time that a person does not want to be coached by you at all. No matter which of the techniques mentioned here you use: they may work well for others but unfortunately do not work with this person. The causes are manifold and there are different ways to proceed, depending on the situation:

1. Your conversational partner remains focused on their problem, for example, and keeps telling you about how unbearable working with the star architect in the team is. In this case, you have probably not fully understood and appreciated the existing problem:

    - This situation seems really difficult for you. Thank you for talking to me about it so frankly. How have you managed to deal with it so far?

    As soon as your conversational partner trusts you to take them and their topic seriously, they will probably be more willing to answer your questions. You can rely on that. Only if you believe it, will they do the same.

2. Do you have the impression that the employee is not willing to develop paths to the preferred future together with you although you honestly appreciated them and their situation? One possible explanation is that it is your preferred future which the employee rejects for personal reasons.

    Coaching will only work if it is voluntary and intentional. Using coaching techniques to achieve your own goals will fail in most cases. It therefore pays off to be honest in this regard and to recognise whose goal it is about. If it is about your own goal, coaching is the wrong way. For this purpose, we recommend using the four steps of the Nonviolent Communication or the potential-focused method as described in section 5.2 "Feedback talks".

3. A third possibility which leads to the fact that a person does not want to be coached is that there are disagreements between the two of you. Only if your conversational partner trusts you will they let you support them in finding their way. This trust can neither be prescribed nor restored at the touch of a button once it has been lost. It takes time and a lot of positive moments between the two of you to regain it.

   If you still want to support the concerned person, suggest that they work with another coach. They might reject this offer. Do not be offended but signal instead that you are willing to talk anytime. This is how you place the next step in your colleague's hands. And this is all you can do at this point.

4. If you have been hired for some coaching and the coaching client comes to the conversation involuntarily, i.e. if they were sent by their superior, for example, you might also get the impression that they are resistant to coaching. In this case, it is important to build a personal and appreciative relationship with the coaching client. Thank them for coming to the appointment and ask them to tell you about their desired goals in this conversation.

   If it turns out that the coaching client does not share the views of their superior, you should take this seriously. There is probably another topic which is relevant to your conversational partner – maybe their relationship with their superior.

   You can trust the systemic principles: if a problem can be solved for the coaching client, no matter which problem, this will also have an impact on other topics. Also, this will probably have a positive effect on the employer's wishes. At least there is a chance. In any case, it does not make any sense to insist on discussing a topic which is irrelevant to the coaching client.

There are other possible scenarios in which resistance to coaching seems to make it impossible to work on solutions together with your conversational partner. However, if the principle that coaching only happens voluntarily is followed, this will not happen.

In all four cases described here, the coaching client is resistant and therefore not willing to participate in a joint coaching process. In such cases, ask yourself *who* really has the problem in the respective situation and whether coaching is the right means to achieve the goal. Do you want your conversational partner to change their behaviour? A clarifying conversation would be much better. Does the employer have a problem with your conversational partner? Maybe you can help the employer with a coaching session.

5.2 Feedback talks

There is a great deal of literature on feedback. One of the reasons might be that feedback involves huge potential for conflict although the reason is usually positive. The feedback provider wants to take the opportunity to support a change in behaviour – which they consider necessary – or convey appreciation. The feedback recipient wants to get valuable information which they can use for their own further development, i.e. gain security with regard to their own behaviour. Both attitudes are undoubtedly important and desirable.

So, how come that feedback is frequently perceived as a threatening scenario by both sides? And how can we deal with it so that feedback becomes helpful and productive for both? Maybe the problem is just the concept of feedback.

Thoughts for the feedback recipient:

For what purpose do you usually want to get feedback? For a lot of people, it is about increasing their own certainty through confirmation (compare section 7.5 "The SCARF model"). This assurance can be needed on several levels: *"Did I do a good job from your point of view? Are you satisfied with me and my performance? Is there something I could do better next time? Do you personally support me and my way? Do you have any more tips for me on how to deal better with situations like this in the future?"* Any of these questions can be a reason for asking for feedback. The feedback provider can only guess the reason if it is not explicitly stated. As a result, there is a great risk that the answer will not take the desired line but instead trigger even greater uncertainty.

For these reasons, we recommend avoiding the word *feedback* and asking concrete questions instead, to get more helpful and goal-oriented answers. "What did you like about my lecture? From your point of view, what should I do differently next time? Do you think that the audience understood XY? Did you feel personally addressed? What would have helped you to follow my lecture even more attentively?"

Thoughts for the feedback provider:

In which situations do you use the word *feedback*? Our experience is that the term almost always leads to a speech on a desired change in behaviour, for example: *"Peter, may I give you feedback on your lecture today? I think you could have done a few things differently."* In many cases, Peter will hear: *"I messed up!"*, although this was not what was said and often not meant.

Whenever the word feedback is used, a lot of people are resisting internally because they fear that they will have to endure negative criticism [Dixon et al., 2010]. Hufnagl [2014, p. 58] describes how, in anticipation of an unpleasant conversation, much that is said is already interpreted unilaterally and that neutral listening is hardly possible anymore.

Most people do not ask whether they are allowed to give positive feedback. They just do it. And they usually do not call it positive feedback either. They say, for example: *"Peter, your lecture today was great! Congratulations! You managed well to get the important information across, and you also had the right sense of humour. Bravo!"* Did you notice? The term feedback was not mentioned at all.

As a consequence, we would like to suggest that the word feedback should no longer be used at all. Formulate appreciative requests with the *potential-focused communication* method (see below: the subsection on "Potential-focused communication") if you want your conversational partner to change their behaviour. Use the first person to formulate a personal statement of appreciation (compare section 3.3 "More linguistic interventions") if you want to give a positive acknowledgement.

Expressing criticism is often difficult and unpleasant. After all, you can expect that the employee concerned will consider your criticism an attack on their professionalism, for example. They may resist, feel misunderstood or even launch a (counter-)attack. Your request in the end will often be unheard – if you even get the chance to make it at all.

5.2.1 The four steps of Nonviolent Communication

With his Nonviolent Communication, Marshall B. Rosenberg [Rosenberg, 2015] provides an opportunity to express criticism and make a corresponding request in a way that enables the employee to remain as cooperative as possible. Rosenberg's method is very extensive; it will certainly take years of intense study to learn and perfect it.

The part of his method which seems particularly helpful for "expressing criticism" is called *The four steps of Nonviolent Communication*. We will briefly introduce these four steps here. They show clearly how important the cautious use of language is when criticism is expressed. With a little practice, this technique can be applied directly.

Step 1: Describe perceptions and observations

Start the conversation with a concrete description of the behaviour you have observed. Be careful not to make an interpretation.

When people hear or see something, they inevitably develop hypotheses based on their own experiences. If they express their interpretations as an observation, the other person will – very legitimately – show resistance. It is therefore important to describe only *real* observations that are not subject to evaluation. You can say, for example: "I have not yet received the report you promised me for 9 o'clock this morning" instead of: "You are completely unreliable!"

There is a simple test to find out whether you expressed an observation or made an interpretation: if the other person can say: "This is not true", you did not express an observation but made interpretations and evaluations.

Step 2: Express feelings

A feeling is an emotional state or reaction. When you express the feeling the observation described above triggers in you, you point out that you are personally affected. So, this is about a matter which means something to you. It is not about some rules that were broken.

Most people are not used to being asked about their feelings and therefore find it difficult to express them. Statements often disguise themselves as feelings but are not feelings at all. Rosenberg [2015, p. 41ff] distinguishes

- feelings from thoughts
- between what we feel and what we think we are
- between what we feel and how we think others react or behave towards us.

Distinguish feelings from thoughts

The sentence: "I feel that we will not be able to do the user story in this Sprint", for example, does not describe a feeling but a thought. If you can replace "I feel" with "I think" then you express a thought rather than a feeling. Also, if "I feel" is followed by *that, like, as if* or by pronouns, *I, you, he, she, they, it* or by a name or noun referring to others, like *Jim, our* or *my*, then a thought rather than feeling is expressed. For example:

- that, like, as if:
  - I feel that you could do more.
  - I feel like a beginner.
  - I feel as if I'm given no chance.
- I, you, he, she, they, it:
  - I feel I am pushed to a decision.
  - I feel it is worthless.
- Names or nouns referring to people:
  - I feel Jim has been rather irresponsible.
  - I feel our Product Owner is being overwhelming.

Rosenberg adds that in English, it is not necessary to use the word *feel* at all when we are expressing a feeling. Instead of saying "I'm feeling happy" we can simply say, "I'm happy".

Another mistake when describing feelings is that comparisons are made. A lot of people understand the sentences: "I feel like it is my birthday today" or: "I feel like dancing," in a positive sense, but there are also some people who hate their birthdays or dancing and therefore get a completely wrong picture of the feeling that is being described here. Sentences that begin with: "I feel like …", and are followed by a pictorial comparison, should be avoided, because they can be misinterpreted.

Distinguish between what we feel and what we think we are

What is also important here, too, is to distinguish between actual feelings and words that describe what we think we are.

- What we think we are:
  - I feel inadequate as a programmer.

In this example, I am assessing my ability as a programmer, rather than expressing my feelings.

- Actual feelings might be:
  - I feel helpless as a programmer.
  - I feel uncomfortable as a programmer.

Distinguish between what we feel and how we think others react or behave towards us

Moreover, Rosenberg points out that there is a difference between words that describe what we think others are doing, or our interpretation of their thoughts or actions, and actual feelings.

- I feel unimportant to the people with whom I work.

The actual feeling here could be, for example, "I feel sad."

- I feel misunderstood.

The actual feeling here could be, for example, "I feel helpless."

- I feel ignored.

The actual feeling here could be, for example, "I feel lonely."

The kind of emotional description that can be understood as a hidden accusation usually has a particularly unfavourable effect. It results from the formulation "I feel …" followed by a past participle. The sentence "I feel *hurt*", for example, involves the accusation that the other person has apparently actively contributed to the concerned person being hurt. You can also expect the recipient to understand this statement as unjust accusation and go into resistance.

If the sentence: "This makes me …", followed by your emotional word, makes sense, you have a good chance that your counterpart will remain cooperative. On the other hand, if the sentence "You [*feeling*] me," makes sense, the opposite is probably true.

- Example 1: "I feel sad."
  - Test 1: "This makes me sad."
  - Test 2: "You sad me."

In this case, Test 1 passes and Test 2 fails. "You *sad* me," makes no sense. It is unlikely that your conversational partner will hear an accusation in this case.

- Example 2: "I feel exploited."
  - Test 1: "This makes me exploited."
  - Test 2: "You exploited me."

Here, Test 1 fails, as it makes no sense. So exploited is not a genuine feeling. However, Test 2, "You *exploited* me," makes sense. Therefore, it is very likely that your conversational partner will hear an accusation in this case.

There are also words that match both tests, which we call *hermaphrodite-feelings*. Use these words with caution. Even if they are meant as a feeling, they can be understood as accusation.

- Example 3: "I feel disappointed."
  - Test 1: "This makes me disappointed."
  - Test 2: "You disappointed me."

Smith [2010] uses a self-reflective question, asked in a gentle and kind inquiring manner, to uncover the real feeling underneath false-feelings, by asking herself: "Peggy, when you tell yourself that you are _____, how do you feel?".

A lot of people have learned from early childhood onwards that they are responsible for the feelings of others. This is wrong. No one can make anyone else angry or sad. And no one can make another person happy or cheerful either. Everyone is responsible for their own feelings. After all, feelings arise when you evaluate an observation, that is, when you think about something in a certain way.

One colleague is annoyed because he has been interrupted in his work without warning when someone asked him a question. The other colleague is happy in the same situation because her expertise has been recognised and others trust her to be open about being asked for advice at any time.

So, nobody else can be held responsible for feelings but the person concerned. Some people might have difficulties in understanding this at first, and yet it opens up the possibility of looking at people and situations with a multitude of interpretations.

Step 3: Explain needs and values

After you described your observations and the resulting feeling, the third step is to explain the needs and values behind your concern. If your conversational partner understands what they should change their behaviour for, and if that makes sense to them, only then they will actually do it. By explaining your need or value, you can help them see the purpose in your subsequent request.

The terms used to describe needs and values are always abstract and not concrete. Needs and values are, for example, protection, success, health, as well as status, certainty, autonomy, relatedness and fairness (compare section 7.5 "The SCARF model").

Needs, and strategies to satisfy needs, are often confused in terms of both language and content. For example, the sentence: "I need a coffee," is a strategy to satisfy one need. Only the speaker knows which need is to be satisfied, i.e. increased attention, recreation or warmth. Others can only speculate about it ...

If your conversational partner knows your need, i.e. the purpose of your concern, it will be easier for them to meet that need in many ways. There will be more flexibility in requests if needs, and strategies to satisfy needs, are clearly separated – there will be countless other ways to satisfy a need if one strategy is rejected.

So, if the coffee machine does not work at the moment and your conversational partner has understood that you need something to increase your attention, they will not have to reject your request. They could open the window to let in fresh air, offer you a cup of black tea or give you an energy drink.

By expressing needs, you show what is important to you. Your needs therefore correspond to your values. Expressing values increases the probability of getting what you want. Needs are always formulated in the first person.

A practical example of "formulating needs"

Imagine the following scenario: There has been a huge mistake in development. The customer noticed it after delivery. The Product Owner is annoyed, and justifiably so. The statement: "I need employees who do not mess up," would be understandable at this point but is not suitable for the goal. The development team would react with resistance and withdrawal instead of increased attention and willingness to cooperate. After all, the team members gave their best at the time from their point of view. And mistakes happen. The team would probably feel devalued, threatened and unfairly

> treated by such a statement. In their anger, the team members would hardly be able to hear the request which follows in Step 4.
>
> The phrase: "It is important for me to be able to rely on you," however, would address the Product Owner's need which sounds honest and comprehensible. There is neither an accusation nor a threat in this statement. If you want, you can even hear something like confidence that improvement is possible. The team's attention will probably remain intact and the team members will hear the following request.

Step 4: Making requests

The fourth and final step is to express what you want. Similar to defining goals, Rosenberg names criteria which must be observed here:

- Formulate requests positively. It is about what should be instead of what should not be.
- Ask for concrete behaviour instead of feelings.
- Your request must be feasible.
- Your request must not contain comparisons because they can be interpreted individually.
- Your requests must allow freedom of decision – your conversational partner must be allowed to reject them. Otherwise, it would be a demand, not a request. The difference lies in losing or maintaining appreciation for the other person when they reject your request.

In the example mentioned above, with the mistake discovered by the customer, the Product Owner might say, for example: "Make sure that never happens again!" If a request is rejected, there are three possible reasons for a "No." Each of the reasons is valid and therefore needs to be accepted.

- The request cannot be granted: "… that never happens again." – "No, we cannot promise that."
- Fulfilling the request contradicts an individual need of the other person: "No, we have to take care of another huge problem as ordered by the management. We will be happy to repair the most serious damage but we will not be able to make lasting improvements before next week."

- The request is understood as a demand: "Why should we take care of it? If you had given us more detailed information about the requirements and if you had been available for questions, this would not have happened."

Especially the last reason for a "No" can turn misunderstandings into conflicts quickly. A short explanation for which purpose the request is made can prevent this. The Product Owner might say, for example:

- I am asking you for your ideas on how to avoid such mistakes in the future, so we can do things differently in the next Sprint.

Summary

The integration of the four steps in the following short version we know from Tyrolean coach and school director Andreas Wurzrainer proves to be helpful in many cases:

1. When I see (hear ...) that (observation),
2. I feel ... (feeling),
3. because it is important to me that ... (need).
4. Would you be willing to ... (request)?

Example 1: "When I hear from the customer that a huge mistake has been made, I feel angry, because it is important to me that I can rely on you and that I also have the reputation with the customer of being reliable. Would you be willing to give me some ideas on how we must proceed differently in the next Sprint so that something like this does not happen again?"

Example 2: "When I see that today's meeting was interrupted by deliveries three times, I feel annoyed, because it is important to me that we can discuss our topics in quiet and with concentration. Would you be willing to organise another meeting room for us?"

5.2.2 Potential-focused communication

When working on the further development of *potential-focused pedagogy*, Andreas Wurzrainer discovered the possibility of formulating the four steps of *Nonviolent Communication* in a solution-focused way. He developed the idea in 2014, a few weeks before the first edition of the German version of our book was written.

Step 1: The preferred observation

The first step is to describe what future observation is preferred instead of describing the real, undesired observation. This approach has several major advantages. The wish is clearly expressed right at the beginning. The person addressed therefore knows immediately what it is all about. Since the statement is about a positive future situation, risks of mis-interpretation and misunderstandings are excluded:

- When all the stories are finished at the end of the next Sprint …
- When the quality of the product is so good with the next delivery that our customer calls to congratulate us …
- When you are on time for tomorrow's stand-up meeting …

Step 2: The preferred feeling

The described feeling that is expected when the preferred future situation occurs is – just like the preferred observation – positive. The rules that must be observed when formulating feelings to avoid accusing or insulting someone involuntarily – as it can easily happen when expressing negative feelings – are obsolete:

- Instead of "I feel bad …" a possible expression is: "… then I will feel good …"
- Instead of "I am sad …" you might say: "… then I will be happy …"
- Instead of "I am worried …" a possible statement is: "… then I will be sure …"

Step 3: The need that will be met then

Expressing the need which can be met in the new situation is similar to the one proposed by Marshall B. Rosenberg in his third step. It is a matter of explaining why it is important to the speaker that the wish is met:

- It is important to me that I can rely on you.
- I need to be certain that the quality of our work is high.
- It is important to me that I know that everyone has all the necessary information required for our work.

Step 4: The solution-focused question

Instead of a request – the wish has already been expressed in the first step – Wurzrainer suggests the formulation of a suitable solution-focused question as the fourth step. The conversational partner's willingness to cooperate is a prerequisite for the fulfilment of the wish. Of course, the conversational partner can still reject it. Experience has shown, however, that the probability of an agreement is significantly higher:

- How could we do this together?
- How can you manage to deliver even higher quality?
- How could you manage to be there at the agreed time?

> **Summarised, the formulation would be as follows:**
>
> 1. When I observe ... (preferred observation),
> 2. then I will feel/be ... (positive preferred feeling),
> 3. because I need/it is important to me that ... (need).
> 4. How/when/where could you ...? (solution-focused question).
>
> Example 1: "When the next delivery to the customer is flawless, then I will feel more confident that they continue to regard us as a reliable partner for their orders. How could we do that in the next Sprint and in the future?"
>
> Example 2: "When we can work through the next meeting without being disturbed, then I will be very content because it is important to me that we have peace and concentration for working on our topics. How could we do that?"

5.3 Supporting further development

People basically strive to become better in their respective areas of interest. These are not necessarily hobbies or activities that are fun. They include all fields where the person considers an improvement reasonable, useful or necessary. Planning your own further development is a pleasure and prompts energy if it is voluntary. If you have been told to do it, you will do it half-heartedly, if you do it at all. And the results are often unsatisfactory.

You can support the further development of skills of employees, colleagues or customers in a solution-focused manner. Participating in such development talks can also be obligatory. The direction of further development, the steps to be made and the planned pace of implementation, however, should remain the responsibility of the person concerned.

We will present a solution-focused approach for conducting development talks below. This has also proved to be successful in an agile environment. It requires willingness to listen, to ask questions and to perceive the conversational partner as an expert in their own situation.

The Solution-Focused Rating

Scales are very well suited for making differences visible. The way scales are usually used in forms for employee performance interviews, however, prevents differences from being displayed. Choosing one single value on a scale rather suggests stability instead of change.

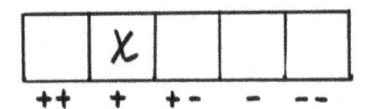

Sometimes it is easier, sometimes less so, to deliver the same performance in a particular area. The difference cannot be displayed with a single cross in the scale. By entering several values, however, the difference can be better displayed and taken into account. In the Solution-Focused Rating (SFR) [Lueger, 2006; 2012], the conversational partner is asked to distribute a total of 100 points in increments of ten on the scale, corresponding to their subjective assessment of performance in the period under review.

```
| 10 | 70 |    | 20 |    |
| ++ |  + | +- |  - | -- |
```

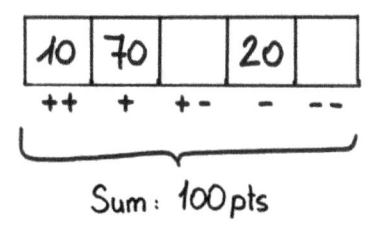

Sum: 100 pts

After the self-assessment, the coach or the superior supports the development of an action plan with solution-focused questions such as:

- What should continue to happen so that the value at + remains at least the same next year (or even rises slightly)?

This question is necessary because the things that are working well need also attention and effort to keep working well. Then continue with ++, if there is a value:

- What ideas do you have on how there could be a value again at ++ next year?
- What should stay the way it is so the value at – remains as small as it is now?
- In your opinion, what could make the value at – smaller or even make it disappear completely next year?
- Assuming that you do not enter a value in the fields with – and – –, respectively, next year, what would be different?
- And how would you achieve that?
- And what would your contribution be?
- What else can you think of?
- How confident are you that you will actually realise your ideas (on a scale from 0 to 10)?
- What needs to happen so that you become a little more confident?

The answers to these questions result in a list of concrete steps developed by the conversational partner. These steps therefore have a great chance of actually being made. The focus is on both the positive and the negative exceptions. The conversational partner writes each single action under the scale in their own handwriting. After the conversation, they will take the sheet with them so they can implement the actions.

In 2006, Veronika wrote her master thesis on evaluating this method. For this purpose, she carried out a small study with ten managers and their employees [Kotrba, 2006]. The interviews with the test individuals showed that the development talks using the SFR were perceived as fairer, more motivating and more trust-building than the talks held using familiar models. The managers stated that all employees had assessed themselves more strictly than the managers would have done. Moreover, the talks had lasted longer than previous talks but had been significantly more relaxed; there was even energy left after the talks for private activities such as sports.

In the beginning, handling SFR requires good training of the conversational partners. Asking solution-focused questions requires some practice too. The results speak for themselves – also with regard to the rate of actual change afterwards.

SFR talks can also be held between colleagues. Since no external assessment takes place, it does not matter who leads the conversation and how much this person knows about the performance of the conversational partner from their own experience. Teams working independently often leads to managers having little insight into the daily performance of individual team members. This circumstance makes the approach especially applicable in an agile environment.

A practical example of using "Solution-Focused Rating"

A: "Let us talk about your ability to work in a team. When you look at yourself over the last six months, how would you rate yourself when it comes to your ability to work in a team? Please distribute 100 points in increments of ten on the scale."

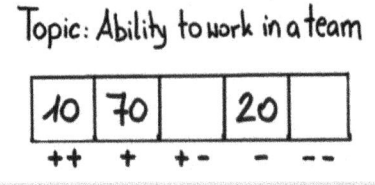

Topic: Ability to work in a team

10	70		20	
++	+	+-	-	--

A: "I see a high value of 70 at +. What do you think you need to do in the future to keep the value at least at the same level for the next six months?"

Individual coaching – the team and its individuals

B: "Well, I think that all team members know that I am always there for them whenever they need something from me. I am rarely ill, do my work diligently and I am on time for all meetings. If I cannot meet a deadline, I will say so as soon as possible, so my colleagues can react in time and provide support."

A: "And what else?"

B: "What else? Let me think ... I frequently bring snacks. Does that count?"

A: "I would say, definitely, yes. Would you like to take notes?" A waits for B to finish writing. "You have a value of 10 at ++. What ideas do you have about what you could try in the next observation period to be able to enter a value here again?"

B: "Perhaps I could volunteer to accompany a new employee once again so that they can integrate well with us. I think I am good at this and it is helpful for the whole team. Nobody else wants to do it anyway. That is all I can think of right now."

A: "Well, it is an idea. And you have a value of 20 at -. What could you do in the next six months to keep this value so small or maybe make it even smaller?"

B: "Hmmm, that is a good question. It is about working with Nik. He is the only one in the team who gives me a hard time when it comes to cooperation. He always wants to be the centre of attention, he thinks he is better than anyone else and he does not want anyone else involved."

A: "And what could you do differently in the next six months compared to the last six months, so that the situation could improve slightly?"

B: "Maybe I could try not to get angry with him anymore. That might help ..."

A: "And what would you do instead of getting angry?"

B: "Maybe I can find out what Nik needs to be more cooperative. I mean, he is not a bad guy. Perhaps he had bad experiences with former teammates and needs to come to trust us. That reminds me. I don't think anyone has asked him yet whether he wants to join us for a drink on Thursday night. Not that everyone participates every time, but we could ask him."

A: "Check the list of concrete actions you have compiled so far. Can you think of anything else you want to add?"

B: "No, the list looks good. Thank you very much. I am looking forward to the teamwork in the next six months."

A: "On a scale from 0 to 10, how confident are you that you will actually implement these actions?"

B: "Very confident, 10. I cannot promise that I will never get angry with Nik again. Anyway, this is not on my list."

Here is the list of actions which B compiled in this conversation:

1. Be there for the team members whenever they need something in the future as well.
2. Continue doing my work diligently.
3. Continue to be on time for meetings in the future.
4. Inform the team members in good time whenever I need help or more time.
5. Volunteer for introducing and accompanying new employees.
6. Find out what Nik needs to cooperate.
7. Ask Nik whether he wants to join us for a drink Thursday night.

5.4 Self-reflection

- What was new/exciting/helpful for you in this chapter?
- How can you use SFR in your daily work?
- Can you think of any situation in your past in which individual coaching made or would have made sense?
- Who in your professional environment could potentially benefit from individual coaching?
- How could you arrange the right setting for an individual coaching in your professional environment?
- How could you provide your colleagues/employees/customers with the opportunity of individual coaching without putting the principle of voluntariness at risk?

5.5 Experiments and exercises

- Find a topic in which you want to improve slightly – and which is important to you – and write it down. Then distribute 100 points in increments of ten on the scale. Now ask yourself the questions mentioned in section 5.3 "Supporting further development" on Solution-Focused Rating.
- Ask a friend to have such a conversation with you. After the conversation, talk about both the process and the result.
- Find a conversational partner who is searching for a meaning at the next team meeting. Do you manage to get him on board?
- Is there someone who, in your opinion, should change their behaviour? Try to express your request with the four steps based on Wurzrainer's potential-focused communication.

6. Team development

Team development is a constant process and cannot be replaced by a workshop or seminar. A lot of managers try to pass this responsibility on to external trainers and coaches. Even if a team building workshop can help eliminate current misunderstandings, sustainable results will only be achieved by continuous team development work integrated into the everyday working life.

6.1 Goals of team development

Teams are formed to achieve results together which individuals would not be able to achieve [Sprenger, 2012, p. 51 ff.]. This requires the combination of existing resources such as skills and abilities, creativity and the experience of the individual team members in a way that they can excel together. The interaction of these strengths is only possible when caution, distrust and competitiveness have given way to good and trustful teamwork. Achieving this is the primary goal of team development processes.

6.1.1 High-performance teams

Who would not want them, the so-called high-performance teams? The question is: what makes a high-performance team? Losada and Heaphy [2004] characterise high-performance teams based on three criteria:

- Economic viability (profit/loss)
- Customer satisfaction (surveys and interviews)
- 360-degree evaluations (assessments by team members, superiors, peers and employees)

This seems to be appropriate as it is contextual. Losada and Heaphy [2004] found that the following three indicators correlate with team performance:

- Positive/negative statements (positivity/negativity)
- Exploring and examining a position versus arguing in favour of the speaker's viewpoint (inquiry/ advocacy)
- Speaker refers to a person or group within versus outside the team, department or company (self/other)

High-performance teams have balanced conversations when it comes to asking for others' and taking their own points of view. They also talk equally about themselves and about others. Moreover, they make significantly more positive statements than negative ones. This knowledge can be used in team development by specifically promoting the strengthening of characteristic qualities in the team; after all, positive thinking also leads to success [Lyubomirsky et al., [2005; Achor, 2010].

Practical Tip

There are a lot of ways to increase the number of positive statements in team communication. We have listed some examples here:

- Tell success stories on a regular basis and ask your teammates to do the same.
- Pass on positive feedback you have received.
- Celebrate team achievements.
- Talk about what has already worked, before looking for something which has to change.
- Say "Thank you!" – and mean it.
- Provide for regular opportunities to talk about private topics as well.

You will certainly find more opportunities to actively promote positive statements in your team if you look for them. To balance the inquiry/advocacy ratio, you can ask "What instead?" when you hear negative statements, i.e. when it includes words such as *not* or *no*.

Teams are groups of people who share a common goal which makes sense for everyone involved. They want to do good teamwork, achieve effective results and, by doing so, use all the talents available in the team. The team members feel collectively responsible for their success. Successful teams observe what works well in cooperation and continue improving their cooperation. They agree that they want to achieve a good reputation with all partners. That means that all team members come to work with the firm intention and attitude to achieve top results together with the team.

Every joint project starts with the question: "For whom do we produce that, for what purpose and with what benefit (for the customer, the team members, the team as a whole, the company or organisation, or another environment)?" Only if this question is answered comprehensively can an attractive goal develop and meaning can be found in both the task and the cooperation. A joint task which makes sense for all team members is a necessary requirement for a working team (see also Gerber & Gruner, 1999).

Another requirement is that the team is in a constant exchange with its environment and has relationships with partners, customers and suppliers. The team ensures that all people involved in the project are integrated in the work process at least temporarily.

As already mentioned, successful teams use the talents of all team members. To be able to do that, however, these talents need to be recognised and known first. Open and appreciative interaction with each other and a good culture of communication bring this knowledge to light and make it usable again and again.

Successful teams keep their boundaries open, so they can expand and add to the team in a reasonable way at any time. For example, presentations of results to customers, superiors or partners are characterised by including the ideas of the audience. Instead of convincing people otherwise, their inputs are recognised as valuable additions and included in the results to achieve further improvement.

Practical example of team development – "My personal style"

In November 2016, Veronika carried out the following exercise in a team development workshop:

A team of five sat down in a circle of chairs. Veronika asked Alex (name changed), who was next to her, to listen carefully, without talking, for the next few minutes. In addition, he was asked to nod or shake his head to evaluate statements made by his colleagues.

"Let's start with Alex. What do you think you already know about what Alex needs in order to work well and feel comfortable at work?"

The colleagues started saying everything they could think of. Alex evaluated each of their statements with a nod or by shaking his head. Each statement he approved of was written down on the Alex flipchart. Afterwards, Alex had the opportunity to correct mistakes and complete the statements. To learn relevant additions, Veronika also asked questions such as: "When someone needs something from you, do you prefer a phone call, an e-mail or being addressed in person?"

Once everything Alex considers relevant has been written down, it is the turn of the next colleague. This exercise takes some time and needs mutual understanding as well as understanding of individual working preferences. However, it helps considerably to look out for each other, particularly in stressful working phases.

My personal style — Alex
- needs coffee in the morning
- likes personal communication more than emails or phone calls
- chocolate helps, when angry or tired
- starts early in the morning (at about 7) and leaves at 3 p.m. to collect his son from playschool
- loves to have so. to share his thoughts with regularly
- needs 2 hours of uninterrupted working time daily (7 to 9 a.m.)

6.1.2 Self-organisation in agile teams

Agile teams are often characterised by the fact that they are self-organising. At least this is the idea that has been preached successfully in the Agile world for years. We had the same opinion as well, until recently. And then the following happened: one of our customers asked us for a training day on "systemic thinking and acting".

To prepare for the training, we delved into the basic books, for the first time in a long time, looking for relevant statements on that topic. During this research, we came across texts written by biologists Maturana and Varela who, among other things, did research on the characteristics of dead and living systems [Maturana & Varela, 1987; Ludewig & Maturana, 1992]. What we read in their texts opened up a completely new view with far-reaching consequences for our daily work: Maturana and Varela claim that every living system – and that is every group of living beings – is self-organising, and that this is what distinguishes them from dead systems.

So, while Agile Coaches do everything they can to support teams in becoming self-organising, the teams have always been there. Therefore, it becomes clear that any well-meant attempt at change is often met with resistance by the respective team. So, if it is not about promoting self-organisation, what is it about when it comes to establishing agile teams?

It becomes clear with the following example: you are at an IT conference and enter the main conference room along with about 400 other participants. The chairs in the room are arranged in neat rows. What will you do? You probably choose one of the free seats and, in doing so, will take various needs into consideration. You might want to take pictures of the speaker and their slides, so you will opt for a seat in one of the front rows where you have an unobstructed view. Perhaps you prefer sitting at the end of the row because your legs are long, and you appreciate being comfortable. Maybe you prefer sitting in the last row so you can leave the room in case you do not like the keynote. And what do the other participants do? They do just the same, that is choosing a seat which meets their needs. In the end, everyone – or most of the participants – sit on their seats, in rows, facing the stage, in this very room, waiting for the conference to start. Nobody sits with their back turned on the stage. Nobody sits on the floor or even on the stage. And all of this works without information signs, a team building sequence or an usher. A clear proof of working self-organisation in living systems.

What would have happened if the chairs in the conference room had been arranged in a circle? You might suspect it: the participants would have sat down in the circle of chairs, facing the centre.

The impact of this thought experiment on agile coaching is huge. It is not simply about teaching the team members to become self-organising when supporting them to become more agile in cooperation. Rather, it is about reviewing the existing conditions and modifying them in a way that the team can and will be self-organising in a more goal-oriented way than before.

> ### *Practical Tip*
>
> Ask the following questions when you look at the given conditions for self-organisation:
>
> - What team behaviour is desirable and for what purpose?
> - Who or what already supports this behaviour?
> - On a scale from 0 to 10, with 10 meaning that the team behaviour already is at the desired level, and 0 meaning the opposite, where would you say the current reality is?
> - What already works that made you choose this value?
> - What changes would occur for whom if the team was already one step further on its way?
>
> Consider both positive and negative consequences for the people concerned. Would this step mean gaining or losing competence for someone? Would costs be saved or new costs occur? Would logistical measures be necessary? Would compliance with official channels be in danger?

The answers to these or similar questions can provide information about current obstacles a team might be confronted with on its way towards more agility. We often encounter long-term habits, unspoken fears, informal rules or resigned acceptance as the learned results of unfavourable surrounding conditions. These are often the real obstacles to agile success stories, they are difficult to detect, and they are persistent. Also, they often cause signs of visible rigidity, reluctance and even aggression among individual team members. The truth is, however, that it is only a kind of working self-organisation which has established itself according to the actual experiences.

Living systems learn and adapt constantly. The good news is that learned behaviour can be relearned again when conditions change permanently. For this purpose, it is necessary to have new experiences. In the beginning, these new experiences will feel unfamiliar and will cause distrust. It is understandable that freedom suddenly offered in teams which were strictly led before is rejected at first. If, despite the rejection, the offer is honest and remains open, however, and if the first cautious use of freedom is encouraged, again and again, new trust can develop. So, it is not the team members but the surrounding conditions of a team which have to be changed permanently if you want another form of self-organisation.

The Scrum Guide of November 2020 [Schwaber & Sutherland, 2020] stopped talking about self-organising teams and refers now to self-managing teams.

6.2 Our R.E.S.U.L.T. model for team development

Our R.E.S.U.L.T. model is a means of support as well as a checklist for daily team development. The model includes tools and interventions that turn teams into winning teams.

R. – Recognise achievements

"Do good and talk about it", says a well-known proverb which deserves much more attention. Addressing achievements leads to self-confidence, motivation and recognition – new achievements are inevitable as a result. Still, most news of the day is about anger, difficulties and problems. Why? It is probably a cultural issue. A lot of people have learned to pay attention to what is wrong. It starts in school: whatever a child does in terms of performance, the teacher corrects the mistakes with a red pen. So, how can the child ever learn that the correct and good parts of their performance are more important?

> **Practical Tip**
>
> You can help your colleagues, employees or customers get out of the circle of troubleshooting by asking questions. Show constant interest in what works. Ask for achievements and comment on them in an appreciative way whenever you observe them by chance.
>
> Start each meeting and each conversation with something positive. That can be positive news for the participants, a positive report on the team's performance or a question about a nice or successful experience your conversational partner had.

E. – Encourage in case of setbacks

The business world is changing faster and faster. This is neither a secret nor a new insight. It is a fact. Progress, improvement and acceleration are thought of as factors of success in the global economy. This opinion starts in the top management and continues right to the heart of every single employee. Hardly anyone can escape it. This is exactly why each obstacle is regarded with suspicion and considered the enemy. Everything that slows things down is unwanted.

An alternative option could be that you appreciate all external obstacles and see them as early warning indicators. They might show you that you need to step on the brake when you enter a tight bend, so you will not go off the road. Whenever you cannot follow a path as planned due to changing external circumstances, it is time to recall your goal. By doing so, you can take the new conditions into consideration, and find and embark on the new path – much in the spirit of the agile idea of "inspect and adapt".

> ### Practical Tip
>
> Take your time to listen to complaints about and displeasure at unforeseen changes. It helps when you understand and honestly appreciate the underlying concern rather than thinking about solutions. Do not play down the incidents you are told about. Those incidents seem important and drastic to your agitated conversational partner. If you play them down, you will experience immediate resistance from your conversational partner, and it will no longer be possible to work on helpful solutions together. Instead, think again about what it is all about in the end. Then, find new ways of working together so you can achieve what you want.

S. – Support Learning

When it comes to *dealing with failure* – particularly failed attempts – it is helpful to change your way of thinking. Mistakes inevitably happen when you work. And whenever someone tries a new approach, failure is a possibility. Of course, you can name and shame the person responsible for the mistake; this is very common in many teams. You can roll your eyes and vent your anger. All of these reactions are very understandable when mistakes and failure are considered something negative in the culture of a company. People tend to behave in a way that they think others expect them to. By doing so, they expect invaluable gain – recognition, belonging and harmony.

However, this is also a great opportunity. Try to turn the tables and see mistakes as a starting point for improvements. Whenever someone makes a failed attempt, it is essential to gain new insights and embrace it as progress. It is about the inner attitude towards experiments – and the associated failed attempts. If a constructive culture of learning is successfully established in a team, you will observe that team members more often dare to try something new and be more creative. You will also observe that the team members will be able to make unexpected achievements together while being very self-confident. This is a new, value-adding way to achieve the major goal of being recognised, belonging and harmony.

A special kind of celebrating mistakes has become established in a lot of companies: the fuck-up nights (*fuckupnights.com*). During the fuck-up nights, people tell their stories about failed attempts and failures and the learnings from these mistakes are celebrated then. The aim of such an event is to initiate a cultural change in dealing with failure.

Practical Tip

Pay attention to your language! Dweck [2006] writes in her book *Mindset* about two different ways of thinking which are also influenced by our language. She refers to one way of thinking as Fixed Mindset. It prevents learning from mistakes and is nourished, among other things, by the following linguistic expressions which suggest stability:

- This is right. This is wrong.
- You are good at that! You are not good at that!
- You are a good programmer! You are a bad listener.

The second way of thinking – Growth Mindset – allows for opportunities to grow personally. Difficult situations are appreciated as challenges, and failure is understood as learning steps. This way of thinking can also be supported by language by emphasising the way and the respective progress:

- I think that you have already managed that well. You should do that again.
- You are doing well already, I think. You can get even better.
- It seems you have already managed well to work out programming. If you focus on it and practise it, you will also find it easier to listen carefully.

U. – Uphold meaningful rules

To uphold meaningful rules means here:

1. ensuring that all employees know and comply with the non-negotiable framework,
2. that institutional rules are adhered to in principle but that they are regularly scrutinised and adjusted, if necessary, and
3. that there is room for continually negotiating selectively necessary team rules.

For effective team development, a clear framework and a few limits set from the outside are needed. Within these limits, everyone should be able to develop freely. This is referred to the *non-negotiable framework*. As the name suggests, these limits are not negotiable. They are firmly established, and any transgression will be penalised. The non-negotiable framework must be known and carefully considered. It should not include more than four points (just like the four sides of a frame). For example, sentences such as

- *I respect and uphold the good name of the company, or*
- *I treat our customers with respect and esteem*

can be part of a non-negotiable framework. Another example of such non-negotiable framework is the Code of Honour mentioned by Linda Webb, as introduced in Franklin et al., [2018, p. 152]:

- *demonstrate personal honour and integrity at all times*
- *choose peace over conflict, and*
- *[demonstrate] respect for ourselves and others.*

Institutional rules are established additionally, and monitoring them should provide a more flexible framework to allow further development. Those rules serve as a basic orientation for cooperation and mutual understanding within a company or organisation. They are to promote confidence and security. If this system of rules becomes inflexible, however, it will prevent this intention from becoming reality. Everyone who is afraid of consequences and who has no opportunity to contribute their own ideas for better cooperation in a company will become aligned, inconspicuous employees who do their job resignedly. You cannot expect an extraordinary commitment from such an employee. Therefore, Sprenger [2012] demands that management challenge institutional rules regularly. That means that managers are to engage actively in making a system unstable from time to time to prevent it from freezing.

The institutional framework might include the following points:

- *No pets are allowed in the office,*

or

- *It is mandatory for every employee apart from the field staff to be present during the core working hours (Mon. to Thu. from 10.00 a.m. to 3.00 p.m. as well as Fri. from 10.00 a.m. to 1.00 p.m.).*

And then there are a lot of negotiable *team rules* which make for good cooperation. The team is to develop these rules together, and the rules should be negotiable at all times. Whenever there is a problem in the team's cooperation, it is important to create space which allows for scrutinising existing rules and, if necessary, modifying them or adding new ones. Team rules can be, for example:

- *Coffee drinking is allowed during a meeting, as long as everyone arrives on time,*

or

- *Whenever a team member asks for help, the others give it.*

> **Practical Tip**
>
> Establish only a few (a maximum of four) rules which are very clear. These rules are the so-called *non-negotiable framework* and serve as guidelines for cooperation.
>
> Whenever situations arise in which someone does not like something, discuss together whether a new rule is needed and what it should be called or if an existing rule needs to be adjusted. Make sure that new rules are introduced only if everyone concerned consents. Otherwise, compliance will not work.
>
> Each rule should apply only as long as it is functional. Therefore, rethink the set of rules again and again at appropriate intervals and together with your team, and keep the set of rules as lean as possible.

L. – Let them solve it

When is a manager, a coach or a person in any other leading role such as a Scrum Master helpful to others? This question leads to different answers today than it did a few years ago. It has always been clear that leaders do a good job when they can solve other people's problems as quickly as possible so that they can continue to work in a good way.

This expectation has led to the fact – and this is still an issue today – that management positions were filled with people who were the greatest experts in their respective field but who did not have any leadership skills. The result was that the team lost an expert in their daily work and, in exchange, got a manager who was barely able to support them in personal matters. A bad deal.

The new idea of effective support, however, looks different. Neither a manager nor Agile Coach nor Scrum Master has to be the greatest expert in a team. The team has experts among its team members and these experts carry out the daily work.

Today, people sought for leadership positions are those who know how to encourage others, let them grow and, at the same time, create conditions which allow for useful cooperation. They help their colleagues solve problems on their own when the solution is part of their sphere of action. Of course, they also make decisions for the team – with the aim of creating a space where the team can move well. The roles and requirements have changed. This contributes significantly to the team members' self-confidence and, therefore, also to team development.

> ### *Practical Tip*
> Still today, some employees expect their Scrum Master or manager to be more of an expert than themselves. Such an employee considers being an expert a basic prerequisite for accepting the authority of the other person. Many modern Scrum Masters and managers struggle with this old view.
>
> Experience has shown that the best way out of this situation is appreciation, again. Admit openly and with self-confidence that you do not have this or that knowledge. Show your gratitude for the fact that you have your colleagues as top experts for all operational issues and point out that you can only be successful together. Also, emphasise your own expertise, that is: leadership, overview, responsibility, support and networking for the benefit of your working together and your customers.

T. – Trust your people

An essential prerequisite for successful cooperation in a team is mutual trust. Unfortunately, this cannot be established or created in the short term. Trust must grow. It must develop from the experience that people can rely on each other – even when things get difficult. This is exactly where focus comes up again. We have discussed focus quite often in this book. Someone who assumes they cannot trust anybody will constantly find proof that this is the case because they are (unconsciously) looking for it. If you search for evidence that you can trust others, however, you will find enough proof that this is in fact the case and your trust will grow.

So, it depends on the team members' own basic assumption whether trust or rather mistrust will grow in the team. Unfortunately, a positive attitude cannot be prescribed to anyone. However, you can set a good example by always expecting the positive from your colleagues or customers. By doing so, you put your trust in them. There is one thing that trust definitely is: it is contagious.

Practical Tip

Trust is based on positive experience. The more positive things you hear about another person, the more you will trust them. Think about an Agile Coach, for example. Which coach would you put your trust in if you had to involve a coach in a transition? Probably – like we would – the coach you have already had positive experiences with. Or the one who reliable sources told you a lot of positive things about. So, make sure your team members hear a lot of positive things about each other. Always say thank you publicly, even for small things, and ask your colleagues to thank each other whenever possible.

6.3 Tools for team development

All the tools and interventions we present here emphasise the strengths and abilities existing in the team. By focusing on and publicly addressing these resources, the team members' trust in themselves and in others increases.

Resource gossiping

This exercise is based on a well-known and popular phenomenon of human communication: gossiping about others behind their backs. Just describing this activity will already lift the mood in a lot of teams.

Ask the team to form groups of three or four people. The number of people in a group should be the same for all groups if possible. The group members then have to sit down in a way they can talk easily to each other. One person in each group turns their chair around and, by doing so, turns their back to the others while still being able to listen carefully.

At your command, all groups have two minutes to talk about the person turning their back to them. The task is to gossip about everything they like about the respective person, including their resources, skills and abilities, what they admire their colleague for, and so on.

Resource gossiping

When the two minutes are over, the person the group has been gossiping about turns around and the next person turns their back to the group, so the others can gossip about them now. This process is repeated until everyone in the group has had their turn.

If one or two group members are left out because some groups had more people than others, the plenum will then gossip about these people. Participants usually report that this exercise has had a wonderful effect on them. It does everyone good to be appreciated and it does everyone good to appreciate others. In a final reflection, the participants can talk about this effect.

Another way to appreciate each other and focus on what works is gratitude. It is all too often taken for granted when we help and support each other. Saying "thank you" shows that the support is noticed and appreciated. In many cases, thanking others often makes mutual support and cooperation even increase and improve in quality.

The Chocolate tour

This is a simple and short exercise of mutual appreciation that draws attention to the resources within the group. The coach or facilitator prepares the exercise by writing the name of each participant on the back of a sticky note, folding it and putting it into a hat. The hat is then passed around and every team member draws a name. If someone draws their own name, they report it immediately and exchange the note. Afterwards, everyone receives a chocolate.

The participants now have the task of thinking about a serious compliment, thank-you or appreciation for the person whose name they have drawn. The coach or facilitator asks "Who wants to start?". The first one walks over to the person whose name is on the note they drew and gives them their thank-you, appreciation and the chocolate. Then this person continues the tour. If there is a break in the chain, some other volunteer continues.

Appreciation cards

Another way to say "thank you" is with so-called appreciation cards. Martin Heider, Agile Coach and co-organiser of the Agile Coach Camps in Germany for many years, has developed a version of those cards which is perfectly suited for distributing small messages of appreciation and gratitude on many occasions. The cards look similar to this one:

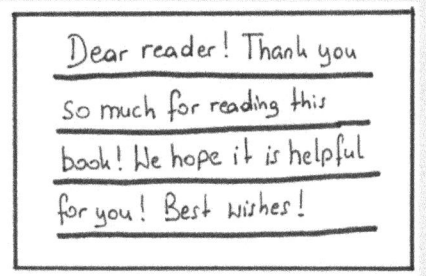

Card 1 (left): A figure holding a sign that reads "Thank you!" with "from: Veronik & Ralph" written below.

Card 2 (right): "Dear reader! Thank you so much for reading this book! We hope it is helpful for you! Best wishes!"

Rolf Dräther told us that in one of his projects, blocks of ten cards were used to start thank-you relays. In these relays, each person who was appreciated received not only the card intended for them but also the remaining pile of empty cards. So, this person now had the relay baton and they wrote the next card and then passed on the pile to the next person.

For a lot of people, it is even more difficult to see their own performance in a positive light than the performance of others. In fact, both need to be seen positively, so that trust can develop and good cooperation becomes possible. Therefore, it makes sense to practice appreciating your own abilities, too.

The Quality Mirror

This exercise by Röhrig [2011] is very useful for team development situations as well as for workshops on optimum cooperation or resource focusing.

Each participant receives a drawing sheet (A3) and is asked to fold it once in the middle and then unfold it again, so two halves in A4 size are created. Everyone writes down their own name in the middle at the top of the page. Then the participants are asked to write down their three most important professional strengths in the left column and the three most important private strengths in the right column. The sheet is then put in an easily accessible position. Everyone walks over to the other sheets and, wherever possible, adds strengths they think the respective person has.

In the end, everyone gets their own sheet back and now has a quality mirror including both a self-view and an external view of their existing resources. A final reflexion in the plenum can even intensify the positive mood after this exercise.

In addition to such short interventions, which can also be used here and there at the beginning or at the end of a meeting or workshop, there are comprehensive solution-focused team development methods designed for long term. We will briefly present the most popular below.

Reteaming

The method of reteaming, developed by Ben Furmanand and Tapani Ahola (Finland) and published in the German-speaking area by Geisbauer [2012], is a solution-focused team building process with a lot of individual stages. Despite this, not a lot of time is needed for this method, which also is highly efficient. With reteaming, you can promote the team spirit, solve problems in cooperation, and get oriented towards the common goal.

The three main aspects are *the method, the tools* and *a special kind of relationship between the coach and the client system*. It is essential that the coach is able to unite all three aspects in harmony. There are specific training courses to become a Reteaming Coach.

We want to present the 15 steps of a "Mission Possible", as described by Geisbauer [2012], as an example. The statements below the various headlines are a possible short version of the introduction. You can use them when working with teams:

1. **Time travel**:
   "Imagine that everything goes very well for you for one or two years. Write a letter together as a team from this *positive future* to inform me about what your life in this future looks like."
2. **Publication**:
   "Show me and some other people in your company this letter afterwards."
3. **Project**:"
   "Find a common goal that will help you reach that future and decide on a project you want to implement to achieve this goal."
4. **Name**:
   "Give your project a special and creative name which you, as a team, like."
5. **Symbol**:
   "Find a symbol, a talisman, which you can use to symbolise your project."

6. **Supporters**:

    "Involve a number of supporters in your project. Who could you ask to actively support your project?"

7. **Benefits**:

    "Find out how the result of your project will help you and other people. Find out what you will get out of it."

8. **Optimism:**

    "Answer the question: 'what makes you believe that you have a good chance of successfully completing your project?'"

9. **Support**:

    "Ask why other people think that you have a good chance to successfully complete your project."

10. **Stairs**:

    "Create stairs of progress. These stairs show you what you have already done, what your next step is and what has already been completed in your project."

11. **Activity**:

    "Take a concrete small step to advance your project."

12. **Report**:

    "Publish your first step and thank others for their support."

13. **Logbook**:

    "Continue your project by taking further small steps. Write a protocol about the things you do and the progress you make."

14. **Celebration**:

    "Plan how you can celebrate the success at the end of your project together."

15. **Setbacks**:

    "Prepare for any setbacks."

16. **Future**:

    "Have a celebration and decide how you strive for your further positive future together."

Mutual trust also develops in joint action. During action, the existing abilities and talents of the team members become directly visible. You can practise producing joint results on a small scale. The recipes for success which are developed there can then be transferred into your daily cooperation.

> **The team advertising brochure**
>
> The team creates one advertising brochure for everyone they are involved with; one brochure for the customer, one for the management, one for other departments, etc. Which of their strengths and talents will make the team the favourite team of other departments? What does the customer need to know so they can see that this team is the best partner for realising great ideas? And how will the management see that this team is really a supporting pillar of the company?
>
> When the idea is developed, all suggestions and contributions are taken seriously and developed further. All ideas and inputs are written down (sticky notes, flipcharts …). By doing so, no contribution is lost, and new team members can be integrated quickly.
>
> Only then is it decided whether a suggestion is profound enough to be actually included in the brochure or not. This brochure is then enriched with texts and pictures, so that the team can actually pass it on to others.

6.4 Working with timelines in a solution-focused way

The timeline is a popular instrument, mainly in retrospectives. The aim is to get a collective view of the events of the past by means of visualisation [Kerth, 2001, p. 121 ff.]. The emotional seismograph [Derby & Larsen, 2006, p. 52 ff.] is a helpful addition. It allows for making the course of the team's mood visible in the period under consideration.

When the team members together see what was in the past, they get to know and understand each other better. Working with a timeline, therefore, is also well suited for promoting team development specifically. The team's concrete goal always needs to be taken into account when working with a timeline.

When it comes to completing a project and a retrospective is requested, other aspects will be highlighted, compared to an agile retrospective which aims at immediate implementation of what was learned. We will take a closer look at two forms of application below.

6.4.1 From the past to the future

The aim is that the team members get an overview of past events and are able to appreciate each other for their success. Moreover, they should take positive experience into the future. Situations which the team would do differently in retrospect should be considered as well. The timeline horizon therefore extends from the past to the present.

Preparation: Take a roll of paper (e.g. white wrapping paper) and put it on a wall. Draw a middle part on the paper. This middle part will be used for displaying the course of the team's mood later on. Mark events such as Easter, Christmas, the beginning of a month and so on, for the participants' orientation.

Prepare presentation cards or large sticky notes, suitable pens and suitable fastening material (e.g. adhesive tape). You will find input for colour codes and other additional visualisations in Derby & Larsen [2006, p. 52 ff.].

Part 1 – Building the timeline

The team members can form small groups or work alone. Ask them to write down the moments which are important to them, and then put them on the timeline according to the chronology. The following questions will help:

- What happened in the period under consideration?
- How would you personally evaluate the moment? Rather positive or rather negative?
- Who was involved?

Then ask each team member to draw in the course of their own mood. It might be helpful if each person chooses their own colour so the respective lines can be distinguished in the discussion. To guarantee subsequent anonymity, the lines should be drawn without names.

If trust within a company is severely compromised, the team members can use the same colour. This will ensure anonymity during the exercise. Hypothesising the content in the timeline together in the subsequent discussion can be helpful. Whenever it is possible, however, we use different colours for drawing the lines on the timeline for more clarity in the following discussion.

Of course, you could have the team make a timeline with positive moments only. Experience has shown, however, that team members reject this idea. They want their problems taken seriously, as described in Chapter 4.

Part 2 – Analysing the timeline

The essential turn to the solution-focus is made afterwards when you ask questions about success:

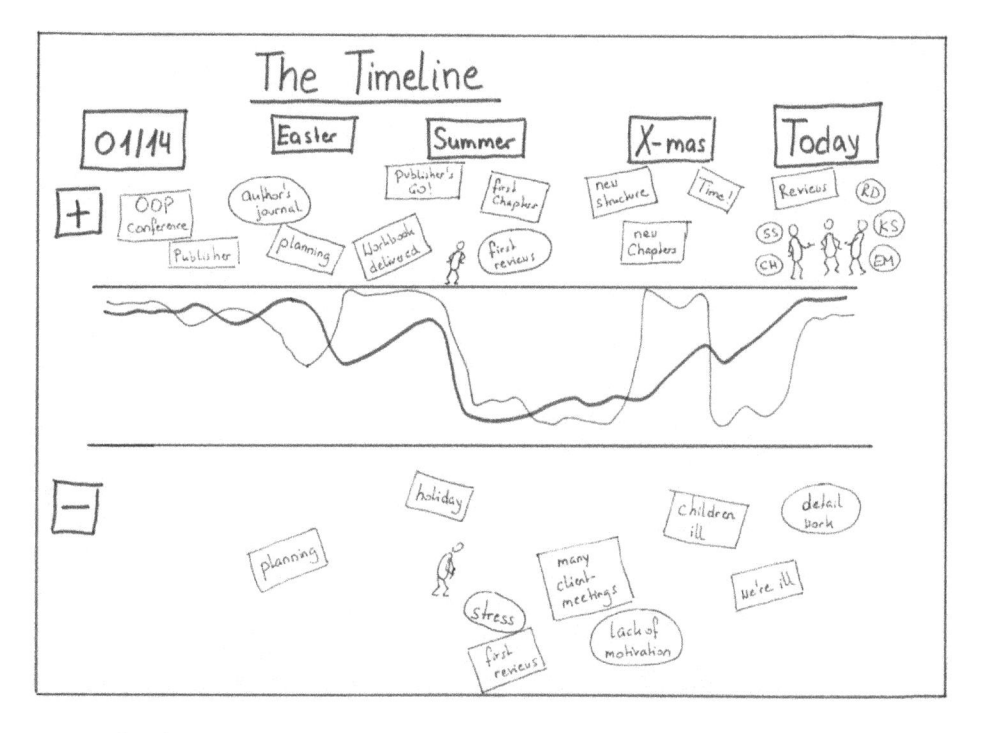

[Figure: The Timeline – a hand-drawn chart showing events from 01/14 through Easter, Summer, X-mas, to Today. Positive events above the line include: OOP Conference, Publisher, author's journal, planning, Publisher's Go!, Workbook delivered, first Chapter, first reviews, new structure, Time!, new Chapters, Reviews, and team member initials (SS, CH, KS, RD, EM). Negative events below the line include: planning, stress, first reviews, holiday, many client-meetings, lack of motivation, Children ill, we're ill, detail work.]

- What have we achieved? What success have we had? How did we do that?
- What was helpful? What do we want to take with us to the future?
- What purpose did this situation have? For whom?
- "How did you manage it so that things went upwards again from there?" – "Who helped you?" (Point at prominent moments in the course of the mood of single persons when asking these questions.)
- Looking back, what would you do differently?

The last questions in particular allow for a solution-focused view of problematic situations. All in all, the idea is to search for gold, as Kerth [2001, p. 124] puts it.

In a project conclusion workshop, you can stop here. Collect important experiences which are to be shared within the company, and write a short report for your management or, if necessary, for your customer.

When you work with teams which will continue working together, it is helpful to take a look at the future as well. Let the team create its future together and find strengths, so that the team considers itself well prepared for its future way. The following questions will help:

- What do we have to get right in the future?
- What special events, which will be important for our cooperation, can take place in the future?

Also, connect the future with the past by asking further questions:

- What can we take with us from the past?
- What can we build on?
- What will we do again?
- What would we do differently – and how?

This approach corresponds to that of Grubert [2014] which was presented at the SOLworld DACH conference. Similar to the course of the conversation according to the Solution Pyramid, you can go back and forth in time when working with a timeline, too.

6.4.2 From the future to the presence

If a current problem needs to be solved, you can start at the end of the timeline, the future [Dierolf, 2013, p. 83]. For this purpose, you can use the miracle question (see section 3.2 "Coaching questions"), the solution talk (see section 8.6.2 "Step 2: Clarify the goal and impact") or any other future-oriented tool. Ask the team members to put all concrete signs of the preferred future on the timeline – again corresponding to the chronology of events:

- What should be at the end? What do we want to achieve?
- What would make us see that we did it?

- What would make our customer see it?
- What makes us see that a miracle has happened? What makes others see it?

Then you can go back in time by asking specific questions:

- How did we achieve …?
- What happened before?
- What difficulties did we have to overcome? How did we do that?

Once the vision of the future has been created, it is worth taking a look at existing strengths and abilities to be able to go into the future with confidence:

- What is at our disposal at the moment?
- Which resources, skills and abilities can we build on?
- Who can help us? And how?
- What would be a concrete first step towards the preferred future?

Have all answers written down on cards and put on the timeline according to the chronology. Checking the results, as described in section 4.5 "The fourth level – review of the results", will be helpful:

- How confident are you that you will reach the desired future?
- What else do you need to be even more confident?

The approach presented here can also be combined with the *Futurespective* of Mackinnon [2005]. The *Futurespective* is based on the exercise *Develop a Time Line* of Kerth [2001, p. 121 ff.] as well as on *Remember the future* of Hohmann [2006]. In essence, the *Futurespective* is a retrospective from the perspective of a successful future.

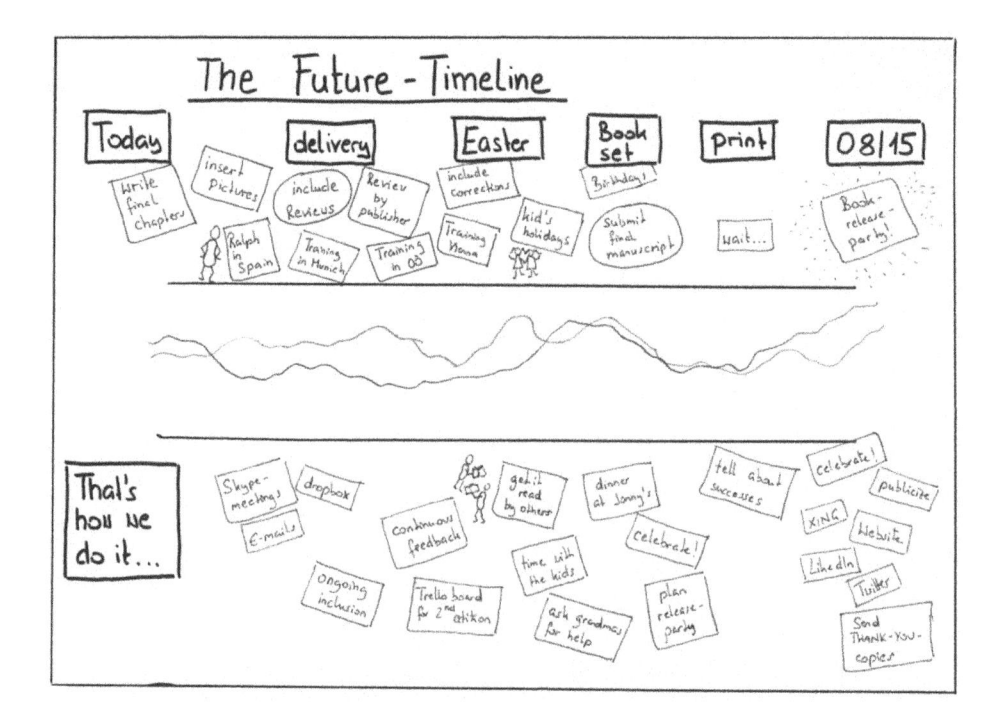

6.5 Developing a team vision

"To achieve the possible, we must attempt the impossible again and again."

[Hesse, 1960]

In addition to the product vision, which is the purpose of a team, the team members should develop a vision of their own future as well. How will they work together, deal with each other, meet each other every day? What will inspire them every working day? What can they rely on and what can others expect from them? What will they appreciate and celebrate in the end?

A jointly developed and supported vision is an important link for all team members. It supports the feeling of belonging to the team; it also helps find a meaning and, therefore, makes a valuable contribution to self-motivation.

The development of such a team vision should not be left to chance. In section 7.5 "The SCARF model", we describe how the human brain always tries to predict a future. This prediction is based on the experiences made in the past; often, those experiences are negative. This is where you should start to allow for solution-focused predictions and, as a result, more positive experiences. For this purpose, we recommend a workshop specifically for developing a team vision. You can start, for example, with an exercise which focuses on the team's strengths.

> ### *Benevolent hypothesising*
>
> This exercise developed by Eberling and Hargens [1996, p. 159] is primarily suitable when the team members do not know each other very well yet. In this case, they will have a lot of helpful lack of knowledge about the each other.
>
> Explain the task as follows: "Everyone expresses benevolent hypotheses about which strengths, skills and abilities the team members might have".
>
> Find someone who volunteers to be the first one to hear positive hypotheses from the others. All participants are now allowed to express their ideas. Sometimes, a hypothesis might not sound benevolent first. Ask: "To what extent is this assumed quality of your colleague a strength or in which situations might it be helpful?"
>
> In the end, ask the volunteer to say which of the mentioned strengths, skills and abilities they think they have and which qualities they were most happy about. Before you move on to the next participant, repeat the instructions again and point out that it is about strengths and favourable qualities.

If the team members already know each other, you can start the workshop with the collection of positive memories and appreciative statements:

- Please tell us about an outstanding moment in a previous project. Something which would make you very happy if it happened again.
- Which of your experiences from a previous project are you grateful for?

A lot of team members consider such a start unusual and regard it as refreshing. Now explain the goal: creating a joint future, even dreaming of it. For this purpose, the team members are also allowed to express seemingly unrealistic ideas and forget current conditions:

- Assuming that you could create your dream team, what would it look like?
- What would your dream work environment look like if there were no guidelines?
- What would your preferred cooperation look like?

The solution talk (see section 8.6.2 "Step 2: Clarify the goal and impact") is also suitable for working on a vision:

- Assuming that we meet in a year from now and you tell me about your dream team, what would you tell me? And what else and what else ...?

The coach has to question the team's assumptions again and again. A world without boundaries is difficult to imagine. After the team has described its preferred future as clearly as possible, the first steps towards this future are defined:

- How can you get there?
- What could you start doing immediately?
- Which aspects might be more realistic to achieve than originally thought?

The collection of ideas can then be the basis of a team charter for the team's cooperation [Larsen & Nies, 2011].

> ### Practical example of "working on a vision" with a real team
>
> The following picture shows the result of working on a vision with an agile team. Plasticine, pens and colours were used to create the picture. In preparation, the team had talked about its future. The picture was then created with the active participation of all team members. Afterwards, the team talked about what the various elements meant for them as a team.

Two team members remember:

It was the process of creating the poster that was exciting and made an impression. It strengthened the team spirit and our shared identity. For us, the picture means departure and forward. The fire illustrates our drive and burns the bugs in the software. At the front is the bridge to the rest of the project world. The hands are helping hands. The helicopter landing site makes it possible for other teams to dock.

Possible titles for the poster were: team mission, mission possible, the commission, to new worlds, the journey is the reward. We hung it up in our team room and we liked to remember the activity regularly and, as a result, the whole workshop.

(Katharina Fritz and Jutta Bednarik)

6.6 Team development with large groups

There are product developments which are no longer made by one team; instead, a lot of sub-teams are involved. Team development measures are also helpful for such a large team, so that everyone has an overview of the big picture and that communication between the sub-teams work. We will briefly present three examples of methods for working with large groups below. For more in-depth information on the topics, please refer to the literature we recommend.

The Solution-Focused-Espresso

The Solution-Focused-(SF-)Espresso by Schenck [2013] is a brief method for large groups based on the World Café concept by Brown et al., [2001].

Schenck describes a workshop for 40 people with a duration of about 2.5 hours. The workshop consists of seven tasks which the participants work on in table groups. The composition of the groups changes with each task:

1. **Personal strengths** – They are remembered based on a situation experienced in the past, discussed with the others and written down. (approx. 40 minutes)
2. **Future Perfect** – "Imagine being voted the best company in our industry in a year from now. What would be different inside your company compared to now?" (approx. 30 minutes)
3. **Scale work** – The participants assess their current position on their way towards this great future perspective with sticky dots on a scale. (approx. 5 minutes)
4. & 5: **"What would make your customers (4) or your colleagues (5) see that you are already one point ahead on your way towards the ten?"**
   The answers are collected on presentation cards and presented on pin boards to the plenary group (each step approx. 15 minutes).
6. **Display of the results** (with fruit cocktails in hand) – The results are viewed on the pin boards and on the tables and discussed in a relaxed atmosphere. (approx. 15 minutes)
7. **Commitment partner** (discussion in pairs) – Each participant chooses one of their own contributions to be achieved and tells a colleague about it. They agree on a date when the commitment partners will remind each other of the realisation. (approx. 10 minutes)

The authors have already had a short SF-Espresso with Klaus Schenck [Schenck, 2014].

The solution-focused future forum

Christiansen [2014] describes a workshop concept for 60 people, with a duration of 3.5 hours including dinner. The aim of the workshop was to support the employees of an institution in a change process while focusing on solutions. The process is divided in five plus two steps:

1. **The preparation e-mail** – It also includes a homework assignment: "From now on until the workshop takes place, please pay attention to what you consider a contribution to joy at work".
2. **Welcome exercises** – 1. Meet the resources (the participants walk through the room and look at each other while thinking of others' possible strengths, approx. 5 minutes) and 2. Sticky names (to create fun and laughter in an atmosphere of ease. Initially, the participants introduce themselves with their own name to someone else. Then, they go around and introduce themselves with the last name they heard. For example, Ralph meets Veronika, then he goes to Sonja and says 'Hi, I'm Veronika' and so on. Approx. 4 minutes).
3. **The future interview** – Working pairs interview other working pairs, asking the question about what they will have achieved in one year and what difference that would make. For this step, Christiansen planned 10 minutes for the introduction and forming of the pairs as well as 35 minutes for the interview (2x15 minutes plus 5 minutes for the switch). His workshop included a 30-minute dinner afterwards.
4. **Back from the future** – After the dinner-break there was a short introduction (5 minutes), groups of a maximum of 6 people exchanged their experiences from the interview exercise and the homework assignment about joy at work (approx. 25 minutes).
5. **Hints & Resource gossiping** – Afterwards, it is about collecting the first hints of success: "Where do I already see hints of the future in my everyday life?" Each team member says something about it and everyone who has shared their experiences then turns their back on the group while the others talk about this person in a positive way. This exercise has a duration of approx. 45 minutes (plus 5 minutes introduction) and aims to strengthen and recognise potentials.

6. **Sharing of knowledge** – One or two discoveries the colleagues can benefit from are written down on coloured sheets of paper. What follows is a snowball fight with the coloured sheets, so that everyone can take away a message from a colleague in the end. This part has a duration of approx. 10 minutes at Christiansen's workshop.
7. **Follow-up e-mail** – It includes several questions based on observations made and will be sent one week after the workshop. The aim is to make participants call the workshop and their findings to mind again.

Great Gatherings

Based on his experiences of designing interventions for large groups in a solution-focused way, Christiansen [2015] developed an approach which he calls Great Gatherings. He was also inspired by the World Café [Brown et al., 2001] and the Open Space [Owen, 2008]. The process of Great Gatherings can be as follows:

1. The goal of the event – setting, focus, desired result – determined with the stakeholders before the event takes place.
2. Personal goals – the individual in the big picture, the personal motivation – are asked about, via e-mail, for example, before the event takes place.
3. Success stories from everyday work are shared; as a result, existing resources become visible.
4. Successful future – A preferred future is described together in detail, including all consequences.
5. First signs – Based on the description of the future, the participants search for first signs of similar things already beginning to happen in the organisation.
6. Next steps – The participants think about the preferred future. They tell each other what is different then and how that could have been achieved. These steps are collected afterwards with an action plan, for example.

> **Practical Tip**
>
> At the Scrum Gathering 2012 in Barcelona, Veronika had the following experience. The idea was to have an initial exercise for the 200+ participants at the opening of the Open Space [Owen, 2008]. It was noisy in the hall. Suddenly, one person raised their hand; soon, a second person followed, then another one, and so on. Within seconds, almost all people present had raised their hands and there was silence in the room. The participants looked at the facilitator who was then able to introduce the exercise. Veronika had never experienced anything like this before. This was it – the dream of everyone facilitating large groups coming true.
>
> This method seems to be quite known in the agile movement. If the participants in your workshop are not yet familiar with this kind of intervention, explain it at the beginning of the event: "If you see a raised hand, please quickly finish what you are doing. As a sign that you are ready now, raise your hand as well, so other participants can see it, too." This is how the group becomes silent in a very short time and you can continue your moderation.

6.7 Self-reflection

- What was exciting/new/helpful in this chapter?
- Which points of the R.E.S.U.L.T. model are already natural in your practice? Which points do you want to tackle next? What exactly do you want to do?
- What would the consequences of transgressing the non-negotiable framework be for the team members?
- Which of your colleagues did you recently thank personally? And how did you do it? What was their reaction?
- Which of your colleagues have you not appreciated personally for a long time? How could you do it? What would their reaction be?

6.8 Experiments and exercises

- Show your interest in what the team did well. Ask about it first thing in the morning tomorrow.
- Set a good example and talk about your achievements – especially the small ones.
- Try answering each question with a solution-focused counter-question for half a day. How many problems do you see being solved?
- Write a list of your personal strengths and abilities. Then ask a good friend (or two) to make additions to this list together with you. Maybe they want to write a list of their own strengths, too?

7. Dealing with Conflicts

Conflicts cannot be avoided wherever there are people. Whether these conflicts are useful or harmful depends on how we deal with them and the parties involved. However, what is a conflict? In this book, we use a definition which fits our own context.

The solution-focused approach of de Shazer and Berg considers a problem as the starting point of reaching a preferred future. The idea of *something better* is, so to speak, already in the problem; otherwise, a situation would not be considered a problem. This leads to the question about *what instead*. What should there be instead of the problem? It is about the presence of something desired instead of something that is not desired; after all, the solution-focused approach avoids analysing the problem and quickly turns to the process of finding a solution.

It should be similar in case of a conflict. Instead of analysing where the conflict has come from, how long it has existed, which type of conflict it is, who started it and who is to blame, the focus is on the time after the conflict – on what will be different then and how this will be achieved. The four phases of the Solution Pyramid represent a kind of guideline and will hopefully lead, step by step, to mutual understanding and cooperation.

7.1 The concept of conflict

Are you currently experiencing a conflict? Can you remember one? What are or were the fundamental factors which turned the situation into a conflict?

It may have started with a few differences in perception, thinking, imagination, feeling and/or wanting. One person thinks that the code must be documented completely, while the other person thinks that good class and method names are sufficient. According to the respective ideas, different actions are taken. One person adds changes to the code of the other person. This behaviour is considered impairment, obstruction or even a threat. According to Berkel [2003, p. 399], this is already enough for a conflict to arise. Often, there are even further actions or counteractions which intensify the conflict [Mack & Snyder, 1957, p. 217 ff.].

Based on Montada and Kals [2001b, p. 67], Milek [2006] wrote: *"For a social conflict to arise between two parties, there must be a subjective or objective discrepancy of concerns, with at least one party feeling impaired or threatened and holding the other party responsible for this threat or considering the other party consciously accepts the threat without apology or comprehensible justification despite demands for reparation or omission".* The feeling of threat is often mutual.

In addition, it is assumed that the act was intentional. It then comes to attribution of blame. One party believes that the other party had a choice or opportunity to act differently, and there was no convincing justification for what happened. In a conflict, both parties believe they are right. Therefore, most intentions are not necessarily malicious; rather, both individuals think they serve the goals.

Stangl adds yet another aspect to the concept of conflict: the presence of feelings. This is about negative feelings which enflame the conflict. These feelings lead to willingness to act. The stronger the feelings are, the stronger is the willingness to act. Strong feelings also have the side effect that they reduce critical judgement [Dörner, 2010].

As you can see, many definitions of and approaches to the concept of conflict exist. We use the following definition in this book:

> ### *The concept of conflict*
>
> A conflict requires a combination of three factors:
> 1. There is an experienced incompatibility in thinking, feeling or acting, which appears to be an impairment or threat to at least one party.
> 2. There is a clear assignment of blame – someone is held responsible for the impairment/threat.
> 3. An action is taken against the culprit(s).

Conflicts can be categorised in many ways. One possible distinction is between internal and external conflict. In this section, we will show you how you can act in a solution-focused way in external conflicts, i.e. conflicts which involve more than one person.

The internal conflict (also called intra-personal) involves only one person. The incompatibility refers to the various needs of one individual. One way to work with some kinds of inner conflicts is to use "The Inner Team" of Schulz von Thun [2009], externalising the elements of the inner conflict and then applying techniques for resolving external conflicts.

Differentiation of the term conflict

Since the concept of conflict is very diverse, it might be helpful to distinguish it from other terms.

- A *difference* is a dissimilarity in perception, imagination, thoughts, feelings and/or wanting. This is not a conflict yet – it is a natural part of living together. As described above, however, differences are part of a situation of conflict.
- A *problem* (Greek *próblēma* = the presented, the assigned – scientific – task) describes a difficult, usually unsolved, task or question. A problem can be the starting point for conflict if the solution is approached by different people the approaches obstruct each other, and everyone insists on their own approach. What the people involved have in common is the solution to the problem.
- A *dilemma* offers two possible decisions, with both possibilities having advantages and disadvantages, such that the person involved does not want to choose either of the possibilities. A dilemma can also lead to conflict since an incompatibility of interests exists.
- A *misunderstanding* arises when two or more people develop a different understanding of statements and/or situations. This mostly happens due to different experiences. Unresolved misunderstandings can also lead to conflicts when the misunderstanding leads to incompatibilities and perceived disadvantages. Usually, these incompatibilities only seem to exist and can be removed easily.

7.2 The nine stages of conflict escalation

Friedrich Glasl identified and described a total of nine stages of conflict escalation. His model provides information on which intervention can be helpful in certain situations and the consequences which have to be expected if the situation is not resolved [Glasl, 1998, p. 92 ff.]. We present these stages below. The change from stage 3 to stage 4 is of particular significance in the context of coaching.

1. **Tension:**
The points of views harden and collide. The awareness of existing tension leads to more tensions. Nevertheless, the people involved are convinced that they can still resolve the tensions by talking. There are no fixed parties or sides yet. Cooperation is still stronger than competition.

In most cases, the parties resolve conflicts in this stage on their own. Intervention from outside is usually not necessary. The offer of assistance can nevertheless be made. Often, this makes the conflicting parties sit down on their own and have a clarifying discussion.

2. **Debate:**
There is polarisation in thinking, feeling and wanting. Black-and-white thoughts arise. There are first signs of verbal violence and talking about third parties to win points. There is a discrepancy between overtone and undertone and fighting for superiority starts. Cooperation and competition change constantly.

In this stage, it can be helpful to actively recommend a clarifying talk. If the conflicting parties are not willing to have such a talk despite the recommendation, facilitation should be offered, pointing out the urgency of a positive resolution to the conflict.

3. **Actions:**
The conviction that "talking does not help anymore" becomes more important and the conflicting parties pursue a strategy of fait accompli. A discrepancy between verbal and nonverbal behaviour develops, with the nonverbal dominating. Empathy for the other person is lost; the risk of misinterpretations increases. A pessimistic expectation of mistrust makes the conflict accelerate. Competition is now greater than cooperation.

When a conflict reaches this stage, we urgently recommend omni-partial conflict facilitation, which can be done by a colleague who has the required knowledge and, moreover, is not involved in the conflict either with regard to the content or personally.

> *Attention!*
>
> Find out whether the conflicting parties still have mutual appreciation. If they do not, the conflict has probably reached a point beyond stage 3 and help is required to resolve it.

From this point, professional facilitation by a mediator is almost inevitable. The escalation stages 4 to 9 are used to evaluate the current situation, and contain warning signals which must be observed.

4. Images/Coalitions:
Rumours fly thick and fast; stereotypes and clichés are built. The parties put each other in negative roles and fight them. They also attempt to attract followers. Moreover, they secretly irritate, tease and annoy each other. Self-fulfilling prophecies arise from the fixation on images.

5. Loss of face:
Public and direct (forbidden) attacks, aimed at increasing the opponent's loss of face, take place.

6. Threat strategies:
A spiral of threats and counterthreats arises. Issuing ultimatums accelerates the conflict escalation.

> ***Attention!***
>
> By now at the latest, individual safety is no longer guaranteed in psychological terms and sometimes in physical terms either. For their protection, the conflicting parties must be separated from each other. Changes in staff are now inevitable.

If, despite all efforts, the conflict cannot be resolved positively, and at the latest from stage seven onwards, changes in staff must be made to protect everyone involved. Take any advice from colleagues seriously and talk to those concerned in private. As soon as you suspect that the safety of an employee is at risk, take initial de-escalation measures quickly. If you wait too long, the consequences not only for those involved but also for the entire team might be irreparable.

7. Limited destruction:
The opponent is no longer seen as a human being. Limited blows are carried out as a "suitable" answer. Reversal of values: a relatively small personal loss is already considered a win.

8. Total annihilation:
The complete destruction and dissolution of the hostile system are intensely pursued as a goal.

9. Together into the abyss:
There is total confrontation without a way back. The annihilation of the opponent at the price of self-destruction is accepted. This even includes the joy of self-destruction as long as the opponent perishes as well.

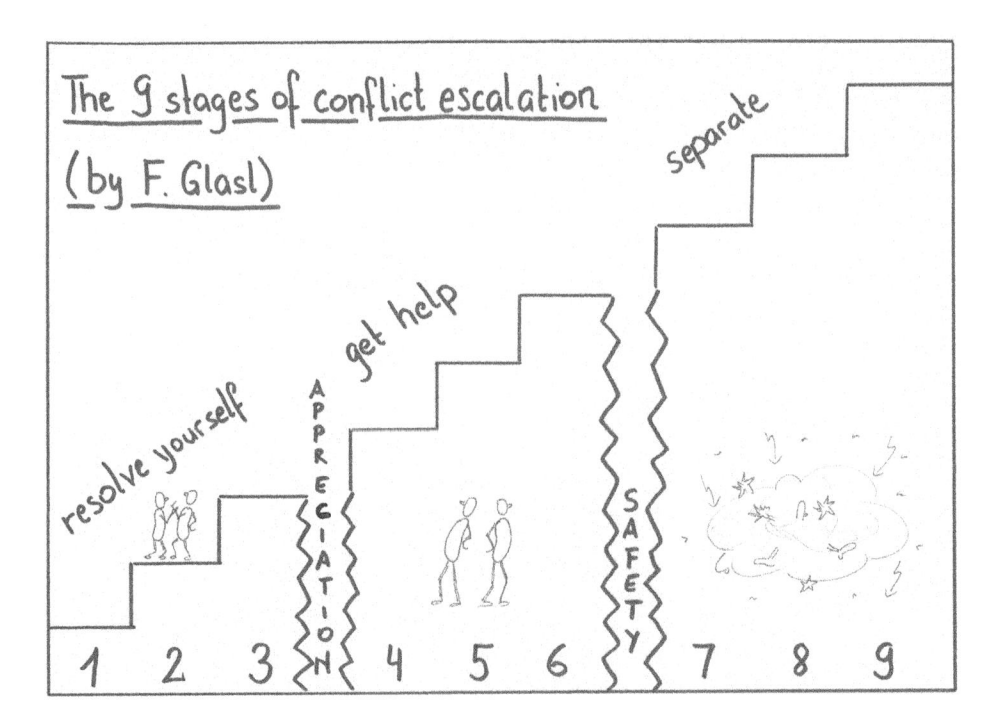

7.3 The benefits of conflict

If you look at the stages of conflict escalation, you will see why conflicts are mostly seen as negative, even feared and, therefore, mostly avoided.

We want to put in a good word for conflict. If you succeed in dealing with conflict-laden situations in a positive and clarifying way, conflicts have their good sides, too. Without them, there would be less progress, less communication and, therefore, more indifference. And – we assume you see it the same way – indifference has never led to outstanding results!

A starting point for positive change

At the beginning of every change, there is a feeling of dissatisfaction with the current situation. As soon as someone takes action to change the situation, there is almost always a conflict with the one who favours the status quo and thus feels threatened by the change. If the conflict is resolved constructively, a new and better situation for everyone involved develops.

Looking at similarities

It may sound like a paradox, but the common interest in resolving a conflict also makes those involved become clear about their shared goals and needs. As a result, they can develop a common picture of the preferred future.

Insight and access to different points of view

In conflict resolution, each conflict party must observe themselves, find out what their fundamental needs are and then be able to articulate them. It is also important and helpful to put oneself in the position of the other person to be able to understand their role and perspective. This ability leads to more mutual understanding and, therefore, to a lower potential of conflict escalation. It is helpful in many situations in life.

Preserving what exists and is desirable

If a new idea is rejected, this also means that the existing structure is consolidated. The conflict leads to awareness of what needs to be preserved. This leads to the development of norms and rules for good coexistence.

More possibilities to react to external influences

Simple models or answers often do not correspond to reality. Discussing them brings new insights to light, thus increasing their complexity. This has happened with the model of the atom, for example, and the Copernican view of the position of the world in the solar system. Both were rejected at first because the imagination was missing. Only intensive common discussions led in each case to a model which could finally be understood and accepted. Through such negotiation processes, a group acquires a better and more realistic picture, as well as the ability to respond more quickly to changes.

> **A practical example of the "Benefit of conflict"**
>
> The same can be observed when estimating complexity and effort in product development. First, there is a conflict due to different perceptions of the task. Discussion clarifies differences in describing the task, allowing common understanding of the actual effort involved.

Long-term connection

As a result of successful conflict intervention, the conflicting parties feel more closely connected. They have received important information about the other party and were able to learn how to deal with each other in a more understanding way. The optimum outcome, therefore, is that individuals who have been exposed in the course of the conflict are reintegrated.

Think, for example, of a tester who has fallen out of favour with the development team due to seemingly excessive care. If communication about the different goals and needs of the team members is supported professionally, mutual understanding of the other's behaviour can grow, and the team can consolidate again. The developers, for example, recognise that the careful tester wants to protect the team from future problems by finding mistakes before the customer does. The tester, on the other hand, understands that the developers want to receive feedback from the customer fast so that they can make necessary adjustments. Misunderstandings are cleared up, and the people involved see each other in a new light. Together, they can set up a procedure which takes the interests of everyone into consideration. In their future cooperation, developers and tester will deal with each other more favourably, and eventually, they will celebrate their success together.

7.4 The comprehensible intention

To be able to benefit from all these positive effects it is necessary to turn conflict into new ways of cooperation in a positive and constructive way. Conflicting parties are to become cooperation partners. This process is difficult, of course. Emotions and different needs collide and obstruct the view of common ground.

Viktor Frankl, the founder of logotherapy, has a helpful answer ready. He assumes that everyone strives to do something meaningful and to take responsibility [Frankl, 2012]. Everything we do is based on a comprehensible intention which, at its core, is positive for the individual concerned. If you manage to understand this approach as a basic attitude and search for this comprehensible intention in the case of perceived incompatibilities, conflict potential will become solution potential.

The search for the comprehensible intention

Regardless of whether you are part of a conflict or want to intervene in conflict-laden situations positively – the fastest, best and easiest way to improve the situation noticeably is to search for the comprehensible intention. For this search, it is best to use the toolbox of solution-focused questions:

- What were you trying to achieve with your actions?
- What is it about?
- What do you need from me?
- For what reason did you do that?

Especially in such delicate emotional situations, we recommend avoiding asking *why* entirely (compare section 3.2.6 "Interposed questions"); after all, this question demands justification and, therefore, creates an imbalance in power which is counterproductive to achieving your goal of cooperation.

> **Practical tip**
>
> By asking "what is the purpose?" you directly ask for the intention behind an action and thus promote mutual understanding. At the same time, this minimises the likelihood of misunderstandings arising and makes the escalation of a conflict less likely.

7.5 The SCARF model

For successful collaboration, cooperation is a prerequisite and resistance is an obstacle. Both cooperation and resistance depend on the extent to which a person considers their fundamental social needs are met or threatened in a certain situation.

The effects of *social pain*, such as rejection, are very similar to physical pain.

The human brain hardly discerns a difference [Lieberman & Eisenberger, 2008]. If we feel threatened socially, various biochemical processes take place in our body, such as an increase in the testosterone level, a change in the oxygen supply to the brain, etc. It is especially difficult to keep a cool head in stressful situations. On the other hand, positive social interactions are rewarded in our brain with dopamine and oxytocin.

Rock [2008; 2009] assumes, to put it simply, that the brain tries to protect us from danger and maximise the satisfaction of our needs at the same time (Minimise Danger and Maximise Reward). Based on neuroscientific research, he developed a model which can be remembered easily, and which describes five fundamental needs of humans: the SCARF model. SCARF is an acronym for Status, Certainty, Autonomy, Relatedness and Fairness.

As soon as one or more of these needs seem to be at risk, cooperation is difficult. Knowing the SCARF model can help to act in such a way that cooperation becomes more likely.

Rock and Cox [2012] present some updates on the research regarding the SCARF model. You will also find additional exciting explanations on the theoretical background in Hufnagl [2014].

7.5.1 The five factors

The following factors have considerable influence on human beings' willingness to cooperate:

- Status
- Certainty
- Autonomy
- Relatedness
- Fairness

Status refers to the perceived personal position compared to others. *Certainty* means the need for clarity and the possibility of making appropriate predictions about one's future. *Autonomy* is about the need to have control over incidents in one's own life as well as about the fact that one's actions also influence one's situation. *Relatedness* concerns the desire to be connected with other people as well as certainty when dealing with them. *Fairness* refers to the need for just and unbiased exchange between people.

Based on these five factors, people decide whether they face a situation of danger or a situation of reward. At first, we do not have control over this decision since it is made in the subconscious. If several SCARF factors are influenced at the same time, the effects will multiply.

Each person reacts differently to the single factors. Those who have more trust in their skills and abilities deal with uncertain situations more easily than others. Some people feel less rejection towards strangers than others. Therefore, please note that your assessment of a situation can be completely different from the one made by your colleagues or employees.

According to Hufnagl [2014, p. 18], once at least one SCARF factor has been attacked, it takes a minimum of two minutes for the reactive resistance to subside and logical thinking to begin again. For conflict situations, this means that in moments of perceived attacks rational arguments cannot reach the recipient initially. Instead, you should allow time so that negative emotions can subside. As soon as resistance has eased, you can start to meet those affected at their individual SCARF needs:

- appreciate the expertise and strengthen the status of the team members,
- provide certainty by passing on required information,
- allow autonomy in solution development,
- show that the person who has a problem is not left alone, and
- show understanding for the fact that some things are perceived as unfair.

Status

"Where do I stand in relation to other people?" This is a fundamental and motivating question which is even more important than the question of income. Most unsolicited advice or criticism is perceived as an attack on the status of the individual. Saying that someone could do something better, can – from the point of view of the recipient – mean that a person is made *smaller*. Letting employees develop their own ways of change, however, often makes their perceived status and motivation increase.

Back to the agile team: all team members are well-educated experts. It is their job to grasp complex facts and incorporate them into software product development. A book on dealing with such geeks appreciatively was written by Glen [2003]. Show your appreciation by asking your experts about how to cope with certain situations. This will increase their status because they know they are valued as experts.

If you are ever dissatisfied with a person's performance, ask them to evaluate their work instead of criticising them. You will see that the team members are as critical about the performance of others as they are with their own. With such a self-assessment, you will probably discover important details, giving you a better understanding of the situation; for instance, that the person lacked information and was therefore not able to do a better job or evaluate the performance differently. In section 5.3 "Supporting further development", we introduced the Solution Focused Rating as a tool for such a self-assessment.

The solution-focused approach always pays attention to the existing skills and abilities of the other person and always reports them back. This is a way to appreciate the status of people and influence it *from the outside* positively. We would also like to mention that success in competition with oneself leads to a similar reward in the brain as does competing with others. So, if we perform, we receive an *intrinsic* reward. Our status – the self-esteem – increases.

Certainty

Neuroscientific research shows that human beings react to perceived uncertainty in any form in a similar way to their reaction to a situation of danger. People constantly try to predict what will happen next. Therefore, it is important that clear expectations are stated at any time and that it is transparent what will happen. In still unclear situations, it helps to say when more information can be expected in order to reduce uncertainty.

Providing certainty works best with clarity and transparency. Be clear in your statements and, as a precaution, ask what was heard and understood. Bad news is always to be addressed directly as well. This is the only way the bad news can be processed and used as a basis for a new goal. Let your team members find the way towards the goal. You will sometimes observe uncertainty despite all transparency. In such situations, it is best to ask what information is still missing and add it as soon as you have it.

According to Rock and Cox [2012], the need for certainty is the strongest one. Personal perception is different with each person, and everyone deals with perceived uncertainty in a different way.

An example from the agile context is dealing with the certainty of development results. Instead of defining the requirements in advance, many feedback loops are built into the process models, and cooperation is promoted. The aim is to ensure that everyone involved receives sufficient certainty.

The solution-focused approach achieves certainty by closely observing the preferred future, among other things. The effects of change are explored, and first clear steps are developed.

Autonomy

The brain reacts with stress signals whenever someone feels they have no control over a situation. If control and choice exist despite a difficult situation, however, the stress level is significantly lower. Therefore, always give employees the feeling that they can choose. This feeling of autonomy alone is intrinsically motivating.

Rasmusson [2009] created the *Drucker exercise* based on an article by Drucker [2005]. It is about promoting autonomy and status by asking the team members what their strengths are, what values they have, what can be expected of them, and how they work best. Disclosing these personal traits promotes the team members' insight into their various working preferences and, on that basis, allows for a more factual discussion about future team organisation. Give your employees enough space to design their working system based on the findings of this exercise.

> ### *A practical example of better cooperation*
>
> Ralph likes to use the Drucker exercise in his team workshops. He briefly points out that cooperation also depends on individual work preferences. For this purpose, he tells the story of John F. Kennedy, who was a good free speaker and only needed keywords for his speeches. His successor, Lyndon B. Johnson, on the other hand, preferred to give prepared speeches. After Kennedy's death, Johnson took over the existing staff, which led to several problems since the people continued working with him in the same way they had worked with his predecessor, assuming they were doing the right thing.
>
> The team members have about 10 minutes to clarify for themselves: what am I really good at? (listening, attention to detail, quickly delivering ideas, etc.) How do I work best? (Am I a morning person? Do I need quiet or rather coworking?) What values are important to me? (for example honesty, quality, punctuality, trust, …) What results can I contribute or what can be expected of me? (e.g. quality work etc.)
>
> Afterwards, everyone presents the answers they want to share with the team.

Autonomy requires certainty. Only when one's freedom and limits of action are known, and mistakes are allowed, can we act freely and without fear. Status can also lead to more autonomy: a successful team is usually controlled less.

With agile working a lot of autonomy lies with the teams. They act on their own responsibility and determine autonomously how they solve a task. Within the team, the individual autonomy of every single person needs to be harmonised with the team goals. For this purpose, it helps to determine shared team rules and talk to each other frequently.

In solution-focused coaching, the team members are considered and appreciated as experts in their own situation. They are encouraged to develop their solutions – autonomously and guided by their intrinsic motivation.

Relatedness

It's a human need to belong, to be part of something bigger. We categorise people into *not-like-us* and *like-us*. This is how clusters of *others* and *us* emerge in companies, i.e. a subdivision into *enemies* and *friends*, to put it bluntly.

To facilitate cooperation and coworking, it is, therefore, necessary to promote mutual contact. This strengthens trust and understanding, and regrouping from *not-like-us* to *like-us* becomes possible. Damian et al. [2009] provides an example: a social meeting was initiated to make it possible for the team members from different regions to get to know each other better. Each Monday, the team members could have personal and non-technical talks for just 15 minutes. This led to better mutual understanding, stronger feelings of relatedness and, as a result, better and more efficient cooperation.

The feeling of belonging can be harmed, either directly or indirectly. A direct violation can be, for example, the threat of being thrown out of the team or the company. However, if an employee's technical expertise is questioned in front of the entire team, the person concerned might fear that this weakens their status in the team, thus putting their belonging at risk. If such a situation occurs, it helps to apologise for any verbal abuse and appreciate performance delivered publicly and honestly.

By the way, the issue of relatedness is not only about the individual's wellbeing. The "Gallup Engagement Index" [Nink, 2015; Gallup, 2017], for example, attaches great importance to social contacts because it has been proven that socially connected people are more motivated, less likely to fall ill and often live longer than others. Relatedness conveys certainty. On the other hand, uncertainty can weaken the feeling of belonging.

Especially when working in an agile team, communication and, therefore, the team spirit is promoted on many levels: starting with the development of a clear joint vision, through many regular meetings and celebrating the success of the team, to the most stable possible composition of teams.

Fairness

It is important to maintain an appropriate balance, which is considered fair. This includes, for example, an income which is appropriate in terms of workload and responsibility. In addition to financial fairness, however, it is also important to ensure content-related fairness. Especially when an interesting and responsible job was promised in the job interview, the job should actually be like that. Compensation which is perceived as inappropriate and unfair activates the danger areas. It is therefore important to ensure fairness, for example through transparency. In regular talks, you can get the necessary information and work on various ways towards perceived fairness together.

It is hardly surprising that the issue of fairness plays an important role in conflicts. According to Montada and Kals [2001a], however, the literature on mediation barely touches this issue. Montada [2013] states that conflicts arise from the violation of normative expectations and the resulting outrage. Experienced injustice is therefore often the cause of conflicts.

Fairness does not always mean equal treatment, but the appropriate consideration of differences. It is about taking inequalities into account. To achieve this, it is first necessary to clarify what is perceived as just by each person [Montada & Kals, 2001a].

No matter what form of fairness is demanded, as a coach you must always ensure that all conflicting parties have the same chances when it comes to making decisions (procedural fairness). A polite and respectful treatment of everyone involved is the basis for this. Moreover, you have to give the conflicting parties the same attention and recognition for their perspectives, i.e. to be omni-partial (compare section 2.2 "Six fundamental coaching attitudes and positions").

If you are involved in a conflict yourself, give the other party the chance to present their perspectives in detail. Try to understand the underlying intention. An apology or saying "I am sorry" might also create a more cooperative basis for discussion.

Once a good basis for discussion has been restored, it helps to talk about individual values and unspoken norms. If it is known what the conflicting parties expect from each other, future conflicts can possibly be avoided. By the way, justice and fairness are universal concerns though there is no universal consensus about what is fair or unfair [Montada, 2013].

7.5.2 SCARF – and why change projects fail

The SCARF model can be used to explain how internal and external conflicts can arise in change projects and how violation of the five fundamental needs often make Scrum transitions fail. It frequently happens that those involved – the actual experts – are not asked whether they consider such a change reasonable. As a result, they feel their status threatened. Carrying out a change process is usually a management decision, i.e. *ordered from the top*. Many employees see their autonomy at risk as a result. The reason for the decision to change to Scrum often sounds as if the employees might think their work was not good enough and that they are therefore to blame for the new situation. Such hidden blame is rarely considered fair.

To really work in an agile way requires cross-functional teams. These teams combine all the functions, skills and abilities to carry out the tasks autonomously and completely. To achieve that, familiar structures are often torn apart, and teams are reassembled. Since this is mostly not voluntary, individuals' autonomy is attacked, and at the same time, trust and relatedness are abruptly destroyed. Why does one colleague become Scrum Master and the other one Product Owner? The team rarely decides on the new roles. Again, several of the SCARF factors are triggered negatively.

Arising uncertainty can be observed in the form of open questions which are rarely answered by the management: *What about me? How can I meet the new requirements? What is actually expected of me? How long will the change process take?* The answers to these questions might provide the urgently needed feeling of certainty. However, nobody can give these answers. If you think about it, you will find many other examples of how the fundamental needs are violated in change processes.

However, the SCARF model not only explains how so much can go wrong in transitions. It also offers possibilities of designing a change process in such a way that the fulfilment of the needs is explicitly considered and the probability of cooperation is increased. Use this knowledge!

You raise perceived status, for example, by asking questions about each other's opinions, by paying attention and showing interest, by appreciation, and by completely and trustfully transferring responsibilities.

You can provide certainty by being authentic, i.e. by doing what you say and saying what you do. People learn through observation and derive their actions from it. You are a role model for your employees, colleagues and customers.

Autonomy means self-determination. Offering interesting problems, which the employees are allowed to solve on their own, provides for this freedom. Give your employees more say and decision-making authority, for example, when it comes to hiring new employees. Leave such decisions to the team. Allowing others to work autonomously also means providing a secure framework for autonomy. This means that you – whether you are a coach or a manager – have to remain available whenever you are needed. Relatedness is also promoted by shared experiences. Planning next steps together, celebrating success together and solving problems in a cooperative way can all lead to team bonding.

Check your working conditions regarding perceived fairness: What rights and amenities do you enjoy compared with your employees? Do you have different computers, phones or special office furniture while your employees are denied those?

A story from practice

As an Agile Coach, Ralph was invited to his fourth or fifth team in a company. His assignment was planned for three days a week for two weeks with the goal of introducing improvements for this team. In general, the team was well respected throughout the company. However, it showed little enthusiasm for introducing and implementing Scrum.

When Ralph met the team, he encountered resistance to the initiative and to the interference in their usual way of working. He heard sentences such as "Scrum is useless!" and "Just let us work!" Each idea Ralph introduced was either rejected or approved with "Yes, okay …" but nothing happened. The team members would often talk about problems which were not in their sphere of influence and never talked about what they could actually change. The typical stand-up consisted of a series of arguments about why tasks had not been completed, although the person concerned had committed to the tasks just the day before. The team seemed to be united only through their complaints.

When Ralph flew home at the weekend, he was close to throwing in the towel. He could not see a way to work with this team.

At home, Ralph told Veronika about his experiences. She asked him what had gone well – a question he would not have asked himself in this situation. She helped Ralph regain respect for the team members and their hard work. Each one of them had an understandable intention behind their negative attitude.

> The client's top management valued these people and their potential so highly that they flew in an Agile Coach for their support. Everyone wanted to do a good job and be appreciated for it. With these thoughts, the team became the "top team" in Ralph's head, a team which was absolutely worth every effort.
>
> Veronika and Ralph also talked about what he could do on Tuesday morning when he returned to the team. He decided that first he would talk to all the team members individually. He wanted to appreciate and respect what they were currently doing. He wanted to ask them for their challenges and also about their opinion on the Scrum initiative.
>
> In these conversations, Ralph found out that Scrum was not the problem at all. Still, the team members regarded the Scrum initiative as a sign that they had not been working well enough.
>
> Since this assignment, Ralph has been considering each team he works with as his current "top team". That allows him to bring this special recognition again and again. He pays attention to the team members' performance and needs. Together, they discuss the team and company goals and find a suitable approach for the upcoming changes. Ralph actively involves the teams in the process of shaping their future and has been experiencing significantly more cooperation and commitment since then.

Trust in the fact that your employees want to handle change processes as successfully as you. Explain the conditions and allow them freedom in implementation.

> ### *A practical example of the consideration of SCARF*
>
> In one company, the employees were not optimally distributed among the rooms, since team members were in different rooms. This obstructed their cooperation. However, certain privileges were linked to the workplaces – a shaded area, a desk at the window or close to the coffee area.
>
> Everyone in the office was informed that as far as possible teams would be in the same room in the future. For this purpose, a large poster with the rooms and sticky notes with the names of the team members were put up. The teams then had two weeks to allocate themselves to the rooms. Perhaps not everyone was happy in the end. Since everyone had a say in the matter (and everyone made use of it), however, the decisions were finally accepted.

7.5.3. Making SCARF usable

"I use this model at least once a week – either to find out how an idea might come across or why a team member does not like the idea that much."

(Silvan Schär, Scrum Master, 2015)

Knowing the SCARF factors can be helpful in the preparation, implementation and follow-up of challenging situations. For example, think in advance about how you can formulate bad news without making somebody feel personally uncertain. If you notice during the conversation that your conversational partner reacts emotionally, you can explain this reaction to yourself with the SCARF model and act correspondingly. You get a better understanding of the behaviour of the people involved after the challenging situation.

Prediction

If you want to implement a new idea or procedure in the team, you can consider the five SCARF factors in advance. Reflect what the team members' reactions could be. Will this idea or the new procedure raise or lower their perceived status? How can you formulate the idea so that the effect on the people's social status and expertise is as little as possible? How confident can people feel with the new approach? Which skills and abilities are available in the team so that they can handle the change well? What other information might be needed? What choice do the colleagues have? How and what can they decide on their own? By considering these questions, it is possible to recognise and counteract at least some of any negative consequences.

Regulation

With SCARF, it is easier to assess an existing situation. Has something just been said that has put one of the SCARF factors of your conversational partner or yourself at risk? If so, this insight might help keep your appreciation of your conversational partner high despite emerging resistance. Then it will also be possible to address the resulting feelings directly. Rock and Cox [2012] refer to studies which show that feelings are already moderated by addressing them. When everyone has calmed down, it is possible to reassess the situation.

Explanation

After a difficult team meeting, the SCARF model can help you find out which of your team members' basic needs might have been violated and understand individual responses. This might help reduce your uncertainty, avoid long-term conflicts and develop other discussion strategies for the future.

Balance

According to Dixon et al. [2010], the negative impact on one SCARF factor can be compensated by strengthening another. It quite often happens, for example, that in times of uncertainty, the need for relatedness increases. You can use this effect.

If, for example, a manager thinks that their team needs to be supported by a coach (attack on the status), they can let the team participate in the decision who is to support them (strengthening of autonomy). If the manager also takes part in the coaching, they will probably have the team back on their side quickly (fairness, relatedness, status).

7.6 Solving conflicts in a solution-focused way

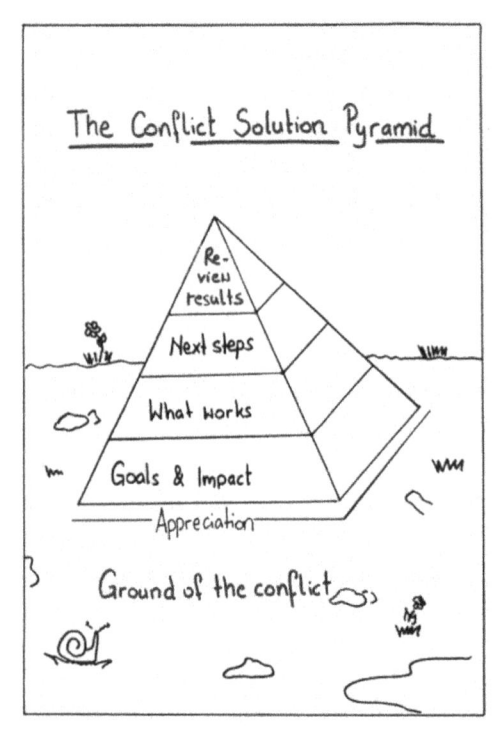

After you have been equipped with all that background information, it now comes to working on existing conflicts beneficially. The Solution Pyramid we presented in in Chapter 4 can be of valuable help here. Let us look at it again, this time from the conflict-solving perspective.

7.6.1 The ground of the conflict

The ground beneath the Conflict Solution Pyramid is the conflict itself, i.e. the emotional topic it is about. In many cases, the ground is ploughed, fertilised and nourished, every stone is turned upside down and closely observed by both parties in the conflict. Alterations of the ground are viewed critically and frequently experienced as attack. The more intense the focus is on the ground of the conflict, the deeper the two parties get into it, and the more difficult it becomes to get out.

Nevertheless, conflicts are important! Without them, there would be no need for changing or improving interpersonal relationships or personal situations. We are forced to deal with important questions and make decisions. What is important? What do we want to achieve? What exactly should not happen? What should be different? And that is what drives our own development in the end.

This is why this ground should be treasured. Each conflict is a new opportunity for personal development and often for further developing mutual understanding and cooperation as well.

7.6.1.1 The ground of the conflict from the participants' point of view

Participants in the conflict pay a lot of attention to the ground, which is quite clear and understandable, given the emotional involvement. Many unanswered questions for the reasons, the focus on everything that makes the conflict escalate further, and our – often strict – goal orientation become the downfall. Whether we can escape the conflict swamp on our own also depends on the extent to which the conflict has already escalated (see section 7.2 "The nine stages of conflict escalation").

If a fundamental appreciation of the conflict partner exists, which means the conflict is rather on a factual level, it is quite possible to seek dialogue and settle the conflict (for example, with the four phases of the Conflict Solution Pyramid). If there is no personal appreciation for the conflict partner, there are two possibilities: either we have to create a new situation in which working well together is no longer necessary (e.g. professional change); or we need an experienced facilitator for a joint clarification process during which we can rebuild mutual appreciation.

7.6.1.2 The ground of the conflict from the facilitator's point of view

If you are called to facilitate a conflict as an uninvolved person, i.e. as manager or coach, you have to be very careful when handling the conflict ground. The goal is to help the parties to leave the ground and enter the first level of the Conflict Solution Pyramid, i.e. the definition of a common goal.

To make this happen, all conflicting parties need certainty and trust in you and your abilities as a facilitator as well as in the fact that their own point of view is well taken care of and represented. It is essential to listen to all points of views without permitting discussion, to honestly appreciate each point of view as a self-consistent view of reality (compare section 2.2.5 "Omni-partiality") and *not* to ask questions about details.

> **Attention!**
> If you are not able to fully stand behind every conflict party, you are the wrong person to facilitate this conflict!

7.6.1.3 Interventions on the ground of the conflict

Attentive listening

The most important tool in this phase is to *listen attentively*. The coach needs the not-knowing position and benevolent acceptance though paying attention to everything that is said. At this stage, both parties to the conflict should be given the opportunity to express their concerns. As a coach, you show your attention with eye contact, physical presence, understanding glances and sometimes with a grunt of approval. If a conflict party could misunderstand statements as attacks, the coach should actively intervene and reformulate what he has heard. In doing so, attention should be paid to esteem, liquefaction (cf. section 3.3 "More linguistic interventions") and understanding.

Whenever you recognise strengths, skills, abilities, values, and needs that should be appreciated, we recommend appreciating them. To achieve this, honesty and authenticity are required. Only then will your appreciation connect with the recipient.

Paraphrasing

Paraphrasing (see also section 3.3 "More linguistic interventions") serves to repeat what was said in a short and neutral way. You can also turn attacks into perceptual statements. If, for example, a conflict partner says: "My colleague constantly disturbs me when I work", you can paraphrase it as follows: "So, you often feel disturbed by your colleague, do you?" This provides a basis for liquefying the conflict later on.

> **Practical tip**
>
> Formulate your re-phrasing as a question, so your conversational partner has the chance to reject your rewording if you do not say what they meant.

Asking questions

Solution-focused questions are, of course, another powerful and important tool for the facilitator. After you have listened carefully and all participants have had the opportunity to present their point of view, offer the conflict partners the chance to show mutual understanding. Questions such as these enable an insight into the conflicting parties' willingness to find a solution and is the first sign of peace for them.

- What do you like about this colleague? What do you appreciate about them?
- What goal might your colleague intend to achieve with their actions?

Providing first aid

In emotionally charged situations, a person may not be able to react to a question or a perceived attack. An omni-partial coach can support this person in such a moment. For this purpose, the coach stands next to the person, puts their hand behind their back (without touching it) as a strengthening gesture and asks for permission: "May I say something for you? And will you let me know afterwards whether this is what you want to say?" If the coach is familiar with this person and if they agree, the coach can put their hand on the person's shoulder blade for moral support. Afterwards, the coach talks in the other person's name. In doing so, the following form should be used:

- I think what XY wants to say is ...

Then, the coach turns to the person they have just supported and asks:

- Is that what you would like to say?

Hopefully, the person concerned has in the meantime found their voice again. They will either agree to what the coach said or make corrections. In any case, the coach has helped ease the situation. This intervention has been derived from the idea of doubling (cf. Thomann & Prior, 2013; Thomann, 2014).

First aid is also needed when there are tears in a conversation. First and foremost, you have remained calm yourself. Remind yourself that tears are an important outlet for accumulated emotions. Tears are a good sign that the concerned person will experience physical relaxation. Therefore, just give them a handkerchief and assure them that this reaction of crying is absolutely okay. Then you wait. In most cases, the person will soon tell you in which direction they want to continue. If they do not, ask after some time: "What would you like to say now?"

Another, perhaps unpleasant, situation to handle is when one conflict party insults the other. Those unpleasant words contain a piece of important information which can and should be used in conflict situations:

I urgently need something, and this person here could help me get it. If only they understood how important this is to me! I am upset that I have not yet managed to make it clear and do not know how to continue. Please help me, dear coach, explain what this is about and that it is important to me!

If you manage to hear this plea behind the apparent insults, you can react in a relaxed and optimistic way: "I hear that you are very upset. Apparently, you want something important from XY, and you have not yet managed to make it clear. Is this the case? If so, what exactly do you want to achieve and for what purpose?" With these, or similar, words you help the verbal abuser reformulate their wish while at the same time you give the other conflict party the chance to save face.

7.6.2 The first level – goals and impact

Different conflicting parties have several goals they pursue, at least at first glance. These goals often seem to contradict each other, which results in a conflict. It is difficult, especially in conflicts, and at the same time essential, to manage the switch in thinking away from the problem towards the preferred goal in the conflicting parties' minds. Expressing what one actually wants to achieve will bring more clarity– and at the same time more understanding for the actions and wishes of the other person.

So, if it is possible to formulate all intentions and goals as well as their positive impact clearly and comprehensibly, the important foundation for better cooperation has already been laid. Moreover, the explanation for which purpose a goal is to be achieved often makes the conflicting parties realise that the interests are more similar than expected. If that happens, searching for a common way is greatly facilitated, and the conflicting parties can become conflict partners.

7.6.2.1 Defining a goal as a participant

As someone who is personally involved in a conflict, it is necessary to distinguish between the conflict itself, the matter at hand and the conflict partner as a person. This is the prerequisite for a clarifying conversation. The deep trust that the other person has acted in this way for understandable reasons is important. Moreover, you should assume that they are willing to understand your needs and goals, i.e. to cooperate in principle. And you should be willing to explain your own goals and needs clearly.

In preparation for such a discussion, it is advisable to consider the following questions and possibly write the answers down:

- What do I want to achieve myself? What is my goal?
- For what purpose do I want to achieve this goal? What else?
- For what purpose do I want a situation or behaviour of someone to change?
- What needs does the other person possibly have?
- What do they need from me? And for what purpose?

At this first level of the Conflict Solution Pyramid, you start by expressing your wishes and needs. Give your conflict partner some credit of trust by openly talking about your feelings regarding the conflict topic as well as about the consequences a resolution of the conflict would have for you. Then ask your conflict partner to tell you about their goals, wishes, needs and feelings openly as well. Take enough time for the first of the four phases. If this phase was processed carefully, the following three phases would be easier to manage.

7.6.2.2 Defining a goal as a facilitator

If you enter a conflict conversation as a facilitator, there is one crucial skill that will help you: the attitude of omni-partiality (see section 2.2 "Six fundamental coaching attitudes and positions"). All conflicting parties need to feel that you back them and represent their interests. Only then can they follow you and cooperate with you in all of the four phases of the Conflict Solution Pyramid. You have already laid the foundation for this trust by actively listening to the ground of the conflict. If you managed to provide certainty back then, you now have the best chance on the first level to get to know the goals, wishes and needs of the conflicting parties. For this purpose, we recommend using solution-focused questioning techniques:

- What is important to you? What do you want to achieve?
- And, if you achieved your goal, what impact would that have on you?
- What is the need behind these goals?
- What new opportunities would open up to you if you achieved your goal?

Pay particular attention to a positive formulation of the answers. If the words *not* or *no* are used, ask: "What instead?" It is about expressing what should be – and not what should not be. Also, use the questions: "For what purpose?" and: "What else?" extensively to find out many useful details.

Another attitude that might be useful for you is persistence. Especially in a conflict-laden situation, it is often difficult for the people involved to express their aims and emotions. Remain patient in such situations. Give the people time and trust in the fact that you will get answers. Please make sure that the conflicting parties only talk about "goals and their impact" on this level. Avoid emerging discussions and interrupt them whenever you feel it is necessary to return to the actual topic. In the best case, you will succeed in identifying a common goal.

7.6.2.3 Interventions for the first level

For what purpose?

In this phase, asking:"For what purpose?" is the most important tool to ask for the conflict partners' goals and intentions. Asking several of these questions in succession can help promote mutual understanding (cf. section 4.2.2 "Asking for meaning").

What else?

This short and simple question is useful when it comes to learning more than what is already obvious. It is hard work to concretise goals, to describe various consequences and to consider possible effects. The question *What else?* supports this effort and can also be asked non-verbally, for example, with an inviting look. We have described this question in detail in section 3.2.6 "Interposed questions".

Other helpful questions are:

- What do you want to achieve?
- What impact would that have on you? And what else?
- What impact would that have on others? And what else?
- What new opportunities would this open up for you? And what else?

7.6.3 The second level – what works despite the conflict

The focus of the people involved in conflicts is usually on what does not work. It is, therefore, a big step to define goals and needs. On this level, we try to achieve an important change in thinking by asking about what is working. Finding what works is usually possible, especially when a common goal has been found. Even if there are different goals, identifying the things that should stay as they are will lead to certainty and trust. The participants' confidence that the next steps towards the goal can be found and taken will increase.

7.6.3.1 Finding out what works as a participant

Congratulations! If you, as a participant, were successful in working on the conflict at the first level, you have already mastered the most difficult obstacle. At the second level, when searching for what works, you can now build on the identified goals and trust in the fact that you will find similarities that are important to you and worth preserving.

Ask your conflict partner what already works well from their point of view so that there is hope that the goal can be achieved. With this question, you show your interest in and openness to their point of view. Take enough time here to address what you think is going well. This will strengthen your conflict partner's trust and willingness to cooperate, which will be the basis for defining the next steps together.

> ### *Practical tip*
>
> If you – or your conversational partner – cannot think of anything else which from your – or their – point of view, works well, this is an indicator that you are at least in Glasl's stage 4 of conflict escalation (cf. section 7.2 "The nine stages of conflict escalation"). In this case, it will be helpful to involve an omni-partial facilitator to support you in resolving the conflict.

7.6.3.2 Finding what works as a facilitator

In your role as a facilitator in a conflict situation, it is your task to encourage all conflicting parties to talk about what is already working well. You will benefit from the fact that the first step of defining goals has already been successful.

And yet it can still be difficult for the conflicting parties to talk about something positive and worth preserving – especially when strong emotions are involved. In this case, for example, you can ask the people present to write down what is already working from their point of view and to present the points they found to the plenary afterwards.

7.6.3.3. Interventions for the second level

The scale question – part 1

Another option is to place the conflicting parties on a scale from 0 to 10, which is depicted on the floor. The value 10 represents the complete achievement of the goal; 0 the moment when the problem or conflict is perceived most strongly. When you ask the people involved to take a position on the scale according to their present point of view, hardly anyone will choose 0.

- Where are you standing right now?

Now ask those involved to explain what is already working well; why they are at their current position and no longer at 0. Write down the answers on a flipchart.

- How come you are already there (and no longer at 0)?
- And how did you do that?

The simple structure of working with scales allows for various points to focus on in the conversation:

1. A realistic description of the preferred future.
2. A list of all those things which already point towards the desired goal – including the success which has already been achieved so far.

Collecting

Give the conflicting parties the chance to write down their thoughts individually. This usually leads to more certainty and also allows them to think without being influenced. Afterwards, the points worked out can be introduced and discussed. The following questions are helpful here, for example:

- What is working well?
- What should stay as it is?

- What is already working?
- What steps towards achieving the goal have already been taken?

7.6.4 The third level – the next steps and their impact

It is a great challenge for everyone involved to develop the willingness to find a way out of the conflict together. On this level, the first thing to do is to encourage the people present to develop as many ideas as possible for the next steps. It will quickly become apparent how successful you have been in restoring the conflicting parties' willingness to cooperate on the first two levels. A clear definition of the goal is as helpful as honestly trusting the conflict partner and their efforts.

7.6.4.1 Defining the next steps as a participant

When you are stuck in a conflict yourself, you probably have a good feeling about whether the time has come to develop the next joint steps. You can feel it if the appreciation towards you is honest.

And even better, you can assess when you are ready to find a joint way towards the goal. If you can answer both questions with *yes*, trust your gut feeling when it comes to the decision of how to develop the next steps.

7.6.4.2 Defining the next steps as a facilitator

Once the first two levels have been processed well, it will be possible from the outset to develop joint ideas for improvement on the third level. As the facilitator, mainly make sure that:

- each point is positively phrased,
- the participants can carry out the actions themselves,
- the steps are concrete,
- the extent of changes is realistic,
- conflicting parties agree on implementing the ideas.

As a facilitator, however, it can also happen that you misjudge a situation. Both on the first level, the formulation of goals, and on the second level, the description of what works, insufficient results can lead to difficulties in finding the next steps. If the participants cannot find any steps towards a better future, it is best to climb down the pyramid and start formulating goals and their effects again.

7.6.4.3 Interventions for the third level

There are various ways to support the definition of the next steps on the way towards the goal. We will explain two of the most frequently used interventions below.

The scale question – part 2

The participants have positioned themselves on a scale from 0 to 10 – remember, 10 stands for the goal – to show how far they already are on their way towards the goal. Now you can continue with the following questions to develop concrete next steps:

- What will make you recognise that you are one point ahead on the scale?
- And what else will make you recognise that?
- And what impact will that have?

The answers to these questions are intended to place the focus on the small signs of progress. It is also about opening up choices and ideas so the participants can plan concrete actions. If these steps are written down, they can be used later to check their effectiveness.

Collecting

The aim here is to obtain as many different possibilities. The following questions can be helpful:

- What would make you recognise the first changes?
- What could be done differently so that …?

The answers are nonbinding at first. It is only about collecting ideas. This should lower the inhibition threshold when developing steps. Then it is helpful to choose concrete, action-oriented language when formulating questions, so the next steps are phrased in a way they can be implemented:

- What could you do differently, so …?
- What would others say about how you could do that?

- What would be a first concrete step towards improvement?
- When will you have taken this first step?
- What will your collaboration look like when the steps have been completed successfully?
- When do you want to achieve this?

7.6.5 The fourth level – review of the results

It may be that confidence in the steps found to resolve the conflict is low, especially if the parties did not come to the conflict resolution meeting voluntarily. The answers then usually lack the necessary openness for successful conflict resolution. A possible reason could be that – despite all efforts – they have not built an honest appreciation for their conflict partner yet; or that they are still worrying that their needs are not understood yet.

So, when you ask the questions: "How confident are you that you will actually implement the next steps?" and: "How confident are you that the implementation will improve your situation?", you make it possible that they can say that they do not believe in the conflict resolution. If a conflict party mentions a low value, for example below 4, you can openly discuss what needs still have to be fulfilled so their confidence in an improvement of the situation increases.

7.6.5.1 Checking confidence as a participant

You would probably have recognised your conflict partner's lack of openness and willingness to cooperate at the beginning of the conversation. Your fine sensors for unspoken resistance would have warned you early on. Nevertheless, you should make sure, and use the opportunity either to dispel any remaining doubts or to increase agreement to the implementation of agreed steps.

If, at this point, your conflict partner's confidence is still low, take their answers very seriously. Ask about their concerns and how the agreement has to be formulated so that their confidence in the implementation increases. If you want, you can also suggest that the agreed steps are written down and then sign the document together. Instead – or in addition – you can set a date for another meeting to discuss the success of the measures taken and which improvements have already been made.

7.6.5.2 Checking confidence as a facilitator

It becomes exciting now, particularly in your role as a facilitator. Asking about confidence allows you to find out how well you have worked in the entire conversation. If the participants' confidence is high, you can rightfully hope that the two conflicting parties will make progress. If their confidence is low, you will now find out whether their mutual trust is high enough to address existing doubts or whether you have to get the participants down to the ground of the conflict once again. We recommend using the confidence scale as a tool here. Appreciate every answer you get.

7.6.5.3 Interventions for the fourth level

We recommend using the confidence scale (as presented and described in detail in section 3.2 "Coaching questions") for an extensive review of results.

- On a scale from 0 to 10 – how confident are you that you will actually implement the next steps (or the next step)?

7.7 Conversational needs in the conflict

The conversational partner's needs, as presented in section 4.6 "Taking conversational needs into account", are also highly relevant for facilitating conflict situations. They draw attention to where the focus should be placed in the course of the conversation.

7.7.1 The conflict partner searching for a meaning

They do not have a direct concern they want to clarify and, therefore, they are either the accused party or they are not directly involved in the conflict. As a result, they often do not participate in the conversation of their own free will, but because they were made to do so.

In this case, the focus in the conflict resolution process is to make sure that this conversational partner recognises the reason for this conversation and what advantages it might have – for them personally, for their work and for collaboration in the team. Being present without having their own reason to be there might lead to a lack of understanding and trigger a form of inner resistance. Therefore, the first and most important task in the conflict resolution process is to establish willingness to cooperate (ground of the conflict).

7.7.2 The conflict partner searching for a goal

They know exactly what does not work and should be changed. Usually, they find many words to describe in detail what problems exist and what damage these problems do to them. What this conflict partner lacks is an awareness of what there should be instead – the goal. It is clear, therefore, that they cannot develop ideas for improvement when they feel like this.

This conflict partner is not ready yet to leave the ground of the pyramid. They need a lot of appreciation for their situation, so they can develop the courage to let go of the problem and go to the first level, which is about defining the goal and its impact. They want something to be different and require support to find out exactly what this something is.

7.7.3 The conflict partner searching for a way

In contrast, the conflict partner searching for a way forward has a clear vision of their goal. They often consider themselves the victim, a role which does not allow them to act. They usually find potential solutions only in the outside world. The others have to change something so that the conflict partner searching for a way can get closer to their idea of a goal.

You will very often find this type of conversational partner when it comes to conflict situations. The facilitator's most important task is to help them to place their focus on what works. In particular, it is about finding out what they were able to do up to now, so that small positive differences were possible (level 2 – what works). This will increase their confidence that their actions will lead to positive changes towards the goal and that the chance of future cooperation increases.

Many conflict partners searching for a way have concrete ideas as to what they could do to achieve their goals. The more urgent the topic is for them, the more important patience and consideration for the other conflict party will become.

Usually, this conflict partner has already thought deeply about their situation – i.e. the goal. The focus in the conflict resolution process, therefore, is on the third level – i.e. the how – and the corresponding next steps.

7.7.4 The challenge

In a team conflict, you usually have to deal with all of these conversational needs. The challenge is to meet every single conversational partner on their own level. In doing so, you need to make sure that those whose interests are on a higher level of the pyramid remain patient and show understanding until the entire team has reached their level. Only then will all of them be ready to take the next step together. Be transparent and explain what you are currently working on so that everyone involved remains patient and confident.

> ### *Practical tip*
>
> Despite all your patience and confidence, you could bite on granite when facilitating a conflict. No matter how hard you try, the key players are simply not willing to cooperate. They close their minds and insist that there is absolutely nothing to talk about.
>
> In such situations, thank everyone present for coming and say that you understand that the trust obviously required for open communication does not exist yet (cf. section 3.3.5 "Liquefying"). Also, apologise for the fact that you have misjudged the situation and announce that you will get back to everyone present individually and in private, in an atmosphere of trust. Explain that it is important to you that cooperation in the team works well and that everyone feels comfortable. Then ask whether this goal is shared by everyone present and get a nod from everyone. End your statement by saying that you think it would be a pity if existing misunderstandings prevented this and that you are sure that it is only about misunderstandings which need to be clarified.
>
> Then end the meeting immediately and leave the room. Stay in sight, however, because it is very likely that the team will be searching for you. Arrange individual meetings then and find out what needs the people involved have.
>
> "Solution-focused lying" sometimes helps in such situations. It was invented by Insoo Kim Berg: she reframed statements about colleagues positively and then passed them on – at least this is the story the solution-focused community tells.
>
> For example:
> Employee: "I cannot focus on my work at all because my boss is constantly monitoring me, and I am worried that I will do something wrong."
> Statement given to the boss: "You are very important to your employee. Their biggest wish is that you are satisfied with their work and they put themselves under a lot of pressure because of this. I think they need your help."

7.8 Self-reflection

- What was exciting/new/helpful in this chapter?
- How do you already strengthen status, certainty, autonomy, relatedness and fairness among your team members? What can you do in the future to support it even more?
- Is there someone in your life with whom you need to work and about whom you cannot find anything to appreciate? Which positive impact would it have for you and others if you were able to cooperate well?

7.9 Experiments and exercises

- Find at least 20 new things which can help you promote the SCARF factors when working with teams, or take these factors into account during the next change process.
- Think of a person whose behaviour you want to change and answer the following questions.
    1. What is the first thing you would like to change regarding this person?
    2. Would you be happy to see these changes?
    3. What would be the difference in your reaction to this person?
    4. Would the other person be pleased about that?
    5. What would be the difference in the other person's reaction?
    6. Would you be pleased about that?

    When you have reached the sixth question, go back to the third. Go through questions 3 to 6 as long as you think is helpful [George, 2012].

    - Think of a person whose behaviour you want to change. Now imagine that this person indeed changes their behaviour. Write down the ten changes you want to see in the other person's behaviour.

        Now think about how you would feel differently about this person and your relationship if they had actually changed. What 20 differences might this person first notice about you? Write them down.

        Now, when you meet the person the next time, act as if this change has actually taken place and behave accordingly. What differences can you observe in the other person?

- The next time you feel verbally attacked by someone, try to react with one of the following questions: "What exactly do you mean by that?" or: "What exactly do you want me to do?" and observe how the other person reacts.
- Is there someone in your environment whom you would like to avoid but have to deal with frequently?
    - Before the next meeting with this person, find three things you could appreciate about them.
    - When you meet this person the next time, look for and find at least three understandable reasons for this person's behaviour and ask whether you are right.

8. Solution-focused meeting design

> *"Meetings are not a bad thing. While we all cringe at the thought of a project centered on a meeting that carries over from one day to the next throughout early development. But our fear of meetings likely comes more from our memories of the ineffectiveness of our meetings, not from their frequency. [...]Project communication, a shared vision, and meetings are important and productive if meetings are properly conducted."*
>
> [Coplien, 1994]

Meetings are a very old way of exchanging information, making decisions, and jointly developing goals and plans. They promote community, because those involved experience each other directly and learn to understand each other better for future cooperation. Of course, this only works if everyone is actively involved.

Facilitating meetings has a lot in common with coaching. Both the facilitator and the coach are responsible for the process, the participants for the content. It is about setting a goal – if none has yet been set. The next step is to identify what can be built on. Then, concrete steps towards achieving the goal are to be defined, and their implementation made as likely as possible. As in coaching, time limits must be adhered to, and structure is needed to achieve the desired meeting goals.

All these tasks require the full and undivided attention of the facilitator. Therefore, the facilitator should not bear any additional responsibility for the content.

In the real world, it often looks different. Most meetings are facilitated by team members or superiors who, in most cases, are also concerned with the content and can, therefore, only partially dedicate themselves to their role as facilitators. This is neither ideal for their technical contributions nor for the meeting.

In this chapter, we will look at some meeting formats from the agile environment through solution-focused glasses. In this context, we present tried and tested interventions for conducting those meetings.

8.1 Considerations for solution-focused meeting facilitation

In this book, you have been introduced to the attitudes and principles of solution-focused work as well as to many tools for facilitating a solution-focused meeting. You know that from such a perspective it is important to appreciate the expertise of everyone present, to challenge assumptions, to promote positive language and, above all, to value those attending. In addition, we will pay special attention to those aspects of a successful facilitation which have not yet been mentioned, which, according to our experience, are always important.

8.1.1 Active involvement of all participants

An important criterion for successful meetings is that everyone is actively involved. Every opinion counts! Every feeling counts! Everyone can contribute something! Experience shows that even people who appear reserved have helpful thoughts and ideas that are often not heard, however. In her book *Time to Think* Kline [1998, p. 102 ff.] describes nine points that lead to successful meetings.

At the beginning:

1. Give *everyone a turn* to speak.
2. Ask everyone to say what is going well in their work, or in the group's work.

During the meeting:

3. Give attention without interruption during open and even fiery discussion.
4. Ask Incisive Questions to reveal and remove assumptions that are limiting ideas.
5. Divide into Thinking Partnerships when thinking stalls and give each person five minutes to think out loud without interruption.
6. Go around from time to time to give everyone a turn to say what they think.
7. Permit also the sharing of truth and information.

8. Permit the expression of feelings.

At the end:

9. Ask everyone what they thought went well in the meeting and what they respect in each other.

Each participant is addressed directly again and again and is directly involved. It is also difficult to completely withdraw when working in pairs.

8.1.2 Monotony versus variety

The purpose of meetings and workshops is to achieve a specific goal. The use of different – sometimes very creative – interventions leads to variety and fun, especially in regular meetings. However, it is important that you take the focus of the participants into account. The more you try to surprise and amuse them with unusual interventions, the more the value of entertainment becomes the centre of attention. Then the focus shifts away from the topic of the meeting and it becomes harder to achieve the content-related goals.

Therefore, meetings should follow a clear, recurring and reasonable structure so that the participants can concentrate on the content itself. Otherwise, there will be uncertainty, expressed in the question: "And what happens next?"

Nevertheless, the course of regular meetings may and should be changed a little from time to time to improve the outcome of the meeting or to avoid boredom in the long run. The situation becomes critical when routine spreads during implementation. This can just lead to mechanical filling in of cards and meaningless phrases when answering questions, instead of thinking and improving in the interest of the desired goal. As soon as you observe such behaviour among the team members, it is time for new interventions.

For most participants, a meeting makes sense when the results are right for them at the end: for example, when they get something out of it, when they are confident that something will change in the desired direction, or when they have had the opportunity to share their worries and problems. All this should be taken into account when designing and facilitating meetings.

8.1.3. Dealing with "unstoppable speakers", "those keeping silent" and "troublemakers"

Questions such as the following arise again and again: "What do I do when …

- someone keeps talking?
- someone says nothing at all?
- someone does not want to participate in exercises?
- someone constantly disturbs what's happening?
- a bad mood pulls everyone down?

We will address these questions below with a few thoughts. There are no universal recipes for every situation you could get into. However, this much is certain: in solution-focused thinking, there are neither unstoppable speakers nor those keeping silent or troublemakers, but only people who pay attention to their needs and try to achieve their respective goals.

"What do I do when someone keeps talking?"

Someone who talks a lot probably has a lot to say. Or they have important things to say and worry that they will not be heard or understood. Veronika once had a participant who turned every statement into a seemingly never-ending monologue. All the other participants rolled their eyes every time this person spoke. At some point, a colleague addressed this issue openly. The participant was visibly embarrassed, apologised for their behaviour and explained that they had been told many times before that they were expressing themselves unclearly. That would be the reason why they were now trying to explain their statements in different ways. They were simply unsure whether they were understood.

There can be various reasons why someone speaks a lot or very little, does not want to participate, or disturbs the group. However, these people have one thing in common: both speaking a lot and remaining silent are personal attempts to find solutions that are intended to have an effect. Appreciate their behaviour and also the person in these situations and take them seriously.

Listen carefully to the person always speaking and thank them for their remarks. Summarise what they have said briefly and ask whether you have understood their statement correctly. This will give them the attention and appreciation they need. Moreover, the other team members have the chance to understand the core of the statement, even if they stopped listening a long time ago.

"What do I do when somebody says nothing at all?"

Invite the participant keeping silent to contribute whenever they want to. Use interventions in which they can express their opinion quietly and in writing, in which they work in small groups and do not have to expose themselves. Experience has shown that if they are appreciated appropriately, silent participants will start speaking.

"What do I do when someone does not want to participate in exercises?"

Basically, as a facilitator, you are responsible for how the meeting is run. This means that you select the appropriate methods and exercises. If someone does not want to participate in exercises, such as those that take place in retrospectives, they should not be forced to do so. Instead, appreciate that they are paying close attention to their needs.

Try to figure out the need behind the refusal. Do they need more clarity about the purpose of the exercise? Does an interpersonal conflict need to be resolved? Does anyone need more understanding? Does the participant want to give priority to other concerns, such as an urgent assignment from the boss or a private challenge? Do they need a break? The person may also have had bad experiences with meetings, exercises and their consequences. Here it is important to pay attention to your gut feeling, to ask helpful questions and to take appropriate measures. Below are some possibilities for handling such situations.

Explain to the person who refuses to participate in the exercise the intention of the particular intervention. This often leads to understanding and participation.

In some situations, it is possible to ask the person concerned about their idea of how the exercise goal could be achieved in another way. When collecting ideas, for example, it may make no difference to the coach whether they work with presentation cards or verbally. If the participant's idea does not seem suitable to you, reject it with good reason.

You could also suggest that the person concerned watches the exercise and then shares their observations with the team. This is a valuable contribution for everyone and is also an approach if participation is not possible for physical reasons, for example.

If, after all your efforts, you cannot find a way to cooperate, a decision must be made as to how you would like to proceed. As an internal facilitator or Scrum Master, it is advisable to seek a one-to-one discussion with the participant to avoid this kind of situation in the future. There will probably be interpersonal disagreements.

"What do I do when someone constantly disturbs the meeting?"

You may remember section 4.1 "The ground – the topic": Disturbances take precedence [Cohn, 2009; Hoffmann, 2017]. Ask the person who seems to *constantly* disturb about their particular concerns and needs. Disturbances are attempts to draw attention to oneself. They want to convey something to you and the team and have not yet found another way to do so. So, give them space and opportunity to express whatever is important to them at that moment. Only then will the chance that this participant can focus on the content of the meeting increase.

"What do I do when a bad mood pulls everyone down?"

So, dealing with someone talking all the time, keeping silent or constantly interrupting is feasible. But what if not only one person is stuck in the problem, but apparently all participants are seized by a bad mood? What if the most beautiful solution-focused intervention does not work because after a few minutes someone falls into problem language again, and others immediately join in?

Something has probably happened that makes the whole group – or at least some people – preoccupied. Another possibility is that a culture of complaining has established itself over a longer period of time. This can be difficult to change.

In such cases, space and opportunity are first needed to let out the accumulated frustration. Below, we will present two of our favourite interventions for such delicate moments. Please use them only in an emergency situation so that the group can get back to work again. We recommend that you continue working with solution- and resource-oriented tools afterwards.

Practical tip: Damn *circle*

We were entrusted with designing the final module with a training group at the end of a two-year management training course. The task was to facilitate a group coaching session with the aim of reflecting on the contents of the course, forging implementation plans and consolidating the network for future cooperation.

After the initial round, we were aware that frustration, dissatisfaction and problem-focus prevailed in this group. The language used between the participants was barely appreciative, and our solution-focused intervention attempts were effective in the short term only. During the lunch break, a participant apologised to us for the behaviour of the other group members. She assured us that it was not because of us, but because communication had been like that since the beginning of the course. And she begged us to do something about the bad mood because she could not stand it any longer. One of her colleagues joined her and agreed with her.

We thought about it for a moment and decided to risk an experiment: After the lunch break – it was a foggy day with a light drizzle – we asked the group to come out into the garden with us. The twelve participants followed us towards the patio door. Only a few of them were wearing jackets while all of them had an anxious look on their faces. Outside we formed a circle. Veronika picked up her mobile phone to use the stopwatch function, and Ralph gave the following speech:

"We learned this morning that you are dissatisfied with many aspects of the course and your company. And that is why we will give you the opportunity here and now to vent your displeasure. We really want to hear every one of you. So, we would like to ask one person after another to speak, without interrupting each other. You get one minute of speaking time to get rid of everything that is bothering you. When the time is up, Veronika will raise her hand. This is the sign that you should finish your speech. The rest of us will then stomp our feet and shout as loudly as we can "Damn!" Then it is the next person's turn – until everyone has spoken."

After a few moments of silence, a participant came forward. There was a lot of emotion in his speech, and within 40 seconds he had said what was important to him. Veronika suggested that he should continue until the time was up. He added two aspects – with much less emotion than at the beginning – until Veronika raised her hand and everyone yelled "damn" out loud. The group laughed. Then it was the turn of the next group member.

The fourth person did not even manage to fill a whole minute with their anger. And from the sixth person onwards, there were hardly any additions. We often had to stop after a few seconds. Everyone responded to Veronika's signs with a bored "damn". We then returned to the seminar room, and the participants wrote down on presentation cards what they thought would be desirable changes. This gave us a useful working basis for the remaining one and a half days and a much better atmosphere.

We want to point out two helpful elements: leave the meeting room with the team – this is the room where improvements are developed – to get rid of excessive resentment. Then return to this "pure" environment. This will make your ongoing work much easier. The second advice refers to the time limit. Set a clear time limit for the participants' speeches and insist on strict adherence. By doing so, you avoid discussions and digressions and instead get concise statements.

Another possibility for getting dissatisfaction out of the solution space is the idea of the anger walk. We were introduced to this form of intervention by John Brooker in a workshop at the SOLworld CEE Conference 2013 in Hungary. Since then, we have been gladly using it from time to time.

Practical tip: Anger walk

Sometimes there are many negative emotions in the team about a specific topic. In such cases, there is a danger that long discussions about the problem will prevent progress. With this intervention, you send the participants out of the room in pairs. Use the following introduction:

"Go for a walk in pairs, equipped with a stopwatch. Walk in one direction for three minutes. Then turn around and walk back the same way for another three minutes. In the first three minutes, one of you will talk about everything that burdens you in connection with the topic. The other one will listen without speaking. On the way back, it will be the other way around. When you come back, you will find two presentation cards on your chairs. Please take your time to write down in silence what you wish for. We will continue to work with these cards afterwards."

While the participants are doing what you told them to do, prepare a flip chart with the instructions for the minutes after they return. Place two presentation cards and a pen on each seat. Ask the returning participants – if necessary – to be quiet so everyone can focus on writing down their wishes.

Objections can be a sign of intensive thought. You may wish to use the technique from the following section for dealing with them. Troublemakers, whatever that means, do not exist in solution-focused work, because everyone is an expert in their situation.

8.1.4 Making decisions

Instead of democratic voting (the majority principle) we prefer to use three other decision-making methods in our work with teams. One is the Systemic Consensus Principle [Visotschnig et al., 2016]; the second is Sociocratic Consent [Buck & Villines, 2017, p. 78ff]; the third decision-making method is the Tetralemma Constellation [Sparrer & Varga von Kibéd, 2009].

The Systemic Consensus Principle

The Systemic Consensus Principle is about finding the solution with the least resistance. All known options are listed, and each team member distributes up to 10 resistance votes per option (10 means I am absolutely against it, and 0 means I have no objections, and any value in between can also be chosen). The option with the lowest group resistance wins.

At first glance, this approach appears to be less solution-focused. On closer inspection, it is: with regard to the goal of, say, having as many colleagues as possible on a trip, the option with the least resistance is the one that is most likely to work.

In the following example, a team uses the Systemic Consensus Principle to decide on the programming language to be used:

	Java	*Ruby*	*C#*	*Scala*	*C++*
John	3	9	2	7	0
Ann	2	7	5	0	4
Frank	0	2	3	10	2
Kelly	4	0	5	5	5
TOTAL	9	18	15	22	11

As you can see from the table, the Java programming language is the preferred one, as there are the fewest votes against it. If a team member with a high individual value is outvoted by consensus, we recommend that you also include the objection handling from the Sociocratic Consent. Behind the apparent resistance is an important piece of information that should be taken up and used.

The Sociocratic Consent

The Sociocratic Consent decision is about finding a suitable solution for everyone. *Consent* means that there is no serious and substantiated objection to a proposed resolution [Buck & Villines, 2017]. Every objection expressed is understood as helpful information and is therefore valued. The person making the objection is actively involved in finding a new, objection-free solution.

Our procedure is usually as follows: a team member submits a proposal for a decision. Everyone in the team may now ask questions of understanding or clarification, which the applicant answers briefly. We ask them: "Are you ready to vote on the proposal?" If the response is positive, the vote will then take place by hand.

We use the following signs: If the thumb is pointed upwards, this means: *Great! I am all for it!* An outstretched arm with an open palm upwards means: *Whatever you decide, I will support the decision!* If a thumb points downwards, this means: *I have a reasonable objection!*

Only if at least half of the thumbs point upwards and everyone else supports the decision (i.e. open palms upwards), will the action in question be included in the action plan in this form. Any thumb pointing downwards effectively prevents the idea from being accepted. Therefore, take every objection seriously and appreciate the courage of the person who has taken a stand. By asking specific questions, you can express your appreciation, obtain valuable information and possibly make important adjustments:

- What do you see that we have not seen yet?
- What do you want to warn us about?
- What should be different in this proposal so that you can at least support it?

Remember – try to assume that everyone has a valid reason for their actions. It is important to discover this and make it usable for the team.

For each decision, we set a timebox of seven minutes. This time span has proven successful in our experience, to keep discussions short and focused. After the seven minutes have elapsed, a decision can be made as to whether the proposal should be postponed – to gather further information – or whether another timebox should be used.

The Tetralemma

In the Tetralemma Constellation, five options are made out of two. The options A (the one thing) and B (the other thing) are joined by the three options neither-nor (not A and not B), both (A and B) and the whole-other-thing (none of the options and not even that). The team moves together to all five positions to see what each of these options could mean in this context.

This method follows the principles of Systemic Structural Constellation [Sparrer, 2009]. So-called ground anchors are used to represent the five possibilities. These anchors are often presentation cards that are labelled with the individual positions. They are placed on the ground for the duration of the intervention, as shown in the diagram. For the start and end of the exercise, the meta-position is also provided as an additional ground anchor.

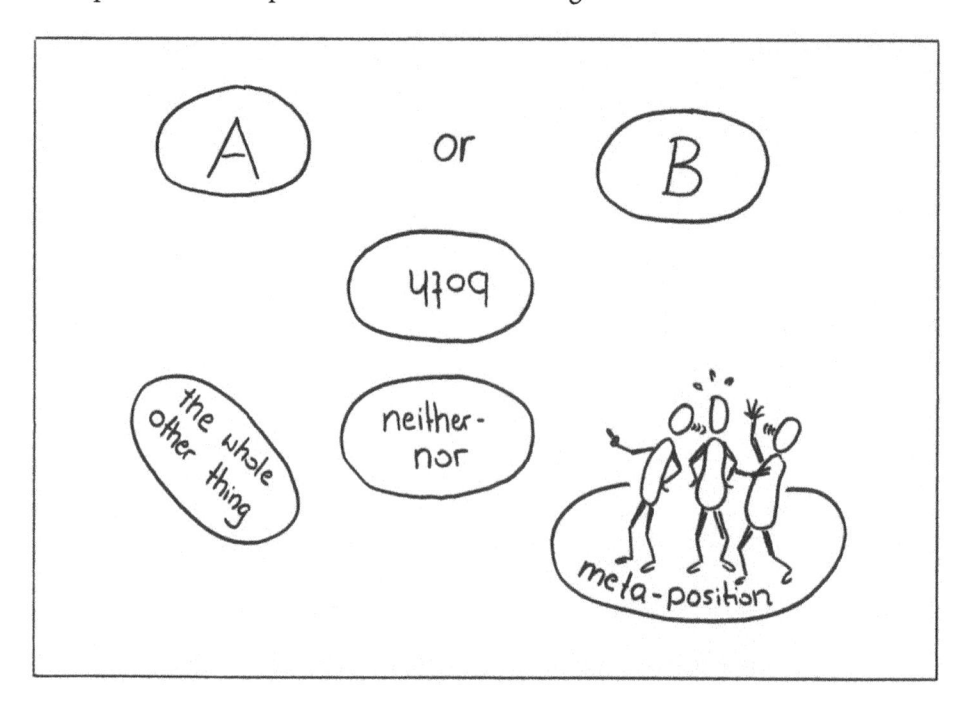

The team first goes to the meta-position together. The process is explained, and then everyone moves to position "A". Once there, the team imagines that they have actually decided in favour of "A" and describes together how life looks after this decision. As a facilitator, you support them with appropriate questions, such as:

"So, you have decided to choose option A. What does this decision mean for you as a team?"

- What effects does the decision have on you?
- What are the advantages of this decision?
- What potential disadvantages do you face here?
- What does this decision make possible for you?
- What else can you tell us about life after this decision?

When as many details as possible have been gathered verbally, ask the team to leave this position, move around a little and shake off the idea of having made this decision. We call this process "to roll off". They can also take a sip of water to facilitate rolling off.

Then ask the team to go to position "B". Proceed in the same way as for the first position. Next come the positions "both" – facing both "A" and "B" –, "neither-nor" – with "A" and "B" at the back – and "the whole other thing" – preferably with a distant view from the window. If the team seems visibly uncomfortable in one position, let them quickly leave it. Unpleasant situations should be as short as possible.

Make sure that all opinions and statements are taken seriously. Of course, laughter can and will occur in some places – this is a good sign and is part of the process. You will see that, in addition to many creative ideas, something like a team spirit develops in the positions. The body language, the voices, the viewpoints of the team members reveal a lot about it. Should it happen that in a position – even after confidently waiting for a long time – only helpless glances are exchanged, release the team from this position.

Finally, ask all participants to return to the meta-position. From there, reflect together which position was perceived most positively. Usually, it is easy now for the team to make a common decision based on what they have just experienced.

8.1.5 Handling objections

Objections from participants of a meeting are also offers of cooperation. The team members reveal an inner conflict and ask the facilitator for support in resolving it.

One possibility that has already been introduced is to ask the one making the objection: "What do you see that the others in the team do not yet see?" Or: "What do you know that your colleagues may not know yet?" This way, this participant and their contribution are taken seriously, and further information is integrated.

Besser [2010, p. 60 ff.] offers a further approach that values the person making the objection as an expert and at the same time invites the entire team to participate in the objection:

- Invite everyone to raise objections right from the start.
- If there is an objection, repeat it. You can also write it down on a flip chart. This is how the attention moves away from the person making the objection to you or the flip chart.
- Now invite each participant to formulate hypotheses about the positive intention behind the objection. Make sure that these hypotheses are phrased positively. If someone has a negative formulation, ask what it might be instead. In this step, the person making the objection and the other team members are asked only to listen to the respective hypotheses.
- Let the person who raised the objection select one of the hypotheses that fits their positive intention best.
- Now invite the team to make offers as to how this intention can otherwise be fulfilled. Again, it is important that ideas are not evaluated, only heard by everyone.
- Let the person who raised the objection select suitable offers. They do not need to justify their selection. You can then ask them whether the positive intention has been adequately taken into account in the selection.
- There is no further reflection, so the person who has made the objection is not forced to give reasons for their decision. Therefore, freedom of choice remains.

A practical example of "Handling objections"

You are enthusiastically talking about test-driven development (TDD) and what advantages this would have for the team. Suddenly Thom, a team member, says: "Yes, but that would not work for us". Now you or others in the team could try to convince Thom to agree nonetheless. However, you can also take his objection seriously and address it appreciatively.

You might say: "Thank you, Thom, for your objection. So, you mean TDD would not work for us?" And further, addressing the team: "Dear team, what positive intention could Thom possibly have with this objection? Thom, please listen first. I will ask you for your opinion afterwards."

"He would like to point out that we do not have the experience yet," Franz, a team member, might say. "He might want to point out that time is too short to learn TDD now," Martin, another colleague, might note. And so many ideas would be put on the table about what Thom could mean with his objection.

You would then ask: "Thom, which of the hypotheses best fits your position?" And Thom might say, "I am worried about the time aspect. I would like us to finish our features for the customer on time."

Now you can invite the team to generate offers on how this concern can be met: "What ideas do you have on how the features can still be completed in time?" Each team member now offers their suggestions.

Afterwards, you can ask Thom: "Which one is right for you? You do not have to justify your answer. I want everyone else to listen to Thom without commenting."

8.1.6 Working with large groups

Meetings with large groups require additional attention when it comes to planning and execution. Usually, you can react less flexibly during the course of the meeting, as too many needs would have to be taken into account.

This means you need to be more active leading the meeting than when working with smaller groups. Provide and communicate a clear set of meaningful rules, get consent on them and ensure that they are followed as far as possible by the participants. If someone does not want to accept the setting, please ask them to comply in the interest of all – if this is possible for the person concerned.

Especially for group work, expect increased noise. Plan for small time-buffers in the process, as it can take a little time for the group to be quiet enough for you to be able to continue with facilitating the meeting and keep the planned duration of the individual exercises as accurate as possible.

Explain your agenda at the beginning so that participants are confident about the breaks. This makes it easier for everyone to keep to the programme – as long as you meet your schedule.

When working, it is advisable to alternate between group exercises, pair exercises and plenary sessions. For the group exercises, it should be considered in advance whether the members of the sub-teams will be mixed up deliberately or left in their traditional sub-teams. This depends on the goals of the meeting and those of the individual exercises.

8.2 Preparation for meetings

When preparing a meeting or a personal talk, there are many things to consider. The following checklist is intended to help you if necessary, even if some of it is not explicitly solution-focused:

- What is the topic?
- What concrete goal is to be achieved? And what for?
- Who are the relevant participants? What strengths and resources does each of them contribute that will help to achieve the goal?
- How many people should be involved? (Note: If you have more than eight participants, you usually need your own facilitator.)
- What are the roles to be assigned? (facilitator, input provider, protocol writer, ...)
- Who can assume which role? Address these people personally and in good time.
- How much space is needed?
- Where can the meeting take place? (in-house or external?)
- Depending on the goal of the meeting, the appropriate choice of room, equipment and seating arrangement must also be taken into account.
- Do you need a circle of chairs, groups of tables or a common table for everyone?
- Is the furniture an obstacle to communication, or does it promote communication? Is it possible for those present to work spontaneously in small groups?
- Are there enough opportunities to capture ideas?

- Does everyone need a laptop or is it enough if only one is in the room in case you want to look up information?
- What materials do you need (e.g. flip chart, pinboards, pens, presentation cards)? Should drinks be available?
- For large groups: are there additional rooms for working in sub-teams or does everyone have to stay in the same room?
- How much time must be planned?
- When can the meeting take place? (During office hours? What day of the week? In the morning, at noon, in the afternoon?)
- Be sure to invite the participants in time and, if possible, personally! (For Scrum teams, it is advisable to announce extraordinary meetings at the latest in the Sprint before the meeting takes place so that the team can take the meeting into account in its Sprint planning.)
- Share the goal and the desired benefit of the meeting in the invitation you send. Also, include an agenda and ask for any additions up to a pre-defined date and time.
- Send the final agenda at least three days before the meeting.
- Prepare the set of meaningful rules on a poster which will then be displayed in the meeting room for everyone to see (start, breaks, end, dealing with secondary topics that are not on the agenda – like a parking lot, decision rules …).

8.3 The planning meeting

The goal of a planning meeting is to agree on what will be developed by the end of the next development cycle, such as a Sprint. If there are a lot of teams, this meeting also clarifies how the goal can be achieved in detail.

Scrum has a structured list of requirements, the so-called Product Backlog. For each item in this list, the implementation effort was estimated by the team. This Product Backlog serves as the starting point for the planning meeting. Each item in the list should meet commonly agreed criteria: the so-called Definition of Ready (DoR) [AgileAlliance, 2014].

The Solution Pyramid in the planning meeting

Below, we will explain how to use the Solution Pyramid in a planning meeting. Many ideas are similar to those of the Scrum Guide [Schwaber & Sutherland, 2020, p. 8 ff]. However, there are also intended deviations in the solution-focused direction.

At the beginning of the meeting, the person responsible for the product value and success briefly discusses the product vision and the current state of development. In Scrum, this person is called the Product Owner. We will continue to use this term as it is common in the Agile world. They also refer to the latest developments in the market and their effects on the company's product development. Moreover, the Product Owner also has the opportunity to thank the team for their work so far if this was not done during the review meeting.

Then clarify what this planning meeting should be about. What goal do we want to reach by x date? What do we want to achieve this goal for? What would be the impact of reaching this goal? What other background information is relevant? Together, all participants develop an understanding of the future work. Only if all team members recognise the meaning of the items under discussion will they be able to unleash their full potential. At the end of this phase, the team decides together on the next (small) development goal, also called the Sprint Goal in Scrum. The following questions may be helpful:

- What will we have achieved by x date?
- How will the customer/Product Owner know that we have been successful?
- What will customers be able to use? How will they be able to use this?
- What will this enable them to do?
- What would be the best feedback we could get at the review meeting?

It can be advantageous if the team now explicitly recalls what is already available to achieve the goal. What can you build on? Who can you cooperate with? What help can you get? This information can then be useful for the later selection of backlog items. Sometimes it is recognised at this point that a backlog item has to be added. It is now also possible to clarify to what extent the team members will be available.

Based on the (Sprint) goal, the team selects the appropriate requirements – called product backlog items in Scrum – and, by doing so, determines the next steps to achieve the goal. For this, it is recommended that each item is approved by each person in the team using thumb voting (see section 8.6.4 "Step 4: Initiate actions"). If the majority is in favour and just one or two team members say they will join the majority, then the backlog item will be selected for the upcoming cycle/Sprint.

If only one person votes against, the item will not be accepted. With the first vote against, a useful question might be:

- What would have to be different for you to opt for this backlog item?

This will tell you what concerns still exist so you can find a solution together afterwards. If the team wants to challenge itself, the following question could also be asked:

- If we were to develop one more story, what would we have to do differently or what would we need for it?

As soon as the team members agree that they will not accept any more items, a final check of the result follows to increase the commitment and remove any remaining doubts. The familiar confidence questions from section 3.2.1, "Scale-Question", can be used here:

- On a scale from 0 to 10: how confident are we that we will meet the goal?
- What would make us even more confident, if necessary?

Now the team has worked out a mutually agreed shortlist of what will be done. The Product Owner should be able to rely on the fact that the corresponding product increment will also be delivered. Often – and this is recommended – the team would then sit down and discuss in detail how the shortlist can be turned into a potentially shippable product increment.

Implementation planning

The team sometimes works in small groups and then gets together again to plan the implementation. The central questions here are:

- How can we achieve what we promised?
- How can everyone contribute to the success?
- What can we build on and what else do we need?

The team repeatedly checks whether all points of the *Definition of Done* and the findings of the last retrospective(s) have been taken into account. At the end of the implementation planning, the confidence question follows again to uncover hidden obstacles and concerns and to work out the first steps to increase confidence. The result is a detailed and operable (Sprint) backlog. In Scrum, implementation planning used to be called *Sprint Planning II*, by the way.

Continuous improvement of the planning meeting

Each meeting should end with questions about satisfaction with the process and ideas for possible improvements. The planning meeting requires a lot of preparation. Therefore, it is important to identify improvements for the next time immediately after the meeting:

- What went well in today's planning meeting?
- What have you contributed to this success?
- What could we possibly do differently next time?

This procedure leads to continuous improvement and, as a result, to more effectiveness and efficiency and therefore also satisfaction for all parties involved.

> **Practical tip**
>
> Such a short reflection should not take more than 5 to 15 minutes.

Planning meetings in large projects

A lot has been written about planning meetings in large projects [Eckstein, 2004; Leffingwell, 2007; Larman & Vodde, 2008; 2010; Pichler, 2010; Larman & Vodde, 2015; Mathis, 2017]. The following is a summary of a few thoughts on this topic. A solution-focused turn is achieved when the team members are sufficiently integrated with their competencies, and the focus is on the successful future. The special feature of working with several teams is that an overall goal and sub-goals are derived from it. Therefore, the steps and the confidence for both goals have to be considered – in the respective team and then with all participants.

> ### A practical example of "goal coordination"
>
> "I once experienced a wonderful example when someone asked, with a scale question, how sure the subproject managers were that their individual goals and the overall goal could be achieved. While the achievement of individual goals seemed quite probable to everyone, this was not the case with the overall goal. Now the focus could shift to the problems that could become dangerous 'between' the overall goal regardless of the sub-goals. It was exciting." (Rolf Dräther, Agile Coach)

In large projects, it is important that everyone involved knows the benefits of the product to be developed and believes in its usefulness, to work as a motivated team. It is, therefore, a good idea to inform all those involved about this benefit and the planned next product step. Such an information meeting creates a feeling of relatedness and community among all participants. After all, something important is created together. The Product Owner, who has overall responsibility, presents the next steps on the product roadmap and explains what they want for the first step and what added value its implementation should bring to the customer.

Once the overall task is clear and meaningful for everyone, more detailed planning can be carried out in the sub-teams. What needs to be clarified is how the sub-teams achieve their respective sub-goals. This question must also be answered collectively. In some companies, for example, the Product Owners of the sub-teams make a preselection in cooperation with team members. This pre-selection should be presented to everyone in the group as a whole so that all sub-teams are informed of the goals with which the other sub-teams are working.

After planning, the detailed plans of the sub-teams should be reviewed again in the large group so that any hidden dependencies can be uncovered and clarified. For example, a "Gallery Walk", extended by the role of a host, as it occurs in the World Café [Brown et al., 2001], can be used. The host is a sub-team member who stays with the planning results of the team while the remaining team members investigate the results of the other sub-teams. The host should be able to answer questions about the detailed plan, take suggestions and report them back to the team afterwards.

Finally, the confidence question, related to the team goals and additionally to the overall goal, should be put to everyone present. There may be concerns and valuable hints that can be considered to actually achieve the goal.

8.4 Solution-focused Daily Stand-ups

How can a team independently coordinate itself on a daily basis so that all team members can work together towards the same goal? And how can you react quickly to changes? Agile approaches include a daily meeting, which has been regarded as a core Agile practice since the mid-2000s [AgileAlliance 2013]. This meeting is limited in time and usually takes place while standing.

The Daily Stand-up Meeting is for team coordination. It involves a discussion about what has been achieved, what is to be achieved, and whether there are any obstacles that need to be overcome. The team should spend more time on planning the upcoming day than on describing the past.

Is a Stand-up Meeting needed?

The Daily Stand-up is often a successful means of promoting team communication. Sometimes team members consider a Daily Stand-up to be unnecessary because, in their view, they coordinate well with each other on a regular basis anyway, or because they do not need to do so. A solution-focused coach takes this expertise of the team members seriously. Questions such as: "How do you coordinate your work?" and: "How do you know who is working on what today?" can increase understanding of the meaning of Stand-up and be helpful in developing alternatives.

Sometimes it even takes two daily Stand-ups – one in the morning and one in the evening. This is the case, for example, when team members are not present every day. In the morning, the plan for the day is devised, and in the evening, the achievements are reflected on.

This approach has some advantages. The direct effects of daily efforts become visible and can be recognised by all and this leads to more motivation and willingness to perform [Hufnagl, 2014]. In addition, you can start directly with the daily planning the next morning. All necessary information is available, even if a team member is not present.

Person- and task-oriented Stand-ups

We basically distinguish between two types of Stand-ups. One type of Stand-up focuses on the team members and, therefore, on the questions: What did I achieve yesterday? What will I do today? What is it that obstructs the team or me? This is a person-oriented approach. The other kind of Stand-up focuses on the tasks to be completed. Starting with the most important open task, the team discusses how things will proceed today and which tasks can be completed during the day. This type is referred to as task-oriented Stand-up. The Scrum Guide November 2020 [Schwaber & Sutherland, 2020] removed the previously well-known *"three questions"* and states now that the structure and techniques of the meeting can be selected freely as long as they focus on progress towards the Sprint Goal.

For the solution-focused turn, we recommend incorporating small changes and additions to the standard questions. In a person-oriented approach, for example, the following questions might be useful in the beginning:

- What did you accomplish that was relevant? What are you proud of?
- What did you do to help others?
- What are you going to do today to help the team get closer to the goal?
- How can you help others today?
- What do you already have and what else do you need to be successful today?

The solution focus is created by concentrating on what has been achieved and on one's own contribution to team success. Making people aware of existing strengths and resources also strengthens each team member.

Person-oriented meetings are more helpful when there are only a few overlaps in the tasks that each person has to perform, and when it is more about exchanging information than team planning. However, instead of coordination, such Stand-ups often lead to status reporting, justifications and apologies if the work has not been done, as well as to micromanagement [Mantsch, 2014]. This distracts from the actual purpose of the meeting, i.e. planning the day.

Therefore, we recommend the task-oriented approach whenever possible. It strengthens the team as a whole and helps to focus on the work to be done. To do this, the team goes through the open tasks in order of importance. Following the Solution Pyramid, the following questions can be asked:

- What was achieved on the task? What are we proud of?
- Who will take part in solving this task today?
- What will be achieved today? What does this mean for you and others? Could the task be completed?
- Who is going to do what today to move the task forward?
- What do you already have and what do you still need to be successful today?

Here, the solution focus is again created by focusing on what has been achieved, on existing strengths and abilities and the successful future. In addition, the experts are actively encouraged to get involved in the completion of the tasks.

Where there is a will, there is a way ...

Sometimes there are circumstances that make it difficult to stand together. Whatever the circumstances, ask the team members for their ideas on how to make the Stand-up successful. You can also see from this discussion whether the team members recognise the significance of the Stand-up and want to act accordingly.

A practical example of "Where there is a will, there is a way ..."

Helmut commutes 150 km every day by train to his workplace and back. He uses his journey as working time because he can carry out many tasks on the train without being disturbed. A Daily Stand-up would have to be scheduled very late in the morning so that Helmut could be present in person. However, a planning phase should take place right at the beginning of the working day to make sense. Therefore, Helmut's team has taken into account his itinerary with all the tunnels, and scheduled the meeting in a way that he can participate by telephone during the entire meeting.

What can be done if ...?

- team members keep coming in late?
- they don't want the discussions?
- the meeting often exceeds 15 minutes?
- the goal of planning the day is not achieved?

A solution-focused coach handles every situation with the conviction that everyone gives their best and is an expert in their situation. Therefore, the coach will ask questions to support the team:

- If you start on time tomorrow, how will you have managed that?
- What do you need to get started on time every day? (Often a postponement of even a few minutes is helpful.)
- What is the positive intention behind your discussions? What needs to be clarified? How can this be better prepared?

Experience has shown that it is more difficult to conduct a Stand-up if important points have not been discussed beforehand in the Planning Meeting. For example, if team members do not need to work together to complete a task, then there is less need for clarification in the Stand-up with regard to team cooperation. Therefore, the coach should already pay attention in the planning meeting to possibilities for co-operation during the implementation phase.

Continuous improvement of the Daily Stand-up

The Stand-up takes place every day. It is therefore important that it is designed in a practical way so that the desired benefit can be achieved. To ensure the optimal flow of the Stand-ups, a brief reflection at the end of such a meeting is recommended from time to time.

> ### *Practical tip – Stand-up short reflection*
>
> "On a scale from 0 to 5 (use your hand to show a fist first and then the five fingers), with 5 meaning this was the best daily Stand-up you can imagine, and 0 the opposite:
>
> Please think about how useful this Stand-up was today. At my signal, show your hand with your evaluation. Ready Steady Go!" Ralph prefers this sports variant to 1-2-3 because he thinks that counting could influence the result.
>
> "What has worked that you makes you show a 1/2/3/4/5?" Ask each participant, from the lowest to the highest rating. "What would have to be different for you to be able to give a higher value?" Again, ask each participant, in the same order as before. We recommend, after one round, the open question: "And what else?" to get more ideas.

> Then ask: "What would you like to do differently tomorrow?" And right before the next Stand-up: "What small change do you want to try out today?" Afterwards, reflect briefly – for example in a timeframe of 5 minutes – with the team what difference the change has made and whether it should be kept.

Cross-team coordination

Like the daily coordination in the team, cross-team agreements are also helpful. How often do sub-teams have to communicate with each other? The sub-teams should clarify this question with each other. The answer depends both on the dynamics of the development and on the external circumstances.

The Scrum of Scrums [Sutherland, 2001] was developed in the Scrum environment. Essentially, delegates of the Scrum teams meet to exchange ideas. The answers to the following, partly solution-focused questions, could be helpful for mutual coordination:

- What have we achieved in the sub-team? What are we proud of?
- Which of the achievements will probably have an effect on others? And what are these effects?
- What impact did the work of others have on us?
- What would we like to thank the others for?
- What do we want to achieve today? What for? How does this support the overall goal?
- What would we need from others?
- What common obstacles would we have to remove?
- How confident are we together that we will achieve the overall goal? What would we have to change to be a little more confident?

These questions strengthen the community and promote a focus on solutions.

8.5 The review meeting

The aim of the review meeting is to learn from each other for further product development. Who wants to learn what from whom?

The customer wants to know what has been achieved, whether the desired work has been done in their interest, and whether a product increment could be delivered. The customer or Product Owner is interested in which plan adjustments they have to make based on the work performed. The team wants to learn whether the work is done in the customer's interest. Together they want to find out how well they understand each other. When the customer says x, will the team understand y or x or X or …?

Richard Sheridan, [Sheridan, 2013, p. 75 ff.] describes this meeting as Show and Tell. The team briefly presents verbally what they have implemented since the last planning meeting. Instead of demonstrating the new functionalities, the team observes the customer using the product with the additional features. In this way, the team learns to understand better the customer's way of thinking to be able to respond even better to the customer's needs in future iterations.

This is followed by a discussion about the new functionalities and their effects. A solution-focused coach could ask the following questions in the review meeting:

- On a scale from 0 to 10, with 10 meaning your boldest hopes have been reached, and 0 meaning the opposite: How do you rate the team's work? From your point of view, what worked well? What else would you have wished for to give only one more point?
- On a scale of 0 to 10, how confident are you that this team will accomplish your project to your satisfaction? What makes you so confident? What would make you even more confident?
- What impact do the results have on further actions?
- A lot went wrong in the last Sprint … still, from your point of view, what has been (a bit) successful?
- What have you (the customer) learned in this review?
- What have you (the team) learned in this review?

[Figure: "Success Slider" — three scales labeled "Meet the expectations", "Product usability", and "Quality of cooperation", each with a − to + slider, flanked by a sad figure on the left and a cheering figure on the right.]

In order to visualise satisfaction and expectations, multi-scaling can also be used. The customer and the team agree on several success factors for the project, the product and/or the cooperation. Such factors might include customer satisfaction, external quality, internal quality or appropriate communication. In project management, this form of multi-scaling is also known as "Success Slider" [Thomsett, 2002, p. 74 ff.]. Based on this information, it can then be asked what it would have taken to give a higher rating.

Review meetings in a large project

The aim of an overall review meeting is to inform customers about the current state of development and to bring the sub-teams together so that everyone can see the big picture again. This is a continuous measure to maintain the project culture and the motivation of all participants. Duration and frequency of overall review meetings depend on the duration of the development, the release dates and the size of the respective team.

A practical example of the benefit of "Review meetings in a large project"

For a customer project, an overall review was carried out every five weeks in the company's foyer. For this purpose, various customers were invited at the same time to watch a demonstration of the software. It was interesting for each team to see what the other teams had achieved in the last review cycle. In some cases, ideas from one part of the software could be transferred to another part. The feedback from the customers was largely motivational for the teams.

Practical tip

Regular in-house trade fairs also offer the opportunity for all teams to present themselves. In addition to the product results, development and test environments can also be shown, and tips and ideas can be exchanged.

8.6 The solution-focused retrospective

The aim of most retrospectives is to look for improvements towards a preferred future within a group or team. Nevertheless, experience shows that a lot of time in retrospectives is spent on discussing the *bad* past. As a result, participants of such retrospectives repeatedly report frustration and demotivation.

The solution-focused approach of Steve de Shazer and Insoo Kim Berg, on the other hand, focuses on the *preferred* future. This approach offers a helpful alternative route for the implementation of retrospectives.

The aim of team retrospectives is to

- achieve better results together,
- improve cooperation,
- adjust working methods to be more successful,
- be able to address problems.

> **Practical tip**
>
> As Scrum Master, am I allowed to introduce topics to the retrospective? As a Scrum Master, you are a part of the Scrum team and therefore co-responsible for continuous improvement, just like any other team member. Therefore, you are allowed to, even have to, bring in your ideas. If you normally play the role of a facilitator in retrospectives, ask a colleague from another team to take on the role of a facilitator so that you can focus fully on the role of a team member when you present your topics.

> **Prime Directive of Retrospectives**
>
> "Regardless of what we discover, we understand and truly believe that everyone did the best job he or she could, given what was known at the time, his or her skills and abilities, the resources available, and the situation at hand."

This statement by Norman Kerth, read through solution-focused glasses, is probably more to be understood as a basic attitude than as an instruction for action. Then it cannot be prescribed by reading it aloud. We rather recommend that you experience what Kerth says in a workshop specially designed for this purpose and thus make it implementable in everyday team life. If this has not been possible so far, the Prime Directive can also be accompanied by the following words:

"Here and now, let us assume the Prime Directive is right. So, let us adjust our behaviour in discussions and evaluations accordingly. Can we do that?"

A solution-focused retrospective in five steps

The following section presents a retrospective based on the attitudes, principles and tools of solution-focused coaching. There is no problem analysis in the procedure; instead, the focus is on the preferred future full of solutions that can be jointly generated. A solution-focused adaptation of the phase model of Derby and Larsen [2006] will be used for this purpose:

1. Opening
2. Clarify the goal and impact
3. Collect what works
4. Initiate actions
5. Review confidence

8.6.1 Step 1: Opening

The aim of the opening is to provide a creative and team-oriented setting. It helps if those present say something true and positive about their own experiences right from the start. This often leads to them being more positive, cooperative, active and creative during the meeting or workshop [Kline, 1998, p. 107 ff.].

In addition, positive thinking expands the mind, and builds resources and resilience [Fredrickson, 2010]. Moreover, everyone present is encouraged to participate right at the beginning of the retrospective.

Tools

You will find here interventions for each of the five steps of solution-focused retrospectives, which you can also use in other meetings as you wish. The amount of time and material required varies greatly.

The chain question is suitable for working with up to ten people. This intervention does not require any preparation and can, therefore, be applied spontaneously.

> **The chain question**
>
> In retrospectives, the chain question is to be preferred to the star question, which is more frequently used. With the star question, the facilitator asks each individual team member a question. Therefore, everyone talks to the facilitator. With the chain question, on the other hand, the facilitator raises the question only with their direct neighbour (person 1). After the answer, person 1 poses the question again to their neighbour (person 2) and so on.

As a result, team members begin to talk and listen to each other, focusing on the positive moments in their lives. This leads to more interest in each other's statements and thoughts and to a good atmosphere to work together on important issues. For example:

- What do you particularly like about your daily work?
- What was your most beautiful experience today?
- Looking back on the last days/two weeks: what are you particularly proud of?

Practical tips

If you send one of these questions around for the first time at the beginning of a retrospective or a meeting, it can happen that, instead of encouraging answers, you will get uncomprehending looks or even massive resistance. The following tips will help you to make good use of the positive effects of this intervention:

- Explain right at the beginning what the purpose of this intervention is, for example: "There are numerous studies that show that, in meetings starting with all participants saying something true and positive about their own experience, everyone is more creative, active, and cooperative. Meetings are then more efficient, and we get more out of the time invested."
- You can also point out in the invitation that you will ask such a question in the starting round. That means your team members will be better prepared and, as experience has shown, will be able to get involved more easily in this kind of start.
- Ask the same question at the beginning for a while. It will become a ritual, and your team members will begin to look for the positive aspects of their work and find them on their own.
- If your team has accepted the starting round well, you could increase the effectiveness even more by having someone else ask a starting question, or even by having each team member ask their neighbour a question about something true and positive. Make sure that the questions are formulated in a way that they can only be answered positively.

> Do not insist on the chain question at all costs. If there is resistance, explain once again what you want to achieve with the start intervention and ask the team to help you find a more suitable form. The team is also an expert for their own situation.

The next intervention can also be carried out at any time without preparation. Here the team members get into motion and make direct contact with each other.

Thank you!

> You could also start by reminding your team of the Prime Directive, i.e. that in the last sprint, everyone gave the best they could. That is why everyone contributed something valuable for which everybody should be grateful. Ask your team members to think, for a few minutes, about what others contributed positively during the last sprint.
>
> Now ask everyone to get up, go around and thank at least three people for their contributions. Anyone who has received and given three thanks can sit down. Make sure that everyone receives their recognition.

The following exercise will also focus on positive and successful aspects. The success of this and any other of the start interventions we presented is reflected in the changed mood and dynamics with which the team continues to work afterwards.

Keep it!

> The next exercise depends a little on the mood after the respective iteration. If it was a normal to good iteration, it could be motivating to collect those things that already work well and should be kept in that way in the future, enabling the team to remain successful.
>
> Get together in pairs and in three minutes collect as many things as possible that should stay that way for future success and write them on cards. Then have the results read out loud in the plenum and cluster the presentation cards. This will reveal the basic strengths on which future improvements can be built.

There are times when everything goes wrong. Neither the focus on the preferred future nor the small steps are useful. The principle "Pay attention to what works" seems somehow bizarre, too, if nothing really works. In such situations, asking for something true and positive at the start is certainly the wrong intervention. Hoping for measures at the end of the retrospective seems downright naïve.

> **Practical tip**
>
> Nevertheless, set up a purposeful retrospective and consider the team's goal. It is now a matter of getting time to suffer together, to talk about the frustration and to get to know each other in the best company. Express this goal clearly at the beginning of the retrospective and ask the participants to tell you when it is enough and how it should continue. Do not pay attention to how long this phase takes.
>
> Just by giving them the chance to suffer, you increase the probability that it will not require the entire retrospective. You will notice when it is enough, and then you can try to steer their thoughts in another direction, for example:
>
> "Let us see together what we can still do, what we have been left with, and what it is still worth coming here for."
>
> Or:
>
> "Yeah, that actually looks pretty gloomy right now. How can we move out of this together?"

8.6.2 Step 2: Clarify the goal and impact

Now that you have created a positive working atmosphere with the team, it is time for the most important point of a retrospective. Setting the goal is sometimes difficult but always necessary! Only a common goal can lead to a satisfactory result.

8.6.2.1 Setting the goal

Start by going over the results of the last retrospective. What has been achieved? What is currently in progress? And what has not been done because it is no longer relevant, or because the change is too complicated?

Based on this review and the current situation, you look together at the goal for this retrospective. In the formulation of a goal, it is important to describe what should be and not what should not be. For negative formulations, use the question "What instead?".

A clear goal is not only an important part of retrospectives but of every form of successful communication. Only if the goal is clear can it be achieved. A well-formulated goal, as described in section 4.2 "The first level – goals and impact", takes into account the REACH TOP factors:

- *R* easonable (as well as motivating)
- *E* xplicit & detailed (formulated as a situation to be reached, not as an action or feeling)
- *A* chievable & verifiable (and within the team's sphere of influence)
- *C* orrectly formulated
- *H* elpful (for everyone involved)
- *T* olerable for others (and takes different needs into consideration)
- *O* bservable
- *P* ositive (formulated as a statement, never as a question).

> ### *Topic – Goal – Measure*
>
> The topic describes what the retrospective is about, for example: improving teamwork.
>
> The goal is the preferred state to be achieved in relation to the topic. For example: What would good teamwork look like in concrete terms?
>
> Measures are concrete activities which, from a current point of view, probably lead to the preferred situation. For example: From now on, we are punctual every day; we let each other finish speaking from now on; we use three hours of pair programming every day to support each other; etc.

It often happens that people have different goals. In the retrospective, however, you want to focus on a common goal. Ask those involved what they want to achieve their goal for and what effects they hope to gain. The exchange about it helps to recognise the underlying needs and to agree on a common goal for the retrospective.

Another option is the goal consolidation [Klein, 2007, p. 190 ff.]. In the first instance, two people work on a common goal. Then two pairs join together and decide in groups of four, based on the two pair goals, on a new common goal.

This can either be one of the goals brought in or a new, third, possibly superordinate goal. This procedure is then repeated with the new group goals. Finally, one or two goals can be worked on in a retrospective. In the concept of Liberating Structures [Lipmanowicz & McCandless, 2014], this activity is known as 1-2-4-all.

Tools

Sometimes it is easier to talk about problems than goals. Problems are well known. Those affected have thought a lot about their problems. All these thoughts need to be put out of the mind and on paper before the next step can be taken. This circumstance is used in the following exercise.

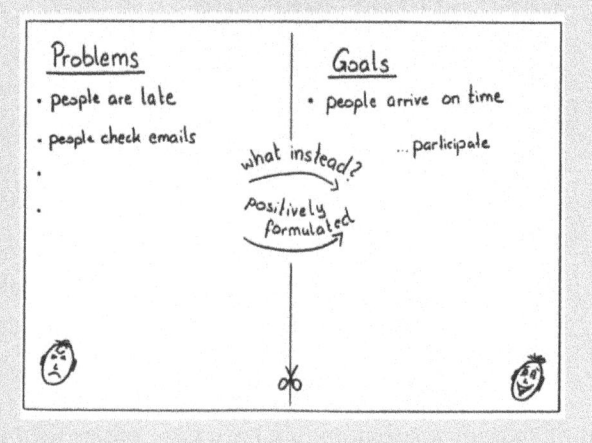

> ### *Problems are disguised goals [Geisbauer, 2012]*
>
> Draw a line on a flip chart so that it is vertically divided into two halves. On the left side, write the word *Problems* as the heading and ask the team to list all known problems below. Allow only a short time for this work – maybe five minutes – to avoid discussions about the individual points.
>
> When the time is up, write the word *Goals* or *Wishes* on the right half of the flip chart as the second heading and ask the following questions: "What would be different if the problem were gone? What do you want instead? Please write down your answers to the right of the problem." For this step of the exercise, it is necessary to allow a little more time.
>
> | Problems | Goals |
> |---|---|
> | · people are late | · people arrive on time |
> | · people check emails | ... participate |
> | · | |
> | · | |
>
> *what instead?* → *positively formulated*
>
> After completing this task, when the right side of the flip chart is also filled, fold the flip chart sheet along the axis and tear or cut it into two parts. As a coach, you now explain that it is your job to look after the team's problems, and that you will take these problems and keep them. You fold the part with the problems and put it carefully aside.

> Attention! Carelessly crumpling and throwing away the problem sheet can very quickly trigger resistance from the team. After all, the work, thoughts and worries of the team have flowed into this list. Hang up the other half of the flip chart so that it is clearly visible again. Now you can continue working with these goals.

One intervention that slightly follows the *Miracle Question* is the *Solution Talk*. The power of fantasy and visionary thought should become the magnet that determines the direction of future work.

Solution Talk

The *Solution Talk* is particularly suitable as an introduction to the target-setting phase with teams. The participants form small groups of two or three people each and have the task of thinking about the future for the following discussion. As a coach, you give the following instructions for this purpose:

"Today is the xx/xx/xxxx (date in the relevant future), and we have managed to achieve our goals successfully. I congratulate us all and ask you to describe to each other in small groups of two or three people exactly what is different now and what effects these changes have had since our workshop on (insert date today), and what has been successful."

Through this method, the participants are invited to create an accurate picture of the preferred future. The most important keywords can then be collected and clustered on presentation cards. In doing so, it quickly becomes clear which goals the team wants to work on.

A similar kind of future jump is used by Hohmann [2006] in his *Remember the Future* innovation game. The Solution Talk could also be used as a first step for a *Futurespective* [Mackinnon, 2005].

Individual, pair and team work: The next intervention changes the setting several times and brings a lot of momentum and vitality to the retrospective. The individual steps are planned in advance and can therefore be easily integrated, depending on the time available.

> ### What do we have to get right? – by McKergow [2008b]
>
> This is another way to work with your team to find goals that the team wants to achieve. You need your team, its experience, a flip chart and pens. Start, for example, with the following introduction:
> "We now want to get an overview of all the aspects of our work that we need to do so that our work improves. Please write a list of all these things. It does not matter how long the list is. You have three minutes."
> After these three minutes, the participants will continue working in pairs. Ask the pairs to merge their lists and mark the most important points on them within the next five minutes. This step may take a little longer if the discussion is really productive.
> Then ask each pair to name the most important item on their common list. If a point is formulated as a problem, you can help to formulate it positively by saying, for example: "Yes, that is an important point. And what do we need to do to achieve that?" Write down exactly those words and phrases the participants use on the flip chart. Collecting should be done quickly, as you have to write down only the most important point of each pair.
> You can then continue working with methods you know to identify the one or two most pressing goals for the next steps.

Even if you have already met it, the following intervention is suitable for any group size. It does not require any preparation and can, therefore, be used at any time.

> ### The Miracle Question
>
> The Miracle Question, as described in detail in section 3.2 "Coaching questions", is also a wonderful choice at this point. It is a creative and effective method of describing the preferred future with all its implications. With a team ask for a team miracle, like: "Suppose you come here on Monday after the weekend and all problems we currently face are gone, like a miracle. How will you notice? What will you discover? What will you do differently in response to the miracle? Please describe this Miracle Monday together." Take some care to get everyone involved in the description and help with questions should they get stuck.

8.6.2.2 Finding meaning and clarifying the impact

The only thing that really motivates people is to find meaning in what they have to do. Nobody can give meaning. Everyone has to find it for themselves. But meaning can be taken away. The will of people can be broken. When this happens, people are like machines: they do what they have to do – without heart, brain or mind (see section 4.2.2 "Asking for meaning").

Therefore, it is important to provide space for the search for meaning. Only when the previously found goals are meaningful for the team members, i.e. when they fully support them, is the achievement of the goals realistic.

The most important question to find meaning is: "What for?". The answer is sometimes not easy to find – and once it is found, you know your goal.

Tools

Get up – change places – contemplate together. For this tool you need enough space for the flip charts and possibly time for upcoming discussions. The effort is worth it!

> ### *Impact Analysis*
>
> Place four empty flip charts in the room.
>
> Ask the team to split among the four flip charts. For small teams, the team can also walk together from one flip chart to the next. Give each group sticky notes and glue as well as some pens. The sticky notes, which are to be put on the respective flip charts, read: I, team, organisation and customer.
>
> Each group now has four minutes to collect and write down the impact that can be expected for the respective target group if the goals are achieved. This means:
>
> - Group 1: What impact does achieving your goals have on you personally?
> - Group 2: What impact does achieving your goals have on the team?
> - Group 3: What impact does achieving your goals have on the organisation?
> - Group 4: What impact does achieving your goals have on the customer?

At the end of the four minutes, let the groups move on to the next flip chart and make additions there until each person was able to add their view to each flip chart. Sometimes negative impacts are also identified. For example, the extra time needed to reach the goal might mean less time with the family. Allow these negative impacts to show up. Those involved will support the achievement of the goal when these impacts are discussed and considered.

The Five What-Fors

This exercise is similar to the "Five Whys" exercise which you might know from Toyota Production System. Kniberg [2009] wrote an informative article about cause-effect diagrams, in which the Five Whys were used.

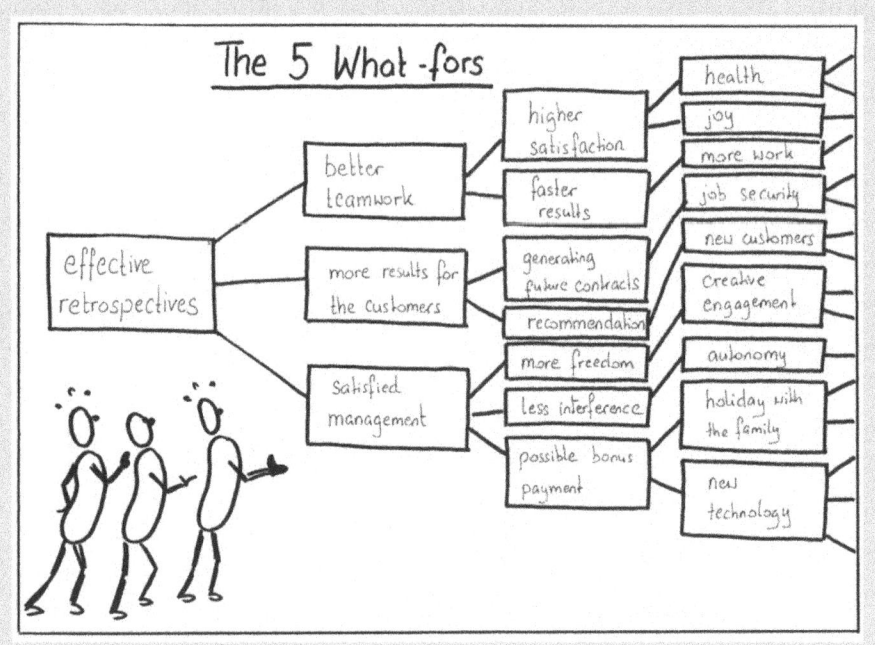

Name the goal and ask: "What is it good for?", then "For what else?" and "For what else?". For each statement, ask again "What is that good for?" and so on. In the end, this technique leads to the formation of a tree with one root and many branches and leaves.

This is where creativity comes in. The following intervention requires a lot of material and time. It is therefore particularly suitable for longer retrospectives.

Team picture

Another approach to arriving at a common picture of the preferred team future is to ask the team to draw one together. Prepare a large sheet of paper, pens, watercolours, and other materials that can be used creatively. The time required for drawing can be adjusted to the time resources available. More time usually means more details in the picture. A good timeframe is about 30 minutes.

Then have a look at the artwork from different perspectives. Let people walk around and describe their impressions and interpretations. Write them down on a separate flip chart.

- What do you notice when you look at this team future?
- What surprises you?
- What catches your eye?
- What pleases you?
- What would you like to be different?
- etc.

If you want to use creativity in shorter retrospectives, you might find your favourite idea in the following exercise. It is also feasible with larger groups, requires little time and material, and is fun. However, the team members must be a little motivated and confident that they can achieve their goals together.

> ### The Hooray-Book
>
> This little exercise is well suited to shifting the focus from the problem towards the preferred future in a short time and with little effort.
>
> Get an A5 notebook with a beautiful and precious-looking cover. Stick the book title Hooray on the first page with golden adhesive letters. Introduce the exercise as follows:
>
> "As you know, we have the next iteration ahead of us. Let us imagine the end of this very successful iteration together and write a book about what is different now. Are you ready?"
>
> Take the book and say, for example: "Hooray, we did it! The work is done and that is really great!" Then pass the book on to your neighbour. They will say a sentence about what is different now and pass the book on to the next person ...
>
> When the book has returned to you, start the second round with the words: "And this is how we succeeded ..." Pass the book on again so that everyone can say a sentence about it.
>
> Afterwards it is recommended to ask each team member to write down the three most important aspects on moderation cards. These aspects can be used in the next steps.

8.6.3 Step 3: Collect what works

Now that the goal and its effects for your retrospective have been agreed, the next phase is about collecting aspects which are already working, at least in part. This refers to everything that has already been undertaken, tried out, achieved or thought through in connection with the goal. In this phase, quality is clearly more important than time. Everything that is already there and on which the team can build should be listed as completely as possible. The question "What else?" is again of great importance here.

Perhaps you are wondering why you and your team should put this effort into the already very tight retrospective timeframe? Often the things that are already working are checked and – symbolically – put into the drawer which says "Done!" No one pays attention to them anymore to save time. However, they are a valuable basis for the future success story on the way to the team goal! The larger the treasure chest of existing resources, the more certainty and confidence all participants have in being able to achieve the goal. Suddenly, the way towards the goal looks much easier, because part of it has already been mastered.

The second positive aspect of this phase is that it is a great preparation for the next one, that is finding suitable next steps: When the goal is known with all its effects and the team knows what has already been achieved, the next necessary steps – as a logical consequence – follow almost by themselves.

Tools

In a solution-focused approach, working with scales is always very important. We want to emphasise them once again here.

> ### *Collecting what works with the scale question technique*
>
> The first part (steps 1 to 3) of the scale question, as described in section 3.2.1, is a useful tool for this phase:
>
> - Display a scale from 0 to 10.
> - Let the participants determine their current position on the scale.
> - Collect as much detail as possible about what has been achieved on the way to reaching this position, plus the resources, helpful information, and everything else that has contributed to the current position on the scale.
>
> **Attention:** Please note that steps 4 to 5 of the scale must also be processed if you have chosen this form. The "scale dance" is a self-contained system, the effectiveness of which can only unfold optimally when used in its entirety.

Evan George of the BRIEF Institute in London introduced us to the use of large lists in 2012 [George, 2012]. Since then, we have been using this method in different contexts, especially when it comes to collecting things that work.

> ### *Large lists*
>
> For this variant, we provide two flip charts and a box of pens. We then ask the team to collect in 10 minutes at least 100 things which they have already done, learned or decided on the way to the desired goal. We leave it up to the participants how they want to organise themselves to achieve this. Over the years, we have been able to observe the most diverse forms of self-organisation in this exercise and always find it exciting.

Collecting what works also goes wonderfully well by asking the team suitable questions. The following questions can be used:

- What have you done/tried/learned so far to get closer to the goal? And what else?
- How have you managed to reach the goals you have set for yourself so far? And what else?
- Who from your environment could help you achieve your goals or be of use to you? And who else?
- What competencies and experiences do you have in your team that you can use to achieve your goals? And what else?
- What questions do you already know that you need to ask or answer to get closer to your goal? And what else?

8.6.4 Step 4: Initiate actions

The hardest part of the work is already behind you. After a meaningful goal has been worked out, it is now time to derive steps towards change. These can be quite small. However, for a successful implementation it is usually important that the team members recognise that they already have the necessary competencies to succeed.

Tools

To collect many already existing ideas for achieving goals in a short period of time, different variations of brainstorming are suitable. However, this method is quite controversial.

Thoughts on Brainstorming

Brainstorming is based on the ideas of Osborn [1948] and quickly became popular worldwide due to its simplicity, both in preparation and implementation. However, there are several scientific studies, such as [Dunnette et al., 1963; Mullen et al., 1991; Furnham, 2000], which show that brainstorming is unsuitable for generating quantitative and qualitative high-end ideas. According to Furnham [2000], when it comes to creativity and efficiency, employees are better off working alone first. Cain [2012] also writes that ideas that are developed calmly and with sufficient time are usually to be classified as of higher quality. Only then should the ideas be merged and jointly evaluated.

An advantage of brainstorming should nevertheless be mentioned, despite all the criticism: most people feel socially integrated into the team during this activity. Depending on the goal, brainstorming can still be used meaningfully.

> ### *Practical tip*
>
> So, the question that you as a facilitator should ask yourself when you think about brainstorming is: What do I want to achieve? Do I want to promote social unity or generate the best ideas? And maybe, in the end, you will decide on the combination of the two, just as we often like to do.

The Idea Competition is a playful form of brainstorming. It fits as a starting point for the generation of feasible measures. Moreover, it requires only a little time and preparation and is also fun to do.

> ### *Idea Competition*
>
> First, small groups of three to four people are formed, each group standing together next to a flip chart. The task for all groups is to collect as many concrete measures as possible to achieve the desired goal. For this task, the groups are given around two minutes, to find at least 20 ideas. The group that generates the most ideas wins. Their prize is the applause of the other groups. Here we go.
>
> In this form, the meta goal of generating as many ideas as possible is achieved. The way in which many points are collected in a very short time is intended to prevent the discussion about the feasibility of individual measures from affecting the creative flow. Experience has shown that the procedures in the groups are different: in some groups, there is a writer; in others, each group member takes a pen to write down ideas. The second version usually generates a higher number of results – and also many duplications.

The next steps emerge when one realises what the next small intermediate goal is. To make the next step visible, you can, for example, work with scales again.

> ### *Continue the "Scale Dance"*
>
> Working with scales has already been described in detail in section 3.2.1. Scales allow for visualising resources and potentials, concrete steps and confidence.
>
> In retrospectives, it is a nice way to perform such working with scales by positioning team members in the room, as described in section 3.2.1.
>
> Variations: Scales can also be done with sticky dots on a flip chart. It is also possible to use different objects on a table, which represent the team members.

Scales and scales again ... The following way of presenting the next steps resembles a map. It provides an overview, orientation and prioritisation for the work to be done at the same time.

> ### *Wishbone [Schenck, 2011]*
>
> Wishbones are a combination of solution-focused scales with Ishikawa's *Fishbone Diagram*. On the *Fishbone*, you collect and sort all current items on the to-do list to reach the desired goal. At the same time, each bone is a scale which indicates how far the particular item is already available and/or the respective completion has already progressed. Improvements are indicated accordingly with a higher value on the scale.
>
> *Wishbone* is helpful in complex situations in which the achievement of goals requires many steps. The diagram takes into account all influences for a solution and provides a good overview. Note that the visualisation requires a lot of space. It is advisable to use at least one pinboard; however, it is better to use even larger surfaces. The use of a Wishbone requires courage and practice to work out the many strings well.

> ### Wishbone (K. Schenck)
>
> [Fishbone/Ishikawa diagram labeled "Wishbone (K. Schenck)" with branches: presence, active help, mentoring, more full-time work, question-techniques, training, buddy-system, sickness-rates, punctuality, meetings, know-how, trainings, flow of information. Each branch marked with "10". Topic: team-cooperation]
>
> You can also use Wishbone as an intervention to find meaning in step 2 by collecting and evaluating all the effects of achieving the goals.

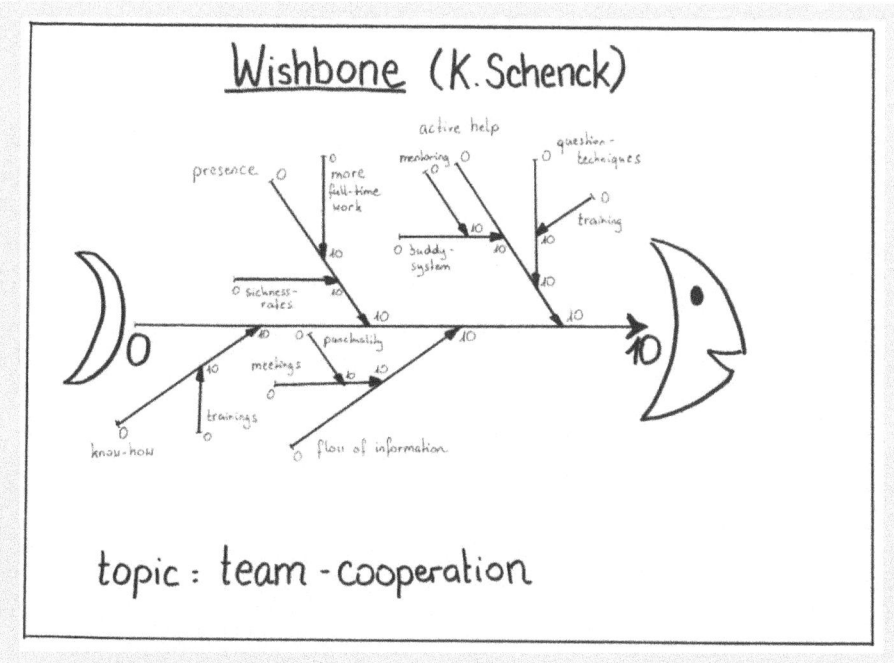

Classic, solution-focused, effective and fair: the last tool for the fourth stage of retrospectives can be used for many meetings. You will need a large sheet of paper, like on a pin board, pens, and the thumbs of your team members.

Action/Experiments plan and consent decision

This is a classic action plan with two small extensions. First, the *What* is accompanied by the corresponding *concrete first step*. When this very first step towards achieving *What* is known, it is easy to start implementing it. And once implementation has begun, the likelihood is high that the remaining steps will follow, so that the action is done.

In addition, the action/experimentation plan is supplemented by the field *Successful if . . .* to describe success criteria. Therefore, there is a clear goal for each individual action.

What	The concrete first step	Who	Until when	Successful if…

To decide which actions and experiments are to be included in the plan, the consent decision by means of hand signals can be used (see section 8.1 "Considerations for solution-focused meeting facilitation", "The Sociocratic Consent")

The "*Who*" is determined by the pull principle. If possible, the plan should include at least half as many actions/experiments as people are present. Start as follows: "We want everyone present to be on the plan at least once. Each action and experiment needs to have a maximum of two "*mentors*". This provides a frame for a helpful kind of self-organisation. The people in the column "*Who*" will then determine "*By when*" there will be a first update and will write this date down.

8.6.5 Step 5: Review confidence

So far, so good. There is now a goal, it makes sense for all concerned, and they know the first steps to reach this goal. After all the work, you want to make sure that the identified actions are put into effect.

How sure can you be that a person or a team will actually realise the set goals? Often there are still small or even bigger doubts that have to be uncovered. Moreover, solutions are needed to deal with them well. It is important to increase the willingness and agreement of the team members.

Tools

The confidence scale, which you have already been introduced to earlier in this book, is useful here. However, here it is interpreted in a different way.

The Confidence Scale

The confidence scale (section 3.2.1 "Scale-Question") can be used here as well. It can also be displayed simply with the fingers and without any other means.

"On a finger scale from 0 to 5: How confident are you that we will actually implement the planned actions (5 means that you are very confident, and 0 means the opposite)?"

Alternatively, you can ask:

- How confident are you that the planned actions will bring us closer to our goal?

Ask those present to think briefly about the appropriate value and then to show their hands at the same time. Depending on the result, ask further questions, such as:

- Assuming you were a little more confident, what would be different?
- What else do you need to be more confident?

The answers will provide important insights for the team to identify pre-requisites that need to be created to achieve the desired changes. Plan about 10 to 15 minutes for this phase to allow time for discussions.

The following intervention is the second part of an exercise by Dominik Godat. It takes about 10 minutes, and needs a flip chart and pens [Godat, 2008].

Footsteps

Draw two footprints on a flip chart. Select the two most important measures from step 4 and write them into the footprints.

Now use the five toes of each foot to write down five things that already exist to implement this measure. This increases trust and confidence that the measure is actually implemented.

The next intervention is a small extension of the previous exercise. It can be carried out with teams of any size and, in addition to confidence, may also add to Step 4 – Initiate Actions.

> ### *What we have – what we need*
>
> To increase confidence in the implementation of actions, it is sometimes helpful to find out what already exists and what is still missing. You can use a small table and facilitation cards to collect this information, for example:
>
> | Action | We have | We need |
> |---|---|---|
> | | | |
> | | | |
> | | | |

8.6.6. A retrospective with Ralph

> ### *Practical example*
>
> The team members sat together in a circle of chairs. I had briefly explained that I wanted to try something different with them today. Their reaction was a slight nod. I started with the positive opening:
>
> - What did you (name) do well in the Sprint? What are you proud of?
>
> Having listened carefully to the answer, I asked the person whom I had addressed to ask their neighbour the same question. Finally, the first round ended with me again. Of course, the person on my right asked me the same question. Everyone laughed and was eagerly awaiting my answer, which I provided, of course.
>
> Then I said: "That worked so well that I would like to add another round. And what else did you do well in the last Sprint?" Surprise! *What, are we not done yet?* This is how I interpreted the participants' expressions on their faces. However, everyone managed to say something again.
>
> And then I asked: "And which of the things you did was helpful for others?

And how?" This, too, was unusual. After all, previous retrospectives had started with: *"What did not go well, what do we have to change?"*

Then I asked everyone to write two or three topics for the day on a sticky note each: "What should be addressed here today to make this retrospective worthwhile for you and the team?" They had about five minutes for this task. The team members presented their topics and attached the notes to the flip chart. Topics were, among others: reducing mistakes, improving communication, starting pair programming, promoting knowledge sharing.

Then I wrote the following on a flip chart:

- Here and today, we want to achieve .... so that ....!

The team was given 10 minutes to complete this sentence. At first, it was a bit quiet, but then the noise level increased, ideas were developed, discarded, reformulated and at the end of the 10 minutes the following sentence was written there:

- Here and today, we want to generate ideas to improve our exchange of know-how so that we reduce mistakes, improve communication, start pair programming and promote knowledge sharing.

Then the team members were allowed to position themselves in the room on a scale from 0 to 10, with 10 meaning that the goal was fully achieved and 0 the opposite. The participants chose positions between 3 and 7. Some were surprised that there were very different views about how close they were to the goal at that time. I interviewed each person individually and started with the one who had chosen the lowest value on the scale. When talking about the respective position, it quickly became clearer that the views on the current status were quite similar, but that the potential for achieving the goals was evaluated completely differently.

Afterwards, we made a leap to the future:

- Where on the scale would you like to be, regarding your goal, in three months?

Everyone took a few steps forward. Again, I asked each person individually:

- What will be different then?

After everyone had had their turn, I asked the team to summarise all the points from the scale on a flip chart.

There was a learning moment for me that I will probably never forget. The flip chart was close to position 0. The team seemed insecure and had no words. Following an inner impulse, I took the flip chart and put it behind position 10, at the other end of the scale. Suddenly the team was busy writing down points. It might have been a coincidence or not. Anyway, since then, I have always made sure that the flip chart finds its place on the goal side of the scale.

Next, we worked out the first steps towards the goal. So, I asked:

- How will you know at the end of the next Sprint that you are already one step further forward?
- What will you have done to get there?

The team collected some measures on a flip chart. At the end I asked the question of confidence:

- On a scale from 0 to 5, how confident are you that you will take these steps?

Their hand signals were from 2 to 4. So, I asked:

- What do you need to be more confident?

The team then added another two points to the measures that were important to them.

In the days following the workshop, I was able to experience an active, committed and motivated team that took great care of the implementation of the measures. So, my top team quickly earned its name. This retrospective design and how I developed it is described in Miarka [2012].

8.6.7 A solution-focused short retrospective

Every now and then it is helpful to carry out a short, intermediate retrospective in approx. 5 to 10 minutes. The following three questions can be asked:

- What did you do well (yesterday)? What are you proud of?
- What of the things you did (yesterday) helped others?
- What would you do differently in retrospect?

To keep it short, just take the first piece of information from each team member. Maybe you use the chain question. If you have a little more time, you can add the "What else?" question to get more information.

8.6.8 Between retrospectives

Retrospectives are merely the beginning of change. Together with your team, observe which aspects change positively. Focus on every positive difference, no matter how small, and share it with others. See how others react to these changes and discuss them with your team. Then you will notice progress. And you will be well prepared for the next retrospective.

Take the time every now and then, maybe every three to six months, to reflect on the retrospective process together with your team and implement improvements if necessary. Talk about what you have achieved through retrospectives and what might be different in order to fulfil hopes that have not yet been fulfilled. Involve all stakeholders in such a meeting. Perhaps you can even show how much time or money the team has saved by having retrospectives so that their approval and funding is secured in the future.

> ### *Practical tip*
>
> Make sure that the commonly created action plan is clearly visible to all participants and can be edited. It should become a living companion for teamwork.
>
> Regularly review the old measures together, tick off what is done, and add new ones. Keep on deciding with the team what is not being done and remove these items from the list. This way, changes become visible, achievements are appreciated, and the purpose of retrospectives becomes noticeable for everyone.

8.6.9 Retrospectives in a large project

A well-known approach for retrospectives in large teams is the *Retrospective of Retrospectives* [Caroli, 2009], also called Project Team Retrospective [Eckstein, 2004]. Delegates of the sub-teams meet to discuss the results of the team retrospectives and adaptations for cross-team cooperation.

There is a risk that these retrospectives will not always be productive. Many of the sub-team experiences are apparently not relevant or helpful for the other teams. Agreeing on a common goal for this retrospective is often quite difficult due to different interests. Moreover, sometimes the right people are missing in this retrospective because it is not clear who is needed for the topics to be discussed. One advantage is that the participants get to know each other and therefore work together better later on.

As an alternative to the Retrospective of Retrospectives, it is possible to hold a quarterly large group meeting with as many project participants as possible. Participation should be voluntary, and the results should be published throughout the company. Topics suggested by the stakeholders can also be taken up. Formats which can be used are Great Gatherings (see also section 6.6 "Team development with large groups"), World Café [Brown et al., 2001] or Open Space [Owen, 2008].

8.7 Facilitating Backlog Refinement Meetings

Estimates are supposed to bring certainty. Firstly, it is about certainty for the customer, because they want to know the time frame in which the result can be expected, and what costs will be incurred. Secondly, estimates also prove helpful for the team. The detailed discussion of the requirements makes the team members develop a more consistent and deeper common understanding of the task at hand. In this short section, we will only refer to the use of coaching in estimation.

There are different estimation methods in the Agile environment, such as Grenning's Planning Poker [Grenning, 2002; Cohn, 2006] or Lindstrom's Affinity Estimation [Mar, 2008; Sterling, 2008]. No matter which method is used, the behaviour of the team members in a Backlog Refinement Meeting usually remains the same. They are reluctant to make estimates as they have often had negative experiences with how their estimates were handled. For example, estimates are often considered a definite promise: "You said it would only take you two days." – "Yes, two days for the implementation, but not for everything…"

The understanding of what an estimate is and what it is made for differs greatly, depending on the role. As in any meeting, it is important to know exactly what the goal is and also its effects:

- What is the purpose of our estimation today?
- What impact will our estimates have?
- How much time can we take for the estimate?
- How much estimation accuracy is required in this particular case?
- What would be the consequences if we were to over- or underestimate?

When preparing the Backlog Refinement Meeting, for example, it is possible to take into account suitable estimates which have been made in the past. What was helpful then? Which of them could be repeated? Which considerations would have to be made anew to be able to make an appropriate estimation?

During the meeting, it is highly recommended that every opinion is taken seriously. Critical team members can point out important risks and obstacles. "What do you see that the others do not see?", "What do you want to warn against?" Low estimators can also provide helpful information. "Which shortcuts or simplifications do you see that the others do not yet see?"

It also proves helpful to add a confidence value to every estimate: "I guess it takes two weeks / I think the story costs five points and I am 40% confident that we can meet that." "Wow, what is the reason that you are 40% confident?" "What do you need to be a little more confident?" This intervention, adding a confidence value, can improve the solution-focused conversation about the requirement.

If necessary, it is also possible to talk to the person responsible for the product about what could be dropped so that the work can be done within a certain time. "Assuming the user needs only half of the functionality, which half would that be?"

So far, only the costs of a requirement have been considered. The anticipated benefit can be determined in a similar way. "How many customers will use the requirement?" "What added value does this have for them?" "What would they be willing to pay?" "How much time does the functionality save?" On the basis of such questions, it can then be calculated or estimated how expensive the feature may be at most to be economically viable. Based on cost and benefit estimates, the scope is iteratively adjusted until the task is reasonable in terms of both content and costs.

As a coach, it is also possible to work with the product-responsible person in advance, so that he comes to the team prepared with a value proposition. Experience has shown that this is also about a bit of fairness: if the team is forced to make an estimate, the person responsible for the product should also be prepared to make an estimate. This is also a way to show that the team is *valued*.

8.8 Follow-up to meetings

After a meeting or a workshop, there are usually still a few things to do. Whenever possible, it is advisable to plan the time for the follow-up directly after the meeting. Then, the contents are still fresh and concrete, and the processing of the to-dos is relatively easy.

- Reflect on the meeting unhurriedly: What went well? What will I pay more attention to at the next meeting? Which planned goals were achieved? What unplanned added value did the meeting bring?
- Take pictures of all visualisations and send the photo protocol together with the written protocol, if there is one, to the participants. A short introductory text with a thank-you note for their active participation and a summary of what has been achieved can help keep the meeting or workshop in positive memory.

Keep in mind that a protocol, similar to a user story, can only be a reminder of discussed content. Ultimately, it is the team members and not the one writing the minutes that are responsible for their own insights, decisions and action plan.

To be able to decide how much effort should be spent on the documentation, Christiansen [2015] proposes asking the customer or the team:

- What will make us realise in six to twelve months that it was worth investing time and energy in the production of this documentation? And what else?
- Discuss any open questions and concerns of participants that could not be addressed during the meeting, and plan how they will be answered or dealt with.

Pitfall
Tried and tripped? No one is born a master ...

We know it, and you know it: every new behaviour needs practice. So, if you want to go the way of solution-focused work in an Agile environment, understand that not everything may work out as you would have expected after reading this book. This is by no means only a result of you being still inexperienced in this field! Your team also has the right to wonder first and then get used to the new manners before screaming hooray. So, practise patience and confidence and please do not give up. It is worth continuing and trying!

Below you will find a few first-aid measures to help you start:

- Start with a little linguistic change. "What else?" and "For what purpose?" (instead of "Why?"), maybe "and" (instead of "but") are ideally suited for inconspicuously and yet purposefully approaching the new method and also for accustoming the environment to it.
- As soon as you feel ready to take a really big, courageous step, such as a whole solution-focused retrospective, do it! Your gut will reliably tell you what you can and cannot expect from your team.
- Should you experience great disbelief when asking for something true and positive instead of sparkling answers, give your conversational partners the scientific background to the chosen intervention. If your team members know the context, their willingness to experiment will increase considerably.
- And if something really goes wrong, the following question helps: What is happening here and what does this have to do with the goal of the question or exercise? You are also welcome to ask your team this question openly. We have experienced that there were really helpful intentions behind seemingly strange behaviour.
- You can also say directly that you are surprised at the outcome of the intervention, which had not been planned like that. Ask your team how it could continue now.

8.9 Self-reflection

- Which of the ideas and questions presented do you already use in your meetings?
- How could you make your meetings more solution-focused?
- Which of the exercises or interventions presented are the most suitable for you?
- Which of them would you like to try out directly with your team in the near future?
- What is your primary goal in the facilitation of your respective meetings?
- Do you know the goal of each team member? If not – what difference would that make to your preparation work?

8.10 Experiments and exercises

- Select one of Nancy Kline's nine points (section 8.1 "Considerations for solution-focused meeting facilitation") and use it in your next meeting to involve everyone present. What differences can you see?
- Is there an unstoppable speaker in your team? At the next opportunity, listen attentively and without interruption. Find out their core message and repeat it in your own words. Appreciate the contribution. How does the team react? How does the colleague in question react?
- Do not consider the objections of your colleagues as disturbances, but as important information which is given to you. What image do you now have of the one making the objection?
- Change your Daily Stand-up tomorrow as a test: At the beginning, ask what the individual team members achieved yesterday that they are proud of. Observe the mood in the team. What changes do you notice?
- For the brave: introduce the law of mobility from Open Space to your meetings. The law says that anyone who believes they cannot contribute or learn anything meaningful at a meeting can and should leave it. Instead, they should move to where they can contribute or learn something meaningful. Watch who comes to the meeting, how it goes, who the meeting would have really needed and what prompted the missing person to engage in something else instead of attending the

meeting. Even if this approach may seem unrealisable at first, Ralph often used it during his time as a project manager. At the beginning, he openly asked individual team members about the benefits they could derive from or contribute to the meeting from their point of view. If no benefit was recognisable, he allowed them to leave the meeting. Later, this approach became normal during internal team meetings. He always invited everyone, and the right people showed up.

9. Tips for the coach

To be able to live up to all the attitudes and principles presented in this book, it is necessary to concentrate and focus on what happens in the coaching process. Distractions and disruptive thoughts, which do not belong to the current process, interfere with the focus, sometimes even completely prevent it. Strong feelings like anger, nervousness, fear, insecurity or aggression make it impossible for a coach to do a good job. Great interest in the topic of the coachee can also quickly become an obstacle.

In this chapter, special attention will be paid to the coach and their strength. How can the coach dissociate themselves from what is happening around them, both personally and in terms of content, so that they do not make other people's problems their own? When is it better to ask for support? To what extent is it possible to take on several roles at the same time, such as when you facilitate a meeting as a team member?

As a coach, you are just as unique as your challenges and needs. A global solution can, therefore, never do justice to this uniqueness. This chapter provides food for thought for you and your situation. With everything you already know about coaching attitudes and techniques, combined with your own experiences, you probably already have great resources to identify the right path for yourself.

9.1 Your role(s)

So, what is your current role anyway? Are you a coach? Or a leader? Maybe a facilitator? Or a team member with a special function? Perhaps even all of these?

In professional life, it often happens that many roles are united in one person. Depending on the situation, your specific tasks change several times a day, sometimes even several times an hour. You facilitate team development measures, manage decision-making processes, coach through conflict situations and personal development steps of individual employees and, in between, work through agenda items together with the team. You juggle around all the different requirements and attitudes to keep all the balls in the air as well as possible at the same time. This much is certain: it is seldom dull in such a working environment.

The challenge is that many of the requirements contradict each other. As a leader, it is necessary, depending on the understanding of leadership, to be decisive, responsible and consistent on the one hand, and trusting and supportive on the other. It is often challenging to keep the balance between: "I make decisions quickly, remain consistent and give my employees the assurance that I am prepared to take responsibility", and: "I involve my employees in all decisions to provide them with the security of being experts and having the right to participate".

Even the balance between content expertise and the not-knowing position is not easy to maintain as an internal coach or team member. This often becomes clear, especially in the facilitation of meetings and in team coaching processes.

9.2 When to act as a coach?

You will find the right balance between unintentional and intentional support of the team and decision-making processes for yourself. Over time, you will learn to feel when you can trust and be patient, and when it is necessary to intervene. Perhaps you have already had this experience. Nevertheless, there are a few simple questions that can help you decide whether to take on the coaching role or apply coaching techniques in your daily work.

9.2.1 What is your assignment?

Whenever others need your support, it is advisable to ask in which form this support is desired or what exactly is to be achieved.

If you are to help develop a solution, the use of coaching techniques is likely to be useful. Is it about resolving a conflict or dealing better with unpleasant changes? Maybe you should just listen and show understanding? Exactly. Coaching is also a good companion here.

Coaching fits here...	...and here, it does not!
> handling conflicts	> making decisions
> accompanying development	> giving professional input
> defining goals	> formulating requests
> developing a vision	> criticizing
> support in personal crisis	> giving feedback
> facilitating meetings	> getting information

Or is it rather a matter of getting information or a decision from you so that work can continue? Then act according to the specific requests instead of using coaching techniques.

The use of coaching techniques, when forced upon others, can quickly lead to resistance. Take the wishes of your partners seriously and act accordingly. Ask again when you are unsure before you risk a misinterpretation of the request.

9.2.2 Contracting

If a coach is appointed to a contract, the first thing to do is a contracting talk with the client. This is the time to exchange all the essential information which the coach needs for the handling of the respective case. Depending on whether an external coach is requested for an assignment or an internal coach is asked to support in a case, different information is required.

As an external coach, you can use the following points as a mental checklist for such an interview. If one of these questions remains unanswered, a professional coach will probably not be able to accept the contract.

- What is it about? How many people are involved?
- What is the role of the sponsor in this case?
- What does the sponsor want? How will they know that the assignment has been carried out to their satisfaction? Do these expectations match my content-related and moral requirements (e.g. professional know-how, confidentiality, etc.)?
- By when should the assignment be completed? Can I meet this deadline?
- What is the budget range? Does it match my fee expectations?
- What should be the course of action? Can I work independently? Is it supported by the sponsor?
- How, when, and by whom are those involved informed?
- Is the sponsor aware of the possible consequences?
- Is the sponsor prepared to bear the possible consequences?
- Is there a written agreement from the sponsor, or do I draw up such an agreement (order confirmation) myself?

An internal coach is a person who works in the company asking for support. So, this person is part of the system and has some advantages over an external coach. For example, they are familiar with the corporate culture, understand how the networks are connected, know many of the employees and enjoy trust because they are well acquainted with them. This situation also results in a number of disadvantages that should not be underestimated. The not-knowing position, for example, is much harder to adopt. It can even happen that the consequences of their coaching work can harm them afterwards in the company – especially if a case cannot be solved positively. The following checklist can be helpful for you to decide whether or not to accept an assignment as an internal coach.

- What is it about? Am I free of my own agenda regarding the content of this topic?
- Who are the people involved, and how do I personally relate to these people? Can I be omni-partial? Do I trust that these people will be able to work out a solution with me and implement it?
- Who is the sponsor in this case? And what is their role?
- What does the sponsor want? How will they know that the assignment has been carried out to their satisfaction? Do these expectations match my content-related and moral requirements (e.g. professional know-how, confidentiality, etc.)?
- By when should the assignment be completed? Can I meet this deadline? Do I have to delay another project to achieve this? What consequences does this have for my direct colleagues and me?
- What should be the course of action? Can I work independently? Is it supported by the sponsor?
- How, when, and by whom are those involved informed?
- Is the sponsor aware of the possible consequences?
- Is the sponsor prepared to bear the possible consequences?
- What possible consequences does this assignment have for me?

9.2.3 Can you stay out of anything content-related?

If you are the one with a concern, you should refrain from coaching others. In such situations, it is better to use the four steps of Potential-focused communication (see section 5.2.2) to express your needs and to ask for cooperation or find someone who is not involved in the issue and can support you with coaching.

Your content-related concerns will distract you from the task of accompanying the process, especially if they are near and dear to you. Meetings at which you want or need to participate in discussions should, therefore, be facilitated by another person if possible.

If, on the other hand, it is important for you that a specific goal is achieved, but you are not involved in the how, and therefore can and want to place it in the hands of the team members, there is no reason why you should not take over the facilitation.

> ### *Practical tip*
>
> Some colleagues also have good experiences with making a small visible change to clarify the role they are currently playing in the meeting. One person, for example, puts on their glasses when they want to contribute something as a team member and takes them off when they switch to their role as facilitator to accompany the process. Such a visible change can be helpful both for the participants and for the facilitator as role clarity is maintained.

9.2.4 Are you omni-partial?

Especially when conflict situations are involved, the question arises as to how much you are part of the conflict system. To be helpful in the coaching role, it is necessary that you can support all parties in the same honest way. You should only accept such an assignment if you can understand all points of view and if you are sure that every single one of the people present gives their best.

It is often difficult to be impartial, particularly if you have known the people involved for a long time. Even if you are entirely sure of your attitude, you should clarify whether the parties to the conflict trust you as well. Only then is it possible to create an atmosphere of openness and trust in which conflict situations can unfold their positive effects.

9.2.5 Do you have support?

Sometimes working with people leads to situations in which a coach cannot make progress without support. It may be that the necessary psychological, medical, or even legal qualification is lacking, that ethical or moral reasons prevent further work, or that partiality about the content gains in importance.

Whenever such cases occur, it is helpful to know people whom you trust as a coach and whom you could ask for support if necessary. You can put such a person in touch with your conversational partners for further work in their specialist area or for answering specific questions. So, make sure you have a good network, even with people from outside the industry such as doctors, industrial psychologists, lawyers or therapists.

Ideally, you should also work together with at least one fellow professional who can assist you in a variety of ways in the event of personal or content-related bias. For this to work well, a high level of mutual professional and personal esteem is imperative:

- For example, your colleague can take on an assignment for you and therefore guarantee your personal and content-related distance.
- Conducting a team coaching session with a second coach can be helpful in a situation where you are biased. The view of the uninvolved colleague on the given situation can open up new perspectives for you and enable you to continue working.
- You can also ask your colleague for intervision. This means that you discuss a situation with them, take advantage of coaching yourself and find a suitable way to deal with your point of view and the assignment.

9.2.6 The appointment agreement and its effects

The appointment agreement is made exclusively between the coaching client and us. This is how we have been doing it for years. We generally reject any coordination with the superior or the HR department. The background of this practice lies in the fact that the step towards a personal appointment already represents the first commitment to cooperation and, therefore, the willingness to change. In a personal conversation with the coaching client, you have the opportunity to create a first positive encounter with them. You both get an initial feeling for the other, and the start of the coaching relationship is made easier for both sides.

Frequently, the request to make an appointment is the beginning of the positive change. This step alone often improves your client's situation. It is a popular solution-focused practice to ask about the positive differences that have arisen since the appointment was made. This phenomenon is known as pre-session change [Weiner-Davis et al., 1987].

9.3 The coach as host

When the role as coach comes into focus, two questions arise: "When should I be a coach?" and: "How should I best fill my role as a coach?" In their book, McKergow and Bailey [2014] have developed a new leadership metaphor, which also seems suitable for the role as coach in many facets: the leader as host.

What makes a good host? As soon as their guests arrive, they welcome each individual. They ensure that those present can meet each other in a positive way by creating a respectful atmosphere. They procure the first drink and introduce the house rules. When the food is ready, they tell all their guests. They make sure that everyone is prepared before the start of the next item on the agenda and that the transitions from one part of the party to the next go smoothly. Of course, the host also mixes with the guests again and again. They make sure that nobody feels lonely and everyone feels good.

Should a glass break or any other mishap happen, the host will be on the spot to take care of it. Finally, when they have said goodbye to all the guests, the host will put things back where they belong and clean the house.

In this sense, the coach also sees themselves as a host of helpful conversations [Hargens, 2000]. They take care of the preparation of the room(s), set the timeframe, and ensure that all discussion partners feel welcome. The coach creates a framework in which the participants get to know each other and can work well together. They ensure that all relevant information is always available and understood. In doing so, they make sure that the prerequisites are met so that everyone present is able to make a valuable contribution to the team. The coach is happy about every small success that the team members achieve.

Moreover, the coach regularly inquires whether all participants are well prepared for the next work step and what their coach can contribute to it. If someone feels left out in terms of content, the coach gives support and mediates in case of misunderstandings in an omni-partial manner. The coach is successful if the others are satisfied with their contribution to the conversation and with the conversation itself.

9.4 Setting and defending boundaries

In section 6.2 "Our R.E.S.U.L.T. model for team development", we have already mentioned the regulatory framework teams need to navigate well in it. Do you remember that? There is a distinction between the non-negotiable framework, which must not be violated under any circumstances; the flexible framework, which is intended to provide security while remaining changeable; and the negotiable set of rules, which is jointly and actively determined by everyone.

You should also set up such a structure for yourself. It helps you determine your boundaries and intervene if they are violated.

9.4.1 Your non-negotiable framework

Can you say *no*? Or *stop*? Especially as a coach or as a supporter of others, you are often tempted to take on too much. After all, it is your task to help others achieve their goals, is it not? That is right indeed, but not at any price, not at any time of the day or night and not in every situation. It is essential that your employees, colleagues and clients know your boundaries and the most important rules for dealing with you so they know where they stand with you. For this purpose, it makes sense that you first think about what is okay for you and what is not.

> ### *Defining your non-negotiable framework*
>
> 1. First of all, you could start by writing down everything that others should take into account when dealing with you. Make a long list and take plenty of time over it.
> 2. Then identify those four points which are essential and which you would not tolerate being violated. These four points constitute your personal *non-negotiable framework*.
> 3. Describe it in as much detail as possible and also consider the consequences of non-compliance.

You alone are responsible for defending your boundaries. Nobody else will do this for you. The better you know your boundaries, the clearer and easier it will be to communicate them. Your security in relation to your non-negotiable framework also leads to more security for others in dealing with you.

9.4.2 First of all, take care of yourself

> *"Be your own chairman, the chairman of yourself. Listen to your inner voices – your different needs, desires, motivations and ideas."*[4]
>
> [Cohn, 2009, p. 122 ff.]

To be able to support other people effectively, you have to take care of yourself as well. Therefore, pay particular attention to your own well-being.

One of the four sides of your non-negotiable framework could be: "I need to feel fine". This means that you are a good coach if you make sure that you are well-balanced inside, secure in your situation and can look at yourself in the mirror with a clear conscience. Consistently reject any assignment that you cannot support ethically [Weinberg, 1986].

Take care of your health and make sure you have a private network in which you feel comfortable and in good hands. Get regular exercise, sleep well and have a healthy diet. Meet friends and read a book that has nothing to do with your job – just for fun. Keep looking for a way to talk to someone about your thoughts. Especially as a leader or if you are self-employed as a single entrepreneur, this exchange is often not or only insufficiently given.

All these are recommendations, you know. And maybe you are like most other people: you know that you should do more for yourself, only at the moment, it is really not possible. So, you postpone looking after yourself until later, when the weather outside is better, when the current time-consuming project is finished, or until summer, when there is generally less going on.

The only right time to start paying more attention to yourself is now. Take just one small step, one that costs you little effort.

- Instead of having a healthy diet from now on, you could start by eating two pieces of fruit or vegetables a day.
- Instead of starting an elaborate fitness program, you could take the stairs once a day instead of using the lift.
- Instead of arranging a meeting with all your friends, you could call one friend and chat with them for ten minutes.
- You could also start by turning off your phone at breakfast and listening to music instead, or …

---

[4] See also [Röhling, 2017]: "Be your own Chairman, the Chairman of your self. That means: (1) Be aware of your inner reality and of your environment. (2) Consider every situation to be a proposition for your decisions. Take and give as befits being responsible for yourself and for others".

- ... by actually having your lunch break every day for at least 20 minutes.
- Perhaps there are some points in your to-do list that you could delete without substitution, or delegate?

Find a little thing that you can start with today to pay more attention to yourself. The reward for this is more satisfaction, balance, energy and joy in doing your daily work. Your health will thank you for it.

9.5 The Scrum Master – a unique role

Scrum is the most widely used Agile framework in large and medium-sized companies today. Within this framework, the role of the Scrum Master is an essential success-factor. The Scrum Master is responsible for ensuring that the team can work together as smoothly and seamlessly as possible. In addition, they are team members themselves; their role description also includes coach, facilitator, problem solver, and contact person for the Product Owner as well as for stakeholders. In some company environments, they also act as an extended arm of management. The Scrum Master has no real decision-making authority. They lead by acting as a role model through indirect influence. Many Scrum Masters struggle with role conflicts and this robs them of strength and energy.

9.5.1 Role clarity

One of the most important tasks is, therefore, to clarify their role and tasks with the team and all those involved in the environment again and again. The Scrum Master should be aware of their own skills and abilities, and especially of their boundaries. Again and again, it is our experience that tasks which should be carried out by the management are passed on to the Scrum Master. Situations like the following are unfortunately more the rule than the exception:

A practical example of "The Scrum Master's non-tasks".

A Scrum Master is repeatedly invited to management meetings. One day, they are also asked to inform their team that the company is about to undergo restructuring. The Scrum Master is now worried about how they can pass this information on to the team in the best way possible. They know that there will be many questions that they cannot answer. There will be uncertainties and perhaps even discrepancies that could have a negative impact on the working climate and therefore on productivity.

> *If you think about a problem for so long that you get headaches, it may not be your problem; it may be someone else's.*
>
> (Unknown source)

As Scrum Master, you should be aware that it is the task of the management to pass on such information to the team. Therefore, you should strictly refuse such assignments and ask your managers to talk to the team directly. Offer to assist in finding a convenient appointment.

Also, Product Owners can make life difficult for a Scrum Master. The goals of a Scrum Master and a Product Owner often contradict each other considerably due to their roles, which can easily lead to discrepancies. While the Product Owner strives to meet the wishes of the customer as quickly as possible, the Scrum Master wants to ensure that the team can work well and undisturbed in the Sprint.

As a Scrum Master, you should learn to distance yourself and say "No!". If you want to avoid this direct kind of confrontation, you can, for example, ask questions for clarification [Bungay Stanier, 2010, p. 90 ff.] or formulate requests such as:

- How should I answer any questions that arise in the team?
- Please ask the team directly if this is possible.
- Please let us schedule this for the next Sprint.
- Which of the previous tasks should the team not complete so that your assignment can be fulfilled?

9.5.2 Appreciation, wishes and further development

Apart from role clarity, the Scrum Master also needs feedback regarding their work from their teammates. It has proven to be helpful if there is a retrospective on a regular basis, e.g. quarterly, that is facilitated by an external Scrum Master so that the team's Scrum Master can become part of the discussion. The agenda should then include the team's satisfaction with the work of the Scrum Master and ideas for improving and changing this work.

The Scrum Master should then also have the opportunity to address their appreciation and wishes to the team. In this way, the Scrum Master can learn how to be helpful for their colleagues and, at the same time, develop the cooperation positively.

As a Scrum Master, you should also give yourself appreciation for your performance every day. At the end of the day, you should know what you have achieved.

It is therefore beneficial to plan the goals for each day in advance. This is best done directly after the Stand-up Meeting. Many Scrum Masters rush to work off the current obstacles. Instead, you should pause for a moment and consider what you would like to have achieved by tonight.

- What is important? – What would support us the most?
- What is urgent? – What must be done immediately?
- What can others do, for example, also the team?
- What can we leave for another day?

And finally:

- If, at the end of the day, I had only managed one thing today, which one should it be?

A day prepared in this way helps with the focused completion of the upcoming tasks. Take ten minutes in the evening and make yourself aware of what you have achieved. The next day, you will be ready for maximum performance and motivated anew.

9.6 Self-reflection

- What roles do you have to take on in your professional environment?
- How do you manage to align these roles with each other?
- What could help you do that even better?
- Which four topics form your non-negotiable framework?
- What do you already do to look after yourself and your health?
- What small step can you easily take to take care of yourself a little better?
- With whom do you discuss your thoughts?
- Who in your company can you ask for help with facilitation or coaching if you have a particular interest in the content?

9.7 Experiments and exercises

- Find four points that are so important to you that you would not tolerate an infringement, no matter by whom. Not even in exceptional situations.
- Stand in front of a mirror and tell yourself these four points loudly and clearly.
- As a coach or facilitator, take part again and again in rounds of appreciation with your teams. Collect, for example, quality mirror information or appreciation cards (see section 6.3 "Tools for team development") that you receive. These memories can help you to maintain courage and self-confidence in difficult times.
- Write yourself a letter from the future, in which you congratulate yourself on what you have already been able to implement. Start, for example, with the words: "Today is the (today's date in one year)". Then describe in as much detail as possible what you would like to have achieved by then and how you will have succeeded. Maybe there are also some ideas from this book. If you like, send a letter to your future me, for example with https://www.futureme.org/, and enjoy receiving it in a year's time.
- Congratulate yourself every day before going to bed from now on about three small or even bigger successes that you have achieved during the day. Repeat this exercise for at least 21 days.
- Alternatively, you can do the same exercise by thinking about which three people you are thankful for each day and what you are grateful for.

- Make a pact with yourself right now: Which tiny bad habit would you like to change immediately in your life, so you pay a little more attention to yourself?
- Did you find anything? Call someone important to you and tell them about your decision. If it is late at night, it is also okay to send an e-mail.

Bibliography

[Achor 2010] S. Achor. *The Happiness Advantage: The Seven Principles of Positive Psychology That Fuel Success and Performance at Work*. Crown Business, New York. 2010.

[Adkins 2010] L. Adkins. *Coaching Agile Teams: A Companion for ScrumMasters, Agile Coaches, and Project Managers in Transition*. Addison-Wesley, Boston, US. 2010.

[AgileAlliance 2013] AgileAlliance. *Daily Meeting*. 2013.
http://guide.agilealliance.org/guide/daily.html (last access: 20150502)

[AgileAlliance 2014] AgileAlliance. *Definition Of Ready*. 2014.
http://guide.agilealliance.org/guide/definition-of-ready.html (last access: 20150525)

[AgileManifesto 2001] Manifesto for Agile Software Development. 2001.
http://agilemanifesto.org/ (last access: 20150503)

[Akers 2016] P. A. Akers. *2 Second Lean – How to Grow People and Build a Fun Lean Culture at Work and at Home*. 3. edition. Leanpub. 2016.

[Bamberger 2010] G. G. Bamberger. *Lösungsorientierte Beratung*. Beltz Verlag, Basel. 2010.

[Bandler & Grinder 1982] R. Bandler, J. Grinder. *Reframing: neuro-linguistic programming and the transformation of meaning*. Real People Press, Utah. 1982.

[Beck 1999] K. Beck. *Embracing Change with Extreme Programming*. IEEE Computer 32 (10). p. 70–77. 1999.
http://ivizlab.sfu.ca/arya/Papers/IEEE/Computer/1999/October/Embracing%20Change%20with%20Extreme%20Programming.pdf (last access: 20150427)

[Beck & Andres 2004] K. Beck, C. Andres. *Extreme Programming Explained: Embrace Change*. Addison-Wesley, Amsterdam. 2004.

[Berg & Szabó 2005] I. K. Berg, P. Szabó. *Brief Coaching for Lasting Solutions*. W. W. Norton & Company, New York, London. 2005.

[Berkel 2003] K. Berkel. *Konflikte in und zwischen Gruppen*. In: Führung von Mitarbeitern. Handbuch für erfolgreiches Personalmanagement. Published by L. v. Rosenstiel, E. Regnet, M. Domsch. Band 5. p. 397–414. Schäffer-Poeschel, Stuttgart. 2003.

[Besser 2010] R. Besser. *Interventionen, die etwas bewegen: Prozesse emotionalisieren, mit Konfrontation aktivieren, über Grenzen gehen, wirksame Rituale gestalten*. Beltz Weiterbildung. Beltz, Weinheim. 2010.

[Böckmann 1987] W. Böckmann. *Sinn-orientierte Führung als Kunst der Motivation*. Verlag Moderne Industrie, Landsberg/Lech. 1987.

[Brown+ 2001] J. Brown, D. Isaacs, T. W. C. Community. *The World Café: Living Knowledge*

Through Conversations That Matter. The Systems Thinker 12 (5). 2001. http://www.theworldcafe.com/articles/STCoverStory.pdf (last access: 20150308)

[Buck & Villines 2017] J. Buck, S. Villines. *We the People: Consenting to a Deeper Democracy: A Handbook for Understanding and Implementing Sociocratic Principles and Practices.* 2nd updated and expanded edition. Sociocratic.info, Washington. 2017.

[Budiu & Anderson 2005] R. Budiu, J. R. Anderson. *Negation in Nonliteral Sentences.* Proceedings of the 27th Annual Conference of the Cognitive Science Society. Stresa, Italy. 2005. http://act-r.psy.cmu.edu/wordpress/wp-content/uploads/2012/12/602p354.pdf (last access: 20150503)

[Bungay Stanier 2010] M. Bungay Stanier. *Do More Great Work.* Workman Publishing, New York. 2010.

[Burgstaller 2015] S. Burgstaller (Ed.). *Lösungsfokus in Organisationen – Zukunftsorientiert beraten und führen.* Carl-Auer Verlag, Heidelberg. 2015.

[Cain 2012] S. Cain. *Quiet: The Power of Introverts in a World That Can't Stop Talking.* Crown Publishing Group, New York. 2012.

[Caroli 2009] P. Caroli. *The Retrospective of Retrospectives.* 2009. http://agiletips.blogspot.co.at/2009/09/retrospective-of-retrospectives.html (last access: 20150502)

[Champion+ 1990] D. P. Champion, D. H. Kiel, J. A. McLendon. *Choosing a Consulting Role.* Training & Development Journal 44 (2). p. 66–69. 1990. http://www.forumzfd-akademie.de/files/va_media/nid1685.media_filename.pdf (last access: 20150226)

[Christiansen 2014] J. H. Christiansen. *Solution Focused Future Forum.* InterAction – The Journal of Solution Focus in Organisations 6 (1). p. 67–74. 2014. http://sfwork.com/resources/interaction/s7.pdf – https://solutionsurfers.dk/wp-content/uploads/2014/11/SF_FutureForum2014_2sided.pdf (last access: 20190817)

[Christiansen 2015] J. H. Christiansen. *The (hand)book of GREAT GATHERINGS – a solution focused approach to working with large groups.* to be published. 2015. http://greatgatherings.net/ (last access: 20190707)

[Clark & Chase 1972] H. H. Clark, W. G. Chase. *On the Process of Comparing Sentences Against Pictures.* Cognitive Psychology 3. p. 472–517. 1972. http://web.stanford.edu/~clark/1970s/Clark.Chase.comparing.72.pdf (last access: 20150216)

[Cohn 2006] M. Cohn. *Agile Estimation and Planning.* Prentice Hall, Massachusetts. 2006.

[Cohn 2009] R. Cohn. *Von der Psychoanalyse zur themenzentrierten Interaktion: Von der Behandlung einzelner zu einer Pädagogik für alle.* 16. edition. Klett-Cotta, Stuttgart. 2009.

[Cooper & Castellino 2012] L. Cooper, M. Castellino. *The Five Minute Coach: Coaching Others to High Performance – In as Little as Five Minutes.* Crown House, Camarthen, Wales, UK. 2012.

[Coplien 1994] J. O. Coplien. *Borland Software Craftsmanship: A New Look at Process, Quality and Productivity.* 5th Annual Borland International Conference. Orlando, Florida. 1994. http://www.cedet.dk/docs/borland-process.pdf (last access: 20150228)

[Damian+ 2009] D. Damian, S. Marczak, M. Dascalu, M. Heiss, A. Liche. *Using a Real-Time Conferencing Tool in Distributed Collaboration: An Experience Report from Siemens IT Solutions and Services.* 4th IEEE International Conference on Global Software Engineering, ICGSE 2009. Limerick, Ireland. 2009.

[Davies & Sedley 2010] R. Davies, L. Sedley. *Agile Coaching.* The Pragmatic Bookshelf, Raleigh, North Carolina and Dallas, Texas. 2010.

[De Jong & Berg 2012] P. De Jong, I. K. Berg. *Interviewing for Solutions.* 4th / International edition. Cengage Learning, Inc. 2012.

[De Shazer 1988] S. De Shazer. *Clues: Investigating Solutions in Brief Therapy.* 11. edition. Norton & Company. 1988.

[De Shazer 1991] S. De Shazer. *Putting Difference To Work.* 5. edition. W. W. Norton, New York. 1991.

[De Shazer & Dolan 2007] S. De Shazer, Y. Dolan. *More Than Miracles: The State of the Art of Solution-Focused Brief Therapy.* Routledge, New York. 2007.

[Derby & Larsen 2006] E. Derby, D. Larsen. *Agile Retrospectives: Making Good Teams Great.* The Pragmatic Bookshelf, Raleigh, North Carolina and Dallas, Texas. 2006.

[Dierolf 2013] K. Dierolf. *Lösungsfokussiertes Teamcoaching.* SolutionsAcademy Verlag, Bad Homburg. 2013.

[Dixon+ 2010] P. Dixon, D. Rock, K. Ochsner. *Turn the 360 around.* NeuroLeadership Journal 3. p. 78-86. 2010. http://www.davidrock.net/files/Turn_the_360_around.pdf (last access: 20150515)

[Dörner 2004] D. Dörner. *Emotion und Wissen.* In: Psychologie des Wissensmanagements. Published by G. Reinmann, H. Mandl. p. 117-132. Hogrefe, Göttingen. 2004.

[Dörner 2010] D. Dörner. *Die Logik des Gelingens? (Vortrag).* Institut für Theoretische Psychologie, Otto-Friedrich-Universität, Bamberg, Wien. 2010.

[Drucker 2005] P. F. Drucker. *Managing Oneself.* Harvard Business Review. 2005. https://hbr.org/2005/01/managing-oneself (last access: 20150503)

[Dunnette+ 1963] M. D. Dunnette, J. Campbell, K. Jaastad. *The Effect of Group Participation on Brainstorming Effectiveness for Two Industrial Samples.* Journal of Applied Psychology 47 (1). p. 30-37. 1963.

[Dweck 2006] C. Dweck. *Mindset: The New Psychology of Success.* Random House, New York. 2006.

[Eberling & Hargens 1996] W. Eberling, J. Hargens. *Einfach kurz und gut. Zur Praxis der lösungsorientierten Kurztherapie.* Borgmann Publishing, Dortmund. 1996.

[Eckstein 2004] J. Eckstein. *Agile Software Development in the Large: Diving Into the Deep.* Dorset House, New York. 2004.

[Frankl 1985] V. E. Frankl. *Man's Search for Meaning.* Revised and Updated edition. Washington Square Press, New York. 1985.
https://www.academia.edu/8147176/Mans_Search_For_Meaning (last access: 20200223)

[Frankl 2012] V. E. Frankl. *Der Wille zum Sinn.* 6. edition. Verlag Hans Huber, Bern. 2012.

[Franklin+ 2018] C. Franklin, C. L. Streeter, L. Webb, S. Guz. *Solution Focused Brief Therapy in Alternative Schools – Ensuring Student Success and Preventing Dropout.* Routledge, New York and London, 2018.

[Fredrickson 2010] B. L. Fredrickson. *Positivity: Top-Notch Research Reveals the Upward Spiral That Will Change Your Life.* Harmony, 2010.

[Furnham 2000] A. Furnham. *The Brainstorming Myth.* Business Strategy Review 11 (4). p. 21-28. 2000.
https://criticalandcreativethinking.files.wordpress.com/2011/07/the-brainstorming-myth1.pdf (last access: 2017-01-22)

[Gallup 2017] Gallup. *State of the Global Workplace.* GALLUP PRESS, New York. 2017.
https://www.gallup.com/workplace/238079/state-global-workplace-2017.aspx (last access: 20200228)

[Geisbauer 2012] W. Geisbauer. *Reteaming: Methodenhandbuch zur lösungsorientierten Beratung.* 3. edition. Carl-Auer Verlag, Heidelberg. 2012.

[George 2012] E. George. *Team Coaching: a Solution Focused Approach (Training Material).* BRIEF Vienna. 2012.

[Gerber & Gruner 1999] M. Gerber, H. Gruner. *FlowTeams – Selbstorganisation in Arbeitsgruppen.* Orientierung (108). 1999.
http://flowteam.com/doc/O_108_D-Gesamt.pdf (last access: 20150503)

[Ghul 2005] R. Ghul. *Moan, Moan, Moan.* In: Education and Training in Solution-Focused Brief Therapy. Published by T. S. Nelson. p. 63–64. Haworth Press, New York. 2005.

[Gingerich & Peterson 2013] W. J. Gingerich, L. T. Peterson. *Effectiveness of Solution-Focused Brief Therapy: A Systematic Qualitative Review of Controlled Outcome Studies.* Research on Social Work Practice 23 (3). p. 266–283. 2013. http://rsw.sagepub.com/content/23/3/266, http://gingerich.net/home/solution-focused-brief-therapy/

[Glasl 1998] F. Glasl. *Selbsthilfe in Konflikten.* Verlag Freies Geistesleben, Stuttgart. 1998.

[Glen 2003] P. Glen. *Leading Geeks: How to Manage and Lead People Who Deliver Technology.* Jossey-Bass, San Francisco. 2003.

[Godat 2008] D. Godat. *Footsteps.* In: 57 SF Activities for Facilitators and Consultants – Putting Solutions Focus into action. Published by P. Röhrig, J. Clarke. p. 253ff. Solutions Books, Cheltenham, United Kingdom. 2008.

[Goethe 1812] J. W. v. Goethe. *Aus meinem Leben: Dichtung und Wahrheit, Bd 2, Buch IX.* J. G. Cottaische Buchhandlung, Tübingen. 1812.
http://www.deutschestextarchiv.de/book/view/goethe_leben02_1812?p=427 (last access: 20150301)

[Grenning 2002] J. Grenning. *Planning Poker or How to avoid analysis paralysis while release planning.* 2002. https://renaissancesoftware.net/files/articles/PlanningPoker-v1.1.pdf (last access: Access Date)

[Grubert 2014] A. Grubert. *Lösungsfokussierte Timeline-Arbeit für Teams.* Workshop bei der SOLworldDACH-Konferenz, Friedrichsdorf (bei Frankfurt/M). 2014. http://solworlddach.files.wordpress.com/2014/06/vb_lforganisationenmai.pdf (last access: 20150203)

[Hargens 2000] J. Hargens (Ed.). *Gastgeber hilfreicher Gespräche.* Borgmann Media, Dortmund. 2000.

[Hargens 2011] J. Hargens. *Aller Anfang ist ein Anfang – Gestaltungsmöglichkeiten hilfreicher systemischer Gespräche.* 4. edition. Vandenhoeck & Ruprecht, Göttingen. 2011.

[Hasson & Glucksberg 2006] U. Hasson, S. Glucksberg. *Does understanding negation entail affirmation? An examination of negated metaphors.* Journal of Pragmatics. 2006. http://www.behaviometrix.com/public_html/Hasson.metneg.pdf (last access: 20150123)

[Hesse 1960] H. Hesse. *Aus einem Brief vom September 1960 an Wilhelm Gundert.* In: Mein Hermann Hesse – Ein Lesebuch. Published by U. Lindenberg. p. 26. Suhrkamp Verlag, Berlin. 1960.

[Hirschhausen 2009] E. v. Hirschhausen. Glück kommt selten allein ... Rowohlt Verlag GmbH, Reinbek. 2009. http://www.hirschhausen.com/glueck/die-pinguingeschichte.php, http://www.hki.uni-koeln.de/sites/all/files/courses/11389/pinguin.pdf, https://www.youtube.com/watch?v=Az7lJfNiSAs (zuletzt geöffnet: 2021-04-03)

[Hochreiter 2012] G. Hochreiter. *Reteaming – lösungsorientierte Teamchoreographien gestalten: Lösungsspielräume für Teams im Kontext von Personen und von Organisation.* In: Reteaming: Methodenhandbuch zur lösungsorientierten Beratung. 3. edition. p. 119–132. Carl-Auer Verlag, Heidelberg. 2012.

[Hoffmann 2017] S. G. Hoffmann. *The Disturbance Postulate.* In: Handbook of Theme-Centered Interaction (TCI) Published by M. Schneider-Landolf, J. Spielmann, W. Zitterbarth. p. Vandenhoeck & Ruprecht, Bristol, CT, U.S.A. 2017.

[Hohmann 2006] L. Hohmann. *Innovation Games: Creating Breakthrough Products Through Collaborative Play.* Addison-Wesley Professional, 2006.

[Hufnagl 2014] B. Hufnagl. *Besser fix als fertig: Hirngerecht arbeiten in der Welt des Multitasking.* Molden Verlag, Wien. 2014.

[Iveson+ 2012] C. Iveson, E. George, H. Ratner. *Brief Coaching – A Solution Focused Approach.* Essential Coaching Skills and Knowledge. Ed. by G. McMahon, S. Palmer, A. Leimon. Routledge, London. 2012.

[Kahneman 2011] D. Kahneman. *Thinking, Fast and Slow.* 1st edition. Farrar, Straus and Giroux, New York. 2011.

[Kaltenecker & Myllerup 2011] S. Kaltenecker, B. Myllerup. *Agile & Systemic Coaching.* 2011.

https://www.scrumalliance.org/community/articles/2011/may/agile-systemic-coaching (last access: 20150503)

[Kaup 2001] B. Kaup. *Negation*. Memory & Cognition 29 (7). p. 960–967. 2001. http://http-server.carleton.ca/~jlogan/PSYC4704/Kaup.pdf (last access: 20150216)

[Kerth 2001] N. L. Kerth. *Project Retrospectives: A Handbook for Team Reviews*. Dorset House Publishing, New York. 2001.

[Kindl-Beilfuß 2011] C. Kindl-Beilfuß. *Fragen können wir Küsse schmecken – Systemische Fragetechniken für Anfänger und Fortgeschrittene*. 3. edition. Carl-Auer Verlag, Heidelberg. 2011.

[Klein 2007] S. Klein. *50 Praxistools für Trainer, Berater, Coachs: Überblick, Anwendungen, Kombinationen*. 3. edition. GABAL Verlag, Offenbach. 2007.

[Kline 1998] N. Kline. *Time To Think: Listening to Ignite the Human Mind*. Cassell Octopus, London. 1998.

[Kniberg 2009] H. Kniberg. *Cause-effect diagrams: A pragmatic way of doing root-cause analysis*. Version 1.1. Crisp, Stockholm. 2009.
https://www.crisp.se/file-uploads/cause-effect-diagrams.pdf (last access: 20150503)

[Koerner 2005] M. Koerner. *Scrum and Brief (Psycho-) Therapy – Traces of an emerging 'systemic' paradigm in the applied sciences?* 2005.

[Kotrba 2006] V. Kotrba. *Solution Focused Rating – Evaluierung einer alternativen Methode für die Mitarbeiterbeurteilung*. Master Thesis, PEF Privatuniversität für Management, Wien. 2006.

[Lamarre 2005] J. Lamarre. *Complaining Exercise*. In: Education and Training in Solution-Focused Brief Therapy. Published by T. S. Nelson. p. 65–66. Haworth Press, New York. 2005.

[Larman & Vodde 2008] C. Larman, B. Vodde. *Scaling Lean & Agile Development: Thinking and Organizational Tools for Large-Scale Scrum*. Addison-Wesley, Massachusetts. 2008.

[Larman & Vodde 2010] C. Larman, B. Vodde. *Practices for Scaling Lean & Agile Development – Large, Multisite, and Offshore Product Development with Large-Scale Scrum*. Addison-Wesley, 2010.

[Larman & Vodde 2015] C. Larman, B. Vodde. *Large-Scale Scrum: More with LeSS*. Addison-Wesley, 2015.

[Larsen 2004] D. Larsen. *Team Planning & Chartering for successful Software Development*. FutureWorks Consulting, LLC. 2004. http://www.futureworksconsulting.com/resources/TeamChartertemplate.pdf (last access: Access Date)

[Larsen & Nies 2016] D. Larsen, A. Nies. *Liftoff: Launching Agile Teams & Projects*. Onyx Neon Press, 2016.

[Leffingwell 2007] D. Leffingwell. *Scaling Software Agility – Best Practices for Large Enterprises*. Ed. by A. Cockburn, J. Highsmith. Addison Wesley, 2007.

[Lichtenberg 1796] G. C. Lichtenberg. *Aphorismen (Sudelbücher)*. Ed. by W. Promies, B. Promies. Carl Hanser Verlag, München. 1796. http://gutenberg.spiegel.de/buch/6445/11

[Lieberman & Eisenberger 2008] M. D. Lieberman, N. Eisenberger. *The pains and pleasures of social life: a social cognitive neuroscience approach*. NeuroLeadership Journal 1. p. 38–43. 2008. http://www.scn.ucla.edu/pdf/Pains&Pleasures(2008).pdf (last access: 20150517)

[Lipmanowicz & McCandless 2014] H. Lipmanowicz, K. McCandless. *The Surprising Power of Liberating Structures: Simple Rules to Unleash A Culture of Innovation*. Liberating Structures Press, 2014.

[Löffler 2014] M. Löffler. Retrospektiven in der Praxis – Veränderungsprozesse in IT-Unternehmen effektiv begleiten. dpunkt.verlag, Heidelberg. 2014.

[Löffler 2018] Mark Löffler. Improving Agile Retrospectives: Helping Teams Become More Efficient. Addison-Wesley. 2008

[Loftus 1998] E. F. Loftus. *Falsche Erinnerungen*. Spektrum der Wissenschaft 1. p. 63 ff. 1998. http://www.spektrum.de/alias/dachzeile/falsche-erinnerungen/823559 (last access: 20150502)

[Loftus & Palmer 1974] E. F. Loftus, J. C. Palmer. *Reconstruction of Automobile Destruction: An Example of the Interaction Between Language and Memory*. Journal of Verbal Learning and Verbal Behavior 13. p. 585–589. 1974.
https://webfiles.uci.edu/eloftus/LoftusPalmer74.pdf (last access: 20150502)

[Losada & Heaphy 2004] M. Losada, E. Heaphy. *The Role of Positivity and Connectivity in the Performance of Business Teams: A Nonlinear Dynamics Model*. American Behavioral Scientist 47 (6). p. 740–765. 2004. http://www.factorhappiness.at/downloads/quellen/S8_Losada.pdf (last access: 20150503)

[Ludewig & Maturana 1992] K. Ludewig, H. R. Maturana. *Gespräche mit Humberto Maturana*. Ediciones Universidad de La Frontera, Temuco, Chile. 1992.

[Lueger 2006] G. Lueger. *Solution-Focused Assessment: New Ways of Developing HR-Instruments*. In: Solution-Focused Management. Published by D. G. Lueger, H.-P. Korn. p. 203–212. Rainer Hampp Verlag, München und Mering. 2006.

[Lueger 2012] G. Lueger. *Leistungsbeurteilung – Die nächste Generation*. 2012. http://solutionmanagement.at/fileadmin/downloads/pdf/2012_13/Loesungsfokussiertes PerformanceManagementErstesKapitel.pdf (last access: Access Date)

[Lueger 2014] G. Lueger. *Potenzial-fokussierte Schule*. Solution Management Center, Wien. 2014.

[Lueger & Korn 2006] G. Lueger, H.-P. Korn. *Solution-Focused-Management*. Band 1. Rainer Hampp Verlag, München und Mering. 2006.

[Lukas 1999] E. Lukas. *Lebensstil und Wohlbefinden: Logotherapie bei psychosomatischen Störungen*. Profil-Verlag, München. 1999.

[Lyubomirsky+ 2005] S. Lyubomirsky, L. King, E. Diener. *The Benefits of Frequent Positive*

Affect: Does Happiness Lead to Success? Psychological Bulletin 131 (6). p. 803-855. 2005. http://www.apa.org/pubs/journals/releases/bul-1316803.pdf (last access: 2017-02-11)

[Mack & Snyder 1957] R. W. Mack, R. C. Snyder. *The analysis of social conflict – toward an overview and synthesis.* Journal of Conflict Resolution 1 (2). p. 212–248. 1957.

[Mackinnon 2005] T. Mackinnon. *Retrospectives ... and Futurespectives.* 2005. http://www.planningcards.com/site/history/thoughts/retrospectives.html (last access: 20150427)

[Mantsch 2014] T. Mantsch. *Focus your daily stand-up meeting on work and not on people.* 2014. http://www.tmantsch.com/wordpress/2014/11/focus-your-daily-stand-up-meeting-on-work-and-not-on-people/ (last access: 20150502)

[Mar 2008] K. Mar. *Scrum Trainers Gathering (4/4): Affinity Estimating.* 2008. http://kanemar.com/2008/04/21/scrum-trainers-gathering-44-affinity-estimating/ (last access: 20150307)

[Mathis 2017] C. Mathis. *SAFe – Das Scaled Agile Framework.* 2., überarbeitete und aktualisierte edition. dpunkt.verlag, Heidelberg. 2017.

[Maturana & Varela 1987] H. R. Maturana, F. J. Varela. *The Tree of Knowledge: The Biological Roots of Human Understanding.* Shambhala Publications, Inc., 1987.

[McKergow 2008a] M. McKergow. *Sparkling Moments.* In: 57 SF Activities for facilitators and consultants: Puttong Solutions Focus into action. Published by P. Röhrig, J. Clarke. p. 48-53. SolutionsBooks, Cheltenham. 2008a.

[McKergow 2008b] M. McKergow. *What do we have to get right?* In: 57 SF Activities for facilitators and consultants: Puttong Solutions Focus into action. Published by P. Röhrig, J. Clarke. p. 44-47. SolutionsBooks, Cheltenham. 2008b.

[McKergow & Bailey 2014] M. McKergow, H. Bailey. *Host: Six new roles of engagement for teams, organisations, communities and movements.* SolutionsBooks, London. 2014.

[Meier & Szabó 2008] D. Meier, P. Szabó. *Coaching – erfrischend einfach: Einführung ins lösungsorientierte Kurzzeitcoaching.* Solutionsurfers, Luzern. 2008.

[Merl 2012] H. Merl. *Lösungsorientiertes ökosystemisches Denken.* In: Reteaming: Methodenhandbuch zur lösungsorientierten Beratung. 3. edition. p. 62–70. Carl-Auer Verlag, Heidelberg. 2012.

[Miarka 2012] R. Miarka. *Coaching als regelmäßige Maßnahme zur Begleitung von „agilen" IT Teams in deren Retrospektiven.* E.S.B.A. – European Systemic Business Academy, Wien. 2012. https://sinnvoll-fuehren.com/wp-content/uploads/Downloads/MSc-Thesis.pdf (last access: 20200223)

[Milek 2006] A. Milek. *Konfliktmanagement: Eine Einführung in die Begrifflichkeiten.* Freie Universität Berlin, Berlin. 2006. http://www.ewi-psy.fu-berlin.de/einrichtungen/arbeitsbereiche/arbpsych/media/lehre/w

s0607/12577/praesentation_konflikte_25102006.pdf (last access: 20150308)

[Montada 2013] L. Montada. *Gerechtigkeitskonflikte und Möglichkeiten ihrer Lösung*. In: Soziale Gerechtigkeit. Published by M. Gollwitzer, S. Lotz, T. Schlösser, B. Streicher. p. 35–54. Hogrefe, Göttingen. 2013.

[Montada & Kals 2001a] L. Montada, E. Kals. *Psychologie der Gerechtigkeit*. In: Mediation – Lehrbuch für Psychologen und Juristen. p. 99–132. Psychologie Verlags Union, Verlagsgruppe Beltz, Weinheim. 2001a.

[Montada & Kals 2001b] L. Montada, E. Kals. *Mediation – Lehrbuch für Psychologen und Juristen*. Psychologie Verlags Union, Verlagsgruppe Beltz, Weinheim. 2001b.

[Mullen+ 1991] B. Mullen, C. Johnson, E. Salas. *Productivity Loss in Brainstorming Groups: A Meta-Analytic Integration*. Basic and Applied Social Psychology 12 (1). p. 3-23. 1991.

[Nink 2015] M. Nink. *Engagement Index Deutschland 2014*. Gallup GmbH, Berlin. 2015. http://www.gallup.com/file/de-de/181859/Pr%C3%A4sentation%20zum%20Engagement%20Index%202014.pdf (last access: 20150708)

[Osborn 1948] A. Osborn. *Your Creative Power*. Purdue University Press, Scribners, New York. 1948.

[Ostberg 2007] P. M. Ostberg. *Führung und Leistung brauchen Werte und Sinn*. Existenz und Logos. Zeitschrift für sinnzentrierte Therapie – Beratung – Bildung. 15 (17). p. 83–99. 2007. http://www.logotherapie-gesellschaft.de/heftarchiv/archiv.html (last access: 20150503)

[Owen 2008] H. Owen. *Open Space Technology: A User's Guide*. 3. edition. Berrett-Koehler Publishers, Inc., San Francisco. 2008.

[Pichler 2010] R. Pichler. *Agile Product Management with Scrum: Creating Products that Customers Love*. Addison-Wesley, Massachusetts. 2010.

[Prior 2009] M. Prior. *MiniMax-Interventionen*. Band 9. Carl-Auer Verlag, Heidelberg. 2009.

[Rasmusson 2009] J. Rasmusson. *The Drucker Exercise*. 2009. https://agilewarrior.wordpress.com/2009/11/27/the-drucker-exercise/ (last access: Access Date)

[Rising 2010] L. Rising. *Offer Appreciations*. Better Software Jan/Feb. p. 76–78. 2010. http://web.lindarising.info/uploads/Offer_Appreciations.pdf (last access: 20150220)

[Rock 2008] D. Rock. *SCARF: a brain-based model for collaborating with and influencing others*. NeuroLeadership Journal 1. 2008. http://www.scarf360.com/files/SCARF-NeuroleadershipArticle.pdf (last access: 20150503)

[Rock 2009] D. Rock. *Managing with the Brain in Mind*. strategy+business 56. 2009. http://www.davidrock.net/files/ManagingWBrainInMind.pdf (last access: 20150503)

[Rock & Cox 2012] D. Rock, C. Cox. *SCARF in 2012: updating the social neuroscience of collaborating with others*. NeuroLeadership Journal 4. 2012. http://www.davidrock.net/files/09_SCARF_in_2012_US.pdf (last access: 20150514)

[Röhling 2017] J. G. Röhling. *The Chairperson Postulate*. In: Handbook of Theme-Centered

Interaction (TCI) Published by M. Schneider-Landolf, J. Spielmann, W. Zitterbarth. p. Vandenhoeck & Ruprecht, Bristol, CT, U.S.A. 2017.

[Röhrig 2011] P. Röhrig (Ed.). *Solution Tools – Die 60 besten, sofort einsetzbaren Workshop-Interventionen mit dem Solution Focus.* managerSeminare Verlags GmbH, Bonn. 2011.

[Rosenberg 2015] M. B. Rosenberg. *Nonviolent Communication – A Language of Life.* 3rd edition. PuddleDancer Press, Encinitas, CA. 2015.

[Scheel+ 2004] M. J. Scheel, W. E. Hanson, T. I. Razzhavaikina. *The Process of Recommending Homework in Psychotherapy: A Review of Therapist Delivery Methods, Client Acceptability, and Factors That Affect Compliance.* Faculty Publications. D. o. Psychology. University of Nebraska. 2004. http://digitalcommons.unl.edu/psychfacpub/372/ (last access: 2017-02-11)

[Schenck 2011] K. Schenck. *„Wishbones": Orientierungshilfe für Lösungen mit „Skalen" und „Gräten"...* In: Solution Focus Home. Published by H. Reisch. Band 1. p. 53–61. Books on Demand GmbH, Norderstedt. 2011.
https://sites.google.com/site/klausschenck/free-resources-articles/veroeffentlichungen-auf-deutsch (last access: 20150218)

[Schenck 2013] K. Schenck. *„SF-Espresso" – Kaffeegemisch als Lösungsmittel: Ein kurzes, lösungsfokussiertes „World Café"-Format.* Focus Five Coaching Solutions 2013. https://sites.google.com/site/klausschenck/free-resources-articles/veroeffentlichungen-auf-deutsch (last access: Access Date)

[Schenck 2014] K. Schenck. *SF-Espresso.* Friedrichsdorf (im Taunus). 2014. https://solworlddach.files.wordpress.com/2014/06/sf-espresso-flipchart-fotokoll-klaus-schenck-140517.pdf (last access: 20150503)

[Schirmer 2014] S. Schirmer. *Eine Frage der Haltung – Lösungsfokussierung im Testing.* Testing Experience DE 6. p. 5–7. 2014.
http://www.testingexperience.de/issues/Testing_Experience_DE_06_Juli_2014.pdf (last access: 20150503)

[Schulz von Thun 2009] F. Schulz von Thun. *Miteinander reden, Band 3: Das "Innere Team" und situationsgerechte Kommunikation.* 18. edition. Rowohlt Taschenbuch Verlag, Hamburg. 2009.

[Schwaber & Sutherland 2020] K. Schwaber, J. Sutherland. *The Scrum Guide.* 2020. https://www.scrumguides.org/docs/scrumguide/v2020/2020-Scrum-Guide-US.pdf (last access: 20210204)

[Sheridan 2013] R. Sheridan. *Joy, Inc.: How We Built a Workplace People Love.* Portfolio/Penguin, New York. 2013.

[Simon & Weber 1988] F. B. Simon, G. Weber. *Das Ding an sich: Wie man "Krankheit" erweicht, verflüssigt, entdinglicht ...* Familiendynamik 13 (1). p. 57–61. 1988.

[Simon & Rech-Simon 2009] F. B. Simon, C. Rech-Simon. *Zirkuläres Fragen – Systemische Therapie in Fallbeispielen: Ein Lehrbuch.* Carl-Auer Verlag, Heidelberg. 2009.

[Simon & Weber 2012] F. B. Simon, G. Weber. *Vom Navigieren beim Driften*. 4. edition. Carl-Auer Verlag, Heidelberg. 2012.

[Smith 2010] P. Smith. *Feelings: The Golden Road*. Phases of the Moon, the newsletter of the Maine NVC Network, Vol 1 (No 4). 2010. http://mainenvcnetwork.org/newsletter4.html and http://www.opencommunication.org/articles/FeelingsGoldenRoad.pdf (last access: 20200308)

[Spaleck 2009] G. M. Spaleck. *Vom Profit zum Sinn – Gedanken zum not-wendigen Paradigmenwechsel in unserem Wirtschaftssystem*. Existenz und Logos. Zeitschrift für sinnzentrierte Therapie – Beratung – Bildung 17 (17). p. 74–108. 2009. http://www.logotherapie-gesellschaft.de/heftarchiv/archiv.html (last access: 20150122)

[Sparrer 2009] I. Sparrer. *Systemische Strukturaufstellungen: Theorie und Praxis*. Carl-Auer Verlag. 2009.

[Sparrer & Varga von Kibéd 2009] I. Sparrer, M. Varga von Kibéd. *Ganz im Gegenteil, Tetralemmaarbeit und andere Grundformen Systemischer Strukturaufstellungen – für Querdenker und solche, die es werden wollen*. 6 edition. Carl Auer Verlag, Heidelberg. 2009.

[Sprenger 2012] R. K. Sprenger. *Radikal führen*. Campus Verlag, Frankfurt/Main. 2012.

[Stangl] W. Stangl. *Was ist ein Konflikt?* http://arbeitsblaetter.stangl-taller.at/KOMMUNIKATION/Konflikte.shtml (last access: 20150218)

[Sterling 2008] C. Sterling. *Affinity Estimating: A How-To*. 2008. http://www.gettingagile.com/2008/07/04/affinity-estimating-a-how-to/ (last access: 20150307)

[Sullivan & Rees 2009] W. Sullivan, J. Rees. *Clean Language – Revealing Metaphors and Opening Minds*. Crown House Publishing Ltd, 2009.

[Sutherland 2001] J. Sutherland. *Agile Can Scale: Inventing and Reinventing SCRUM in Five Companies*. Cutter IT Journal 14 (12). p. 5–11. 2001. http://www.controlchaos.com/storage/scrum-articles/Sutherland%20200111%20proof.pdf (last access: 20150304)

[Sutherland 2013] J. Sutherland. *Labcast: Reaching Your Full Potential with Scrum*. 2013. http://labs.openviewpartners.com/implementing-scrum-reaching-your-full-potential/ (last access: 20150228)

[Sutherland 2014] J. Sutherland. *Scrum: The Art of Doing Twice the Work in Half the Time*. Crown Business, New York. 2014.

[Szabó 2007] P. Szabó. *Skalierungsfragen im Coaching: Ein einfaches und wirksames Instrument für die Praxis*. 2007. http://www.solutionsurfers.ch/wp-content/uploads/2014/08/Skaleboard-Artikel_D1.pdf (last access: 20150503)

[Szabó 2017] P. Szabó. *Multi-Skalierung*. In: Coaching-Tools II – Erfolgreiche Coaches präsentieren Interventionstechniken aus ihrer Coaching-Praxis Published by C. Rauen. 4. edition. p. 316ff. managerSeminare Verlag, 2017.

[Thomann 2014] C. Thomann. *Klärungshilfe 2 – Konflikte im Beruf: Methoden und Modelle klärender Gespräche.* 6. edition. Rowohlt Taschenbuch Verlag, Hamburg. 2014.

[Thomann & Prior 2013] C. Thomann, C. Prior. *Klärungshilfe 3 – Das Praxisbuch.* 3. edition. Rowohlt Taschenbuch Verlag, Hamburg. 2013.

[Thomsett 2002] R. Thomsett. *Radical Project Management.* Prentice Hall, NJ. 2002.

[Visotschnig+ 2016] E. Visotschnig, V. Visotschnig, U. Baumann, D. Berger, E. Hafner, S. Schrotta. *Einführung in Systemisches Konsensieren.* Institut für Systemisches Konsensieren ISYKONSENS International OG, Graz. 2016. http://www.sk-prinzip.eu/ (last access: 2017-02-11)

[Wales & Grieve 1969] R. J. Wales, R. Grieve. *What is so difficult about negation?* Perception & Psychophysics 6 (6A). p. 327-332. 1969.
link.springer.com/article/10.3758%2FBF03212785 (last access: 20150216)

[Weinberg 1986] G. M. Weinberg. *The Secrets of Consulting: A Guide to Giving and Getting Advice Successfully.* Dorset House Publishing, New York. 1986.

[Weiner-Davis+ 1987] M. Weiner-Davis, S. d. Shazer, W. J. Gingerich. *Building on pretreatment change to construct the therapeutic solution: An exploratory study.* Journal of Marital and Family Therapy 13 (4). p. 359–363. 1987.

[Whitmorc 2015] J. Whitmorc. *Coaching for Performance: Potenziale erkennen und Ziele erreichen.* Coaching & Beratung. Junfermann Verlag, Paderborn. 2015.

[Wilhelm] J. Wilhelm. *Reframing: Der Rahmen macht's.* http://www.froschkoenige.ch/sites/default/files/modelle/Refraiming_LR.PDF (last access: Access Date)

[Wiseman 2009] R. Wiseman. *59 Seconds: Think A Little, Change A Lot.* Pan Books, 2009.

[Wittgenstein 1922] L. Wittgenstein. *Tractatus Logico-Philosophicus.* 1922.
http://www.gutenberg.org/files/5740/5740-pdf.pdf (last access: 20150121)

[Wranke 2009] C. Wranke. *Der Einfluss von Emotionen auf das logische Denken.* Justus-Liebig-Universität, Gießen. 2009.
http://geb.uni-giessen.de/geb/volltexte/2010/7426/ (last access: 20150502)

Tool Index

A
Action plan, 231
Anger walk, 193
Annoying moments, 25-26
Appreciation cards, 131

B
Benevolent hypothesising, 141
Brainstorming, 228

C
Chocolate Tour, 131
Chain question, 215
Confidence scale, 48, 233
Consent decision, 195, 231-232
Crossed scales, 46

D
Damn circle, 192-193

E
Experiments plan, 231

F
Five What-Fors, 224
Footsteps, 233

G
Great Gatherings, 146

H
Hooray-Book, 226

I
Idea Competition, 229
Impact Analysis, 223

K
Keep it!, 217

L
Large lists, 227

M
Miracle question, 49, 222
Mission Possible, 133
Multi-scaling, 44-45
My personal style, 119

P
Problems are disguised goals, 220-221

Q
Quality Mirror, 132

R
Resource gossip, 129-130
Reteaming, 133

S
Scale-Question, 41-44
Sociocratic Consent, 195-196
Solution Talk, 221
Solution-focused future forum, 145
Solution-Focused-Espresso, 144
Sparkling Moments, 23-24
Systemic Consensus, 194-195

T
Team advertising brochure, 135
Team picture, 225
Tetralemma, 196-197
Thank you!, 217
Timeline work, 135-140

W
What do we have to get right?, 222
What we have – what we need, 234
Wishbone, 230-231

Index

A
Achievements, 122
Action experiments, 63, 231-232
Action plan, 231
Agile Chartering, 12
Agile Coach, 8-11, 17, 120-121
Agile values, 7
And instead of but, 61-62
Anger walk, 193
Annoying moments, 25-26
Anything else?, 51
Appreciation, 53, 67-68, 131
Appreciation cards, 131
Assignment, 246
Attentive listening, 170
Autonomy, 158, 161

B
Backlog Refinement Meeting, 238-239
Benevolent hypothesising, 141
Brainstorming, 228-229
Breaks, 62

C
Certainty, 158, 160
Chain question, 215-216
Chocolate tour, 131
Circular questions, 50
Clarifying questions, 40-41
Clean Language, 72
Closed question, 39
Coaching attitudes, 16-27
Coaching questions, 41-53
Coconut Model, 19-21
Common goal, 12, 118, 169, 218-219
Comprehensible intention, 156-157
Concept of conflict, 149-151
Confidence, 21-22, 28, 48, 82, 180-181
Confidence scale, 48, 81, 180-181, 233
Confidentiality, 26-27, 93-94
Conflict, 149-185
Conflict escalation by Glasl, 151-154, 176
Context Reframing, 56-57
Contracting, 68, 90, 247-248

Conversational needs, 83-90, 181-183
Coping questions, 48
Corridor conversations, 96-97
Crossed scales, 46-47
Cross-team coordination, 210

D
Daily Stand-up, 206-210
Damn circle, 192-193
Definition of Ready, 201
Difference, 151
Dilemma, 151, 196-197
Directed questions, 39
Disturbances, 68, 191

E
Emotion, 55, 156, 159, 175, 193
Estimation methods, 238-239
Everyday questions, 38-41
Exceptions, 34-35, 49
Experiments, 63-64
Experiments plan, 231
Expert in their situation, 18-21
eXtreme programming, 29

F
Facilitation, 187ff
Facilitator, 169-180, 186ff
Fairness, 158, 163
False memories, 33
Feedback, 30, 99-100
Feelings, 44, 101-104, 150
First aid, 171-173
Five What-Fors, 224
Focus, 27, 67
Focus on resources, 22-26
Follow-up conversation, 90
Footsteps, 233
Futurespective, 139, 221

G
Goal, 69-77, 218-219
Great Gatherings, 146

Index

H
Handling objections, 198-199
High-performance teams, 116-118
Hooray-Book, 226
Host leadership, 251
Hypothetical questions, 41

I
Idea Competition, 229
Impact, 69-78
Impact Analysis, 223-224
Implementation planning, 203-204
Individual coaching, 93-115
Institutional rules, 126
Interposed questions, 50-51

K
Keep it!, 217

L
Large lists, 227
Learning, 123-124
Liquefying, 58-59

M
Meaning, 77-78, 223
Meaning reframing, 56-58
Measure, 219
Meta questions, 52-53
Meta-monologue, 60
Miracle questions, 49-50, 222
Mission Possible, 133
Mistakes, 31, 35-36, 123-124
Misunderstanding, 151
Monotony, 188
Multi-scaling, 44-45
My personal style, 119

N
Needs, 105-106, 109
Next steps, 79-80
Non-directed questions, 39-40
Nonviolent Communication, 100-107
Normalising, 55-56
Not and no, 51, 61, 69, 88
Not-knowing position, 10, 16-17

O
Observation, 63, 101
Observation experiments, 63

Omni-partiality, 26, 152, 170-171, 174, 249
Open questions, 39

P
Pair programming, 29, 31-32, 63
Paraphrasing, 54-55, 170
Patience, 21-22, 62
Perception, 101
Planning meeting, 201-204
Positive wording, 69
Potential-focused communication, 100, 108-109
Preferred feeling, 108
Preferred future, 14, 15, 27-28, 33, 41, 43-44, 49, 50, 69, 108, 146, 213
Preferred observation, 108
Preparation for meetings, 200-201
Prime Directive of Retrospectives, 18, 214
Problem, 14-15, 31-34, 66-67, 149, 151, 220
Problems are disguised goals, 220-221
Product Backlog, 201

Q
Quality Mirror, 132
Questions, 38-64

R
R.E.S.U.L.T. model, 122-129, 251-252,
REACH TOP, 76, 219
Reflecting team, 60
Reframing, 56-58
Relatedness, 158, 162
Requests, 106-107
Resistance, 75, 97-98
Resource gossip, 129-130
Reteaming, 133
Review meeting, 211-213
Ritual experiments, 64

S
Scale-Question, 41-44, 177-180, 227
SCARF model, 78-79, 99, 105, 140, 157-168
Scrum Master, 127-128, 214, 254-256
Sparkling Moments, 23-24
Sprint goal, 17, 202, 207
Status, 158, 189
Sticky names, 145
Strengths and abilities, 22-23, 129, 132, 139, 141
Success Slider, 212

Summarising, 54
Systemic Consensus, 194-195
Systemic Structural Constellation, 196

T
Team advertising brochure, 135
Team development, 26, 116-148
Team picture, 225
Team rules, 125-127
Team vision, 140-143
Tetralemma, 196-197
Timeline, 135-140
Topic, 66, 219
Troublemakers, 189-191
Trust, 93-94, 98, 128-129

U
Unstoppable speakers, 189

V
Voluntary participation, 94-95

W
What do we have to get right?, 222
What else?, 50-51, 64, 79, 175
What instead?, 69-70, 149, 175
What we have – what we need, 234
What works, 78-79, 176
Why?, 52, 157, 241
Wishbone, 230-231

Y
Your role, 245

Lightning Source UK Ltd.
Milton Keynes UK
UKHW020632261021
392864UK00006B/546